LUCASVILLE

LUCASVILLE

THE UNTOLD STORY OF A PRISON UPRISING

STAUGHTON LYND

TEMPLE UNIVERSITY PRESS

Philadelphia

Temple University Press
1601 North Broad Street
Philadelphia PA 19122
www.temple.edu/tempress

Design by: Robin West Morrow/Ox and Company

∞ The paper used in this publication meets the
requirements of the American National Standard
for Information Sciences—Permanence of Paper
for Printed Library Materials, ANSI Z39.48-1984

Library of Congress Cataloging-in-Publication Data

Lynd, Staughton.
    Lucasville : the untold story of a prison upris-
ing / Staughton Lynd.
        p. cm.
    Includes bibliographical references and index.
    ISBN 1-59213-093-3 (alk. paper) –
ISBN 1-59213-094-1 (pbk. : alk. paper)
    1. Southern Ohio Correctional Facility
(Lucasville, Ohio). 2. Prison riots—Ohio—
Lucasville—Case studies. I. Title.

HV9475.O32S68 2004
365′.641–dc22   2004041188

    2 4 6 8 9 7 5 3 1

CONTENTS

R0019984025

LUCASVILLE

INTRODUCTION

PROSECUTORS HAVE CALLED IT "the longest prison riot in
United States history."[1] More accurately, the director of the Ohio
Department of Rehabilitation and Correction (ODRC) refers to "the
longest prison siege in U.S. history where lives were lost." A 1987
rebellion at the United States Penitentiary in Atlanta seems to have
lasted a few hours longer.[2]

The uprising took place in April 1993 in Lucasville, Ohio, a small
community just north of the Ohio River. Two populations, approximately equal in number, confronted one another there. On the one
hand were the maximum security prisoners at the Southern Ohio
Correctional Facility (SOCF), mostly black, mostly from cities like
Cincinnati and Cleveland. On the other hand was the all-white population of the town. Almost everyone in Lucasville worked at the
facility or knew someone who did.[3]

In the course of the 11-day occupation, one correctional officer
and nine prisoners were murdered by prisoners.

My wife, Alice Lynd, and I were living in northern Ohio at the time.
Those 11 days in April 1993 coincided with the much-publicized
siege of the Branch Davidian compound in Waco, Texas. We were
barely aware of the Lucasville disturbance.

In 1996 Alice and I learned that a supermaximum security (or
"supermax") prison was being built in Youngstown. Alice organized a
community forum at a church near the site to explore the question
"What is a supermax prison?" Jackie Bowers from Marion, Ohio, tes-

tified about the experience of 23-hour-a-day isolation. She is the sister of George Skatzes, one of the five men condemned to death after the Lucasville events.

Alice and I became acquainted with "Big George," whom at this writing we have visited monthly for seven years. We became increasingly convinced of his innocence and volunteered to assist his post-conviction counsel. As retired attorneys, we had more time than busy practicing lawyers to read 5,000- or 6,000-page transcripts. Little by little we came to be researchers for several of the Lucasville Five defense teams.

Two things caught my attention at the outset.

First, there has been an extraordinary degree of solidarity among the five men condemned to death. They have shared legal materials to a greater extent than have their attorneys. They have expressed concern about one another's health problems. Together they have engaged in a series of hunger strikes protesting their burdensome conditions of confinement. Yet two of the five were at the time of the uprising members of the Aryan Brotherhood, an organization thought to endorse white supremacy, and the other three are African Americans. I sensed a dynamic quite different from the unchanging—even unchangeable—racism that many historians have recently ascribed to white workers in the United States (see Chapter 7).

Second, emotions in southern Ohio have run so strongly about the Lucasville events that truth has gotten lost in the shuffle.

The *Columbia Journalism Review* published an article about the irresponsible speculations of the media during those 11 days. "Glaring mistakes were reported as fact, and were never corrected," the *Review* declared. "Reporters ... vied for atrocity stories. They ran scary tales—totally false, it was later found—that spread panic and paranoia throughout the region."[4]

Among the examples recounted were these:
- Six days into the riot, a front-page story in the Cleveland *Plain Dealer*, citing anonymous sources, reported that along with seven

inmate deaths, 19 other people in the prison had been killed, including "some pretty barbarous mutilations of the dead."

- A reporter for Channel 4 told viewers that as many as 172 bodies were piled up in the prison. This body count turned out to be a head count of inmates in one of the blocks *not* involved in the riot.

- The *Akron Beacon Journal* reported about the murder of Officer Robert Vallandingham "that his eyes had been gouged out, that his back, arms and legs had been broken, and that his tongue had been cut out." Not one of these details was accurate.[5]

Even on the tenth anniversary of the uprising, in April 2003, media coverage in Ohio dealt almost exclusively with persons outside prison. The highest award given to Ohio correctional officers for bravery was renamed for Officer Vallandingham; his widow, Peggy Vallandingham, accepted the Vallandingham Gold Star Award for Valor in his name; and flags at Ohio prisons flew at half-mast. News stories conveyed next to nothing about the men on Death Row.

This was not wholly the fault of the media. Applying what appears to be a permanent policy, in mid-February 2003 ODRC Director Reginald Wilkinson informed a reporter for the *Columbus Dispatch* that "no inmates convicted of riot crimes will be permitted to speak to" reporters.[6]

I write as both a historian and a lawyer. Both professions claim to be devoted to the search for truth. And because historians and lawyers commonly turn their attention to events after they have occurred, one might suppose that history and law would correct the mistakes of journalists reporting in the heat of the moment.

Yet from a historian's point of view, official narratives about what happened at Lucasville are disturbing in many ways. For example, a historian writing about these events would almost certainly begin by exploring the causes of the riot. But as I will explain more fully in Chapter 8, in the Lucasville capital cases the defense was forbidden to present such evidence, while the prosecution was permitted to expand on this theme at length.

Indeed, my belief in the integrity of truth-seeking in the law has been shaken by the Lucasville judicial proceedings. I have come to feel that the idea that the adversarial process promotes truth-seeking may be as misleading as the assumption that the free-market competition of profit-maximizing corporations will produce adequate public health.

In what follows I present the facts of the Lucasville disturbance as best I can discern them. This is the untold story that the State of Ohio doesn't want you to hear.

A central thesis of this book is that the State of Ohio and its citizens need to face up to the state's share of responsibility for what happened at Lucasville.

It might be argued that the authorities have already conceded their part in the sequence of cause and effect. Prisoners not involved in the disturbance later sued state defendants for negligence in connection with the rebellion. The prisoners' suit alleged in part:

> **17.** In 1990, following an investigation at SOCF, a State Senate Select Committee determined that the security policy and procedures at the institution were "woefully inadequate," and recommended various reforms....
>
> **18.** Also in 1990, in order to rectify overcrowded conditions and to maintain proper security within SOCF, defendants ... announced the implementation of "Operation Shakedown" pursuant to which the entire population of the prison was to be single-celled.
>
> **19.** As of April 11, 1993, single celling had not yet been instituted at SOCF; one thousand eight hundred and twenty (1,820) inmates were still housed in the prison (a number far in excess of the institution's design capacity).

Rather than defend against these and other allegations, the authorities settled with the prisoners for $4.1 million.[7] The correctional officers taken hostage, together with the widow and son of Officer Vallandingham, likewise sued the authorities "for numerous torts before and during the siege." The state once again settled, for more than $2 million.[8]

In addition to the state's role in causing the riot, there were several ways in which its negotiators heightened the peril for the correctional officers held hostage in L block. As I will demonstrate in detail in Chapter 3:

- Sergeant Howard Hudson, who was present throughout the negotiations, conceded that state negotiators deliberately stalled.
- On April 12, apparently in response to communication between prisoners and the media, Warden Arthur Tate cut off water and electricity in L block. This action unnecessarily created a new conflict between the occupiers and the authorities, and the failure to resolve it was the occasion for Officer Vallandingham's murder.
- On the morning of April 14, a state spokesperson named Tessa Unwin denigrated the prisoners' demands and said that the prisoners' threat to kill a guard was "just part of the language of negotiation." Officer Vallandingham was killed the next day while an anguished George Skatzes, negotiating over the telephone, pleaded with the authorities to restore water and electricity.

None of this impressed the Supreme Court of Ohio. In affirming one of the death sentences, the court stated:

Nor was DRC's alleged refusal to "negotiate in good faith" relevant in the guilt phase. Let us be clear: The authorities in lawful charge of a prison have no duty to "negotiate in good faith" with inmates who have seized the prison and taken hostages, and the "failure" of those authorities to negotiate is not an available defense to inmates charged with the murder of a hostage.[9]

I believe these words to be profoundly misguided. To be sure, the authorities negotiated under duress. Moreover, if Sergeant Hudson and Ms. Unwin helped to cause the death of Officer Vallandingham, this does not mean that the leaders of the uprising were necessarily free of guilt.

What I nonetheless find unacceptable in the decisions of the Ohio Supreme Court is the attitude that prisoners in rebellion are "enemy combatants" toward whom the authorities have no obligations at all. For example, one Court of Appeals held that under the plain language of the law existing in 1993, the state had illegally eavesdropped on the conversations of prisoners in L block, and that this crucial evidence should therefore have been excluded at trial. On further appeal, the Ohio Supreme Court held that enforcement of the statute for the benefit of rioting prisoners would be "absurd" (see Chapter 6).

Such a holding, and the attitude prompting it, oversimplify a tangled sequence of cause and effect. Perhaps the law itself is prone to such rigidity. Perhaps legal practitioners are driven to view the world superficially by the desire to win. History, with its constipated academicism, has serious problems of its own. But history at least stands for the proposition that an event can have more than one cause, and that sometimes what happens in life is not a melodrama, with clearcut villains and heroes, but a tragedy in which we all have played a part. Is it too much to ask that before sending five more men to their deaths, we pause and seek to determine what really happened?

Finally, there is the state's misconduct after the prisoners surrendered on April 21. At that point the agency charged with investigating what had occurred—the Ohio State Highway Patrol (OSHP)—and the special prosecutorial team appointed to try the Lucasville cases were free to act calmly and with circumspection.

Instead, as I demonstrate in Chapters 4 and 5, in the absence of physical evidence the state, through its various agencies, targeted those whom it believed to have led the uprising and built cases against them by cutting deals with prisoners willing to become informants. The government threatened prisoners with death if they declined to "cooperate." I believe I can show that the prosecution put witnesses on the stand to offer testimony that the state knew to be false. Like Emile Zola in his celebrated exposé of the Dreyfus case, I accuse the state of deliberately framing innocent men.

I shall argue that Ohio should be guided by the experience of the State of New York after the rebellion at that state's Attica prison in 1971. During the years 1975–76 it came to light that prisoners had been induced to present perjured testimony, and that prosecutors were intentionally suppressing evidence of misconduct by state personnel during the assault on the prison. In the end, New York Governor Hugh Carey declared an amnesty for everyone involved in the Attica tragedy—both prisoners and persons involved in the state's assault on the recreation yard—and extended clemency to prisoners who had already been convicted or had previously entered into plea bargains.

I believe that Ohio should do likewise. The pattern of prosecutorial misconduct should cause Ohio's governor to pardon all Lucasville defendants found guilty of rebellion-related crimes.

It remains to thank the many people who have helped me to bring this book to the light of day.

They include Frances Goldin, friend, literary agent, and negotiator extraordinaire, and Peter Wissoker, senior acquisitions editor for Temple University Press. Three academics to whom the manuscript was sent for peer review provided helpful comments. I am deeply obligated to a number of lawyers, among them Niki Schwartz, who represented the prisoners in L block in settlement negotiations at the end of the disturbance; Dale Baich, who worked on the Lucasville cases while employed by the Office of the Ohio Public Defender; Richard Kerger, one of the lawyers for the supposed principal leader of the rebellion, Siddique Abdullah Hasan; Palmer Singleton of the Southern Center for Human Rights, which represents capital defendants in Georgia and Alabama; and Professor Jules Lobel of the University of Pittsburgh School of Law. I am solely responsible for all errors that nevertheless remain in the text.

In addition to the five men condemned to death, at least eighteen prisoners contributed relevant memories, documents, and insights. I have not named them lest doing so expose them to retaliation. They know who they are, and they will find their contributions in these pages. In most cases, the information provided to me offered no benefit to the prisoner who shared it. In at least one instance, a prisoner conveyed information to clear his conscience at considerable peril to himself.

Like the women who attended Jesus at the cross after the disciples fled, three women—Jackie Bowers, sister of George Skatzes; Angela Merles Lamar, wife of Keith Lamar; and Vincenza Ammar, beloved friend of Namir Abdul Mateen—provided whatever assistance was in their power to give.

Most of all I am indebted to seven persons who labored with me as an ad hoc editorial collective to try to find the truth about these complex events.

My wife, attorney Alice Lynd, spent approximately three years poring over the transcript of the capital proceedings against George Skatzes, indexing and cross-indexing, and identifying issues for appeal. Later, her time was almost wholly taken up by litigation concerning conditions at the supermax prison that opened in Youngstown in 1998. Most of the prisoners who were found guilty of crimes or rule violations connected with the Lucasville uprising, including those sentenced to death, have been housed at the supermax. The pool of prisoner witnesses to what happened in 1993 was thus near at hand. And Alice has had an uncanny ability to retrieve documents that I knew I had once examined but that thereafter seemed to have disappeared.

The five men condemned to death—the "Lucasville Five"—have been extraordinary collaborators. Throughout the process each of these men has been confined alone in a small cell, with little access to any of the others. A meeting between myself and all five around a table has never been permitted. Disagreements among the Five could not be ironed out face to face. Prison mail presented many frustrations. Despite these physical obstacles, all five have shared their legal papers with each other and with me, responded to my requests, and reviewed the manuscript in various stages of its preparation. One at a time, I would probe their recollections, considering documents that very often they had provided. When I have come to conclusions different from what some of these men remember, we have discussed those differences with mutual respect and tried to establish the truth. I alone remain responsible for what is set forth herein.

Mumia Abu-Jamal has played a special role. He is probably the best-known prisoner in the United States, if not in the world. During the period in which I put this book together, Mumia and his attorneys were in the midst of cross appeals from the decision of a federal judge who had for the moment set aside Mumia's death sentence (although he remained on Pennsylvania's Death Row), but left the jury verdict of guilt intact. Mumia stepped back from these pressing personal concerns to help with this book.

Mumia knew of George Skatzes, and there existed respect at a distance between the former Black Panther who had remained silent about the events surrounding the death of Officer Daniel Faulkner in Philadelphia, and the former member of the Aryan Brotherhood who had declined the state's invitation to accuse other prisoners of murdering Officer Robert Vallandingham (see Chapter 5). Mumia said that he thought the book was "doable." Pennsylvania prison regulations prohibited direct correspondence between Mumia and the Lucasville Five, but through me he offered encouragement.

In an unpublished essay on the Lucasville events, Mumia shares his views about what happened there:

Lucasville.

The name is evocative. People who hear it, who may know very little about its recent role in Ohio history, seem to recognize its penal roots.

It has become a site etched upon the American mind that means prison, like Sing Sing, Marion, or Lewisburg.

The name evokes an aura of fear, of foreboding.

In this essay Mumia contrasts what happened at Lucasville with the much greater loss of life at Attica in 1971. The Lucasville Five, he writes,

> worked, against great odds, to prevent an Attica (where over thirty men perished when the state unleashed deadly violence against the hostages taken, and falsely blamed it on the prisoners). They sought to minimize violence, and indeed, according to substantial evidence, saved the lives of several men, prisoner and guard alike.

Like myself, Mumia is particularly struck by the extent to which these five men overcame "easy labels"—Muslim and Aryan, black and white—and began to perceive each other's humanity.

They rose above their status as prisoners, and became, for a few days in April 1993, what rebels in Attica had demanded a generation before them: men. As such, they did not betray each other; they did not dishonor each other; they reached beyond their prison "tribes" to reach commonality.

I concur. I dedicate this book to all persons, in whatever country, on Death Row for political reasons.

Niles, Ohio

Chapter 1

A LONG TRAIN OF ABUSES

THE UPRISING AT THE Southern Ohio Correctional Facility (SOCF) in Lucasville began on Easter Sunday, April 11, 1993. As prisoners returned from recreation in the yard at about 3 p.m., they overpowered correctional officers on duty inside L block (Fig. 1.1). After the release of certain badly injured officers, eight continued to be held as hostages.

In the course of the occupation, two more hostages were set free, and one was murdered. Eventually, with the help of attorney Niki Schwartz, the state and the prisoners came to a 21-point agreement. On Wednesday, April 21, 407 prisoners surrendered and the five remaining hostages were released.

In subsequent legal proceedings, three negotiators and spokesmen for the prisoners—Siddique Abdullah Hasan, formerly known as Carlos Sanders (hereafter "Hasan"), Jason Robb, and George Skatzes—were found guilty of the aggravated murder of Officer Robert Vallandingham. So was Namir Abdul Mateen, also known as James Were (hereafter "Namir"). All four were sentenced to death, along with Keith Lamar, alleged to have organized a "death squad" that killed five supposed prisoner informants in the early hours of the

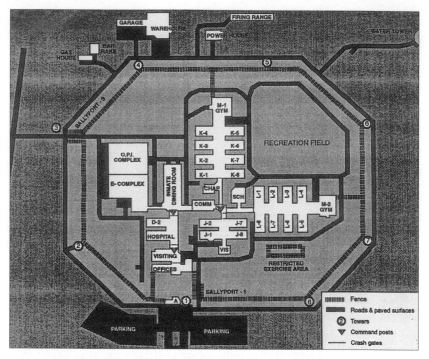

1.1 Layout of Southern Ohio Correctional Facility

uprising. Hasan and Namir are Sunni Muslims; Robb and Skatzes were at the time members of the Aryan Brotherhood.

As this book goes to press, the five capital cases are making their way through the courts. Hasan, Robb, and Lamar are at the last (federal habeas corpus) stage of appeals.

KING ARTHUR

What makes human beings rebel?

Often rebellion seems not to be in the personal interest of the insurgents. This was true in Philadelphia in 1776, where Benjamin Franklin is said to have joked about the need for the signers of the Declaration of Independence to hang together lest they hang separately.[1] It was equally true in Lucasville, Ohio, in April 1993. At least two of the five men later sentenced to death for their alleged roles in the uprising were within sight of release from prison when the "riot" began. Hasan, the supposed mastermind of the rebellion, was in the SOCF honor block.

The words "a long train of abuses" come from the Declaration of Independence. I draw on that history because the American Revolution is the rebellion about which I know most. I taught students about the American Revolution at Spelman College, a college for African American women in Atlanta, and at Yale University. I tried to ask hard questions such as: Why did some tenant farmers support the patriot cause while others hoped for a British victory? (Answer: It depended on the politics of your landlord. You opposed what the landlord was for, in the hope that if he lost you could obtain ownership of your farm.) Why did city artisans, who were radical Sons of Liberty before 1776, vote in 1787 for a constitution drafted by conservatives like Alexander Hamilton? (Answer: Before and after independence, the artisans were concerned to keep British manufactured goods out of America.) And how did it come about that these advocates of inalienable human rights set up a government that protected slavery? (Answer: Both northerners and southerners expected the population in their own part of the country to grow more rapidly than that of the other section, allowing it to dominate the Congress and resolve the issue of slavery in its own interest.)

In writing about the Lucasville uprising, I have viewed it as a rebellion like the American Revolution. I am encouraged in making the comparison by the following words from the country's leading authority on prison riots, Bert Useem: "[T]he principles underlying collective behavior against authorities appear to be fundamentally the same whether one is examining revolution against monarchies and empires or riots against prison authorities."[2]

So what made prisoners at Lucasville rebel? What were the causes of the uprising?

To answer these questions, we must turn to studies conducted both before the disturbance and after it ended; to deposition and court testimony, especially in a subsequent civil suit by victims of the rebellion; and to the collective memory of the rebels themselves.

The drafters of the Declaration of Independence charged King George III with "a long train of abuses" against their rights. Similarly, prisoners at Lucasville had multiple grievances against Warden Arthur Tate, whom they called "King Arthur."

The Southern Ohio Correctional Facility in Lucasville was opened in September 1972 to replace the old Ohio State Penitentiary in Columbus, where there had been riots in 1968.

According to John Perotti, who was a prisoner at SOCF, "Luke" acquired a reputation as one of the most violent prisons in the country.[3] Prisoner Emanuel "Buddy" Newell, testifying in the trial of a fellow prisoner after the surrender, agreed. When he heard the commotion begin in L block on April 11, he said, he first assumed that it was a "normal fight."

Q. When you say a "normal fight," what are you talking about?
A. You know, just inmates, just some inmates fighting, maybe two or three inmates fighting.
Q. Okay.
A. Officers trying to break it up, like all the time.
Q. Is that uncommon at Lucasville?
A. No.[4]

Perotti says that most of the guard-on-prisoner brutality took place in J block, which housed Administrative Control and Disciplinary Control ("the hole"). In 1983, Perotti continues, 12 guards beat to death Jimmy Haynes, a mentally disturbed African American prisoner. While nurses stood watching, one guard jumped on Haynes's neck while another guard held a nightstick behind it. Two other black prisoners, Lincoln Carter and John Ingram, were alleged to have touched white nurses. They were beaten by guards and found dead in their cells in the hole the following day.[5] No criminal charges were pressed.

A group of prisoners known as the "Lucasville 14" sought to give up their United States citizenship and emigrate to other countries. Three of these prisoners cut off one or more fingers and mailed them to President Carter and other officials to prove that they were serious. The United States refused to allow them to renounce their citizenship.[6]

Some prisoners organized a branch of the Industrial Workers of the World to demand the minimum wage for prison labor, Perotti relates. The courts rejected this demand. Perotti also helped to prepare a 38-page petition to Amnesty International. The petition described instances in which prisoners were chained to cell fixtures, subjected to chemical mace and tear gas, forced to sleep on cell floors, and brutally beaten, all in violation of United Nations Minimum Standards for the Treatment of Prisoners. The petition was confiscated as contraband, and its authors were charged with "unauthorized group activity."

In 1989 Warden Terry Morris asked the Correctional Institution Inspection Committee (CIIC)—a body appointed by the Ohio legislature—to prepare a summary of concerns about SOCF to be used by him in discussions with unit managers and department heads.[7] The CIIC based its response on letters from 427 SOCF prisoners received between August 21, 1987, and November 1, 1989. Many of these— 180, or 42 percent—expressed concerns about personal safety. The CIIC report mentioned the murders of prisoners Tim Meachum in December 1988 and Billy Murphy in January 1989, and the stabbing death of prisoner Dino Wallace.

In more than a hundred subsequent interviews with CIIC staff, prisoners—years before April 1993—*"relayed fears and predictions of a major disturbance unlike any ever seen in Ohio prison history."*

It was alleged that knives have been and can be bought or provided from staff, and that a staff person allegedly provided a gun that is reported to be hidden in the institution (whereabouts unknown). Inmates claimed of staff approaching them with suggestions or offering to make it worthwhile if they would stab another inmate. Certain inmates are reportedly allowed to stash or transport knives.

One victim of a stabbing claimed that he knew it was coming, because of a reported pattern in such matters. His cell was targeted for daily consecutive shake downs reportedly to ensure that he had no weapon when the inmates stabbed him. A security staff person reportedly apologized to him afterwards, explaining that he has a family. Incidents were cited in which staff reportedly were present when verbal death threats were relayed from one or more inmates to another, (in one case when

1.2 Warden Arthur Tate

the inmate also displayed his knives by raising his shirt) yet staff were reportedly silent. In another case, after a stabbing, a staff person reportedly approached the inmate who stabbed the inmate and said, "Why didn't you kill the son of a bitch?"[8]

Another prisoner at SOCF in those days, part–Native American "Little Rock" Reed, describes the events that led to the appointment in 1990 of a new warden, Arthur Tate (Fig. 1.2).[9]

Operation Shakedown was the extreme and unjustified result of a horrible incident in which a mentally unstable prisoner killed a young, beautiful school teacher who worked at the prison assisting prisoners to achieve their high school diplomas. Although the prisoner had a documented history of mental instability including violence against women, the administration carelessly assigned him to work as the teacher's aide, where he would be in a room with her at times alone, with no supervision. The prisoner took her hostage and ultimately cut her throat with a coffee can lid, nearly ripping her head from her shoulders. Many prisoners thought highly of the young teacher, and were outraged at her senseless and brutal death....

Nevertheless, immediately following the incident, the prison was placed on lockdown ["lockdown" means confinement of each prisoner in his cell]. The guards came into each cell block, armed in full riot gear, and systematically ransacked every prison cell while the prisoners could only stand helplessly and watch.... Meanwhile, local citizens banned together in front of the prison demanding that the prisoners be stripped of all privileges, holding placards with such proclamations as "Kill the killers."

SOCF housed both maximum security prisoners and prisoners classified as "close security," a status intermediate between "maximum" and "medium." However, prisoners agree that once Arthur Tate became the warden, the whole complexion of the penitentiary changed for everyone imprisoned there.

One of the Lucasville Five, Keith Lamar, remembers that Tate "immediately scrapped all the programs, supposedly as a way to cut down on inmate traffic. Lines were painted on each side of the hallway floors, and we were ordered to stay within those lines as we walked— military style—to and from the kitchen, gym and work areas."[10]

Chrystof Knecht, another Lucasville prisoner, has similar memories: "Under Tate's regime, SOCF prisoners were told how and when to eat, sleep, talk, walk, educate, bathe and recreate. Privileges were taken away on a regular basis. New rules were enforced daily, disregarded, then re-implemented weeks later." Bill Martin, also a SOCF prisoner, thinks the "most bizarre" rule was the one "requiring prisoners to march to chow, recreation, chapel, work, school, commissary, etc." King Arthur wanted prisoners not only to walk within the lines, "but walk in double-file formations. Prisoners who hated each other were forced to march next to each other. Everybody deeply resented this." According to Martin, there were repeated massive shakedowns of

prisoners' personal property and constant transfers of prisoners from
one part of the facility to another.[11]

SNITCH GAMES

A prisoner who becomes an informant is known behind bars as a
"snitch." In its report to Warden Morris, the CIIC concluded that the
main concern of SOCF administrators should be "snitch games,"

> the common denominator reported to be related in one way or
> another to past or present circumstances of the large majority of
> inmates. They spoke of the relationship between snitch games and
> unit management, violence, gangs, racial tension, drug, gambling,
> sex and extortion rings, job assignments, cell assignments, unit
> moves, lack of personal safety, fear of other inmates and distrust of
> staff.[12]

Yet, according to Keith Lamar and an influential Muslim prisoner,
Taymullah Abdul Hakim, also known as Leroy Elmore, after Warden
Tate's appointment SOCF continued to encourage "snitches": "the
only way you could work where you wanted to work, or cell where
you wanted to cell, was to be in cahoots with the administration. This
served to increase the snitch population exponentially." Taymullah
declares that Tate "promoted informing on guards and prisoners.
Prisoners were fitted with 'wires' (recording instruments) and sent at
guards to entrap them in criminal activities. Flyers were printed up
instituting a 'snitch line' where prisoners and visitors could write to
inform on criminal activities inside Lucasville."[13]

Warden Tate's invitation to snitch was conveyed in a memorandum, a copy of which is before me as I write. It is dated May 31, 1991,
and directed to "All Inmates And Visitors." The memo states in part:

> Due to my concern about violations of laws and rules of this insti-
> tution, I feel it necessary to make myself available for persons
> wishing to pass this information on to this office concerning these

things.... I have established a post office box at Lucasville, Ohio for information which could assist our departmental efforts in eliminating violation of institutional rules and criminal conduct. Your letter will be intercepted by this office and will not be processed through normal institutional mail. Your information will be held in strict confidence.... The address is as follows: Operation Shakedown, P.O. Box 411, Lucasville, Ohio 45648.

Prisoners view snitches much as striking workers perceive scabs, only more so. It should not have come as a surprise that at least eight of the nine prisoners later killed in the uprising were perceived by others as "snitches."

L'ÉTAT C'EST MOI (I Am the State)

What did Warden Tate intend? In a document entitled "Situation at the Southern Ohio Correctional Facility as it led up to the riot," dated July 5, 1993, an anonymous prisoner states that he believes that Tate would have liked to lock down the whole institution permanently "and make it another Marion, Ill. supermax" (a prison in which prisoners are confined in single cells for 23 or more hours a day).

There is evidence for this theory. The most comprehensive of the post-uprising studies, *Southern Ohio Correctional Facility: Disturbance Cause Committee Findings* (sometimes called "the Mohr Report" after its chairperson, Gary Mohr) contains in its appendix a memorandum dated March 22, 1993—20 days before the uprising began. The memo, from Tate to Eric Dahlberg, South Region Director is entitled "Request to Construct a Maximum Security Unit at SOCF." Although Tate speaks of constructing a "maximum security" unit, SOCF was already for the most part a maximum security prison, and his request must be understood to seek supermaximum conditions of confinement. The memo states in part:

Over the past several months I have expressed my concerns relative to the need for a maximum security unit at this facility which is suitable to house those prisoners who are high security risks requiring maximum levels of supervision as well as a physical structure designed to effectively house them.... [I]nmates in the highly assaultive, predatory category requiring maximum security confinement, will continue to increase due to lengths of sentences.

Recognizing that the department was unable to finance the construction of a new supermaximum security prison at that time, Tate asked permission to build a "high security unit" at SOCF.

Whether or not Warden Tate consciously wanted to turn SOCF into a supermax, it is certain that he insisted on absolute obedience. Like Bourbon kings before the French Revolution, he acted as if he believed that "I am the State." Bill Martin offers an example of Tate's mindset.[14]

King Arthur followed Otto Bender's advice of closing all the windows during the summer because SOCF was designed to have a flow-through ventilation system to keep the institution cool. Without any investigation, King Arthur signed Bender's decree which ordered all the windows closed.... My supervisor, Pat Burnett, subsequently went into King Arthur's office and inquired about his "window decree." King Arthur ... had the institution's blueprints on his desk and, as he was gently patting them, he told Burnett, "I have it all right here. The institution was designed with flow-through ventilation. It will keep the institution cooler if the windows are kept closed." Burnett then informed King Arthur that the flow-through ventilation will not work because most of the blowers on the roof are burnt out.... [You would think that King Arthur would have rescinded] his "window decree." But he did not want to appear foolish so we all suffered through a very hot summer.

Similar hard-headedness about the best way to test for tuberculosis would trigger the April 11 uprising.

OVERCROWDING, DOUBLE-CELLING,
AND TRANSFERS

A prison is a good deal like a factory. Prisoners, like workers "on the street," may have some voice in small decisions. But just as workers— even unionized workers—have no say in decisions to close the plant, merge with another company, or move the machinery to Mexico, so prisoners have no input in decisions about a prison's security level, who should be retained or transferred, and how many prisoners the facility will be permitted to house.

Lucasville was designed to house 1,540 prisoners. On April 11, 1993, when the uprising began, the prisoner population was 1,820, with 804 prisoners double-celled. Moreover, 75 percent of the prisoners at the highest security level were double-celled. According to the Mohr Report, "double celling of the inmate population was voiced by a vast majority of both staff and inmates as a cause of the disturbance."[15]

This overcrowding was the result of short-sighted decisions by the Ohio Department of Rehabilitation and Correction concerning classification and transfer. After Warden Tate's appointment late in 1990, SOCF made some progress in reducing overcrowding by transferring prisoners to other institutions, especially to the Mansfield Correctional Institution (ManCI) in north central Ohio. Had SOCF become and remained a single-celled institution—as is recommended by the National Institute of Corrections for maximum security prisons—problems resulting from both double-celling and forced racial integration could have been avoided. But an officer was killed at ManCI, and ManCI was reclassified as a "close" rather than "maximum security" institution. As a result, between June 1992 and April 1993, 293 prisoners were transferred from ManCI to SOCF.[16] They were young and, according to prisoner Keith Lamar, "unruly"; 96 percent of them were classified maximum security.[17]

Meantime, getting out of SOCF became very difficult. The Mohr Report found that between January 1992 and April 1993, when the uprising began, 75 percent of the prisoners recommended by SOCF staff for reduction to medium security (and thus, for eventual transfer out of SOCF) were rejected by the department's Central Office in Columbus "with no reasons provided for the rejection."[18]

George Skatzes recalls his personal experience. While imprisoned at SOCF in 1985 or 1986, he was found guilty of possessing one joint of marijuana and $40, and told that he would have to do five more years at SOCF. At the end of the five years, he met with the Lucasville classification committee. The chair said, "You are eligible to transfer. Where do you want to go?" Since his sister and other relatives live in Marion, Ohio, Skatzes replied: "Marion." But he was turned down by Columbus without explanation.[19]

The inability to transfer created hopelessness among SOCF prisoners. So did the fact that prisoners were permitted only one five-minute telephone call per year, at Christmastime.[20] The prison grievance procedure offered no practical relief. Already in 1989 the CIIC reported that "many inmates will not use the grievance procedure due in large part to reported retaliation by staff." In 1991, after Warden Tate's appointment, prisoners told CIIC investigators that staff "always take the word of staff over inmates," and expressed exasperation and anger that prisoners were not permitted to call other prisoners as witnesses and that appeals were reportedly always denied.[21]

THE TRIGGER: TUBERCULOSIS TESTING BY INJECTION

The event that sparked the uprising, all accounts agree, was Warden Tate's insistence on testing for tuberculosis by injecting under the skin a substance that some Muslims objected to, believing that it contained alcohol. Muslim prisoners tried to tell Tate that their religion, as interpreted by the religious authorities to whom they adhered, forbade this, and asked him to consider TB testing by X-ray or sputum sample.

The Sunni Muslims who told the warden that they would refuse to take the TB test by injection were followers of the Hanafi Math-hab as expounded by the Council of Theologians in Port Elizabeth, South Africa. Ohio prison authorities consulted the Islamic Council of Ohio and the Islamic Center of Greater Toledo as to whether "Islam" forbade the injections. But as the South African center remonstrated:

> The Ohio Department of Rehabilitation [and Correction] was aware of the fact that the Sunni Muslims do not follow the Islamic Council of Ohio nor the Islamic Center of Greater Toledo. This fact is confirmed by Arthur Tate's letter dated 7th April 1993 to Eric Dahlberg, South Region Director. Now when the prison authorities were aware of the religious affiliation and allegiance of the Sunni Muslims, why did they seek advice and direction from those who they know are not acceptable to the Sunni Muslims? Will it be proper for the prison authorities to seek advice from the Roman Catholic Church in matters affecting Anglicans? Will it be proper and reasonable to seek direction from the Anglican Church to ascertain the beliefs of members of the Jehovah's Witnesses or of some other Christian sect? Just as it will be incorrect to do so, so too, is it improper to refer to those who are not acceptable to the Ahlus Sunnah. The prison was fully aware that the Sunnis follow our Council.[22]

On Monday, April 5, 1993, Warden Tate and his staff met with three Muslim prisoners: Hasan, Taymullah Abdul Hakim, also known as Leroy Elmore, and Namir. The following dramatization is based on an article by Taymullah and a "synopsis" by Hasan.[23]

Tate: I am Warden Arthur Tate, Jr. This (pointing to each in turn) is Deputy Warden Roger E. Roddy; Deputy Warden Bill G. Seth; Captain Earl P. Kelly; and Chaplain Warren Lewis.[24] Weren't passes sent out for five of you?

Hasan: Only three of us are able to honor our passes. Cornelius Barnes and Isaac Hughes are in segregation. I am Siddique

Abdullah Hasan, whom you call Carlos Sanders. This (pointing to each) is Taymullah Abdul Hakim, also known as Leroy Elmore; and Namir Abdul Mateen, or James Were.

Tate: My staff has informed me that 159 inmates have refused to take the TB test. The largest group out of this 159 are Muslims. That is why I singled you out to send passes to.

The TB test is a health issue. It is mandatory that all prisoners be tested. There will be no exception or deviation from this rule.

I understand that the Muslims' objections to taking the test are religious, and based on a letter that you received from your leader in Port Elizabeth, South Africa. Your concerns have been put forth to Central Office and they, in turn, have contacted various Muslims from the Ohio area. All the religious leaders stated that there was nothing religiously wrong with Muslim inmates taking the TB test.

Therefore, we will be testing all inmates. I expect the Muslims to cooperate. If I allow the Muslims to deviate from taking the test, then the Aryan Brotherhood and other groups will want to deviate from institutional policies. I cannot tolerate that in my prison.

Sanders, do you have anything to say?

Hasan: I have nothing to say. You have already said what is going to happen and I see no reason to waste my breath.

Tate: This is a meeting. I want to hear what you have to say.

Hasan: This is not a meeting where what we say makes a difference. It is a meeting where you are being a dictator, and have adopted a hardline approach. You are not being sensitive and understanding toward our leadership position on the test.

Tate: Elmore, what do you have to say?

Taymullah: The test is unlawful for us to take. We have no intention of taking it, for we would be guilty of a sin. However, if someone forces us to take the test, we will be absolved of the sin.

Chaplain Lewis (smiling): How much force would have to be applied in order for you to be absolved of the sin?

Taymullah: This is not a joking matter. The bottom line is we are not going to take the test.

Tate: Elmore, what will you do if one of my officers grabs you and tries to give you the test?

Taymullah: I can't say what I will do. You do what you have to do, and we will do what we have to do. If I were to tell you, "If one of your officers puts his hands on me I will physically strike him," I know for a fact that you would put me in the hole before I could even leave this so-called meeting.[25] Again, all I can tell you is that it's not permissible for us to take this test.

Namir: I do not trust the prison officials to test us. You have a reputation for using us as guinea pigs.

Tate: Mr. Roddy, when will you finish testing the inmates that are HIV positive?

Roddy: By Friday, April 9.

Tate: Then we will be ready to start testing you early next week. I hope you will change your minds.

As Hasan puts it, when those present rose to leave, "the vibes were somewhat tense."

On Wednesday, April 7, Hasan sent the warden the following message:

> In spite of what the modernist and westernized Muslims say, the TB substance is unlawful for a Muslim and an infringement on his right.
>
> A person can be tested positive or negative by taking an X-ray test and/or spitting into a cup. Hence, we have no legal objections to this form of testing, and pray to the Most High you and your staff will accommodate us in this form of TB testing.

In closing, I was informed that the above optional policy was instituted at ManC.I. [Mansfield Correctional Institution].

We thank you in advance for your time, consideration and mutual cooperation in being of any assistance to the Muslim body here. We anxiously await your response.[26]

Physicians have confirmed to me that, from a medical point of view, Hasan's was a perfectly reasonable request. Robert L. Cohen, M.D., who has extensive experience in monitoring medical care in prisons, states:

The purpose of screening for tuberculosis in a prison is to identify active cases of tuberculosis, so that these prisoners can be isolated and treated. The PPD, an intradermal injection of killed tuberculosis bacteria, is a screening test. If it is positive, it means that the person was exposed to tuberculosis at some time [in his or her] life. It does not mean that they currently have active tuberculosis. If the PPD test is positive, then a chest X-ray must be obtained to determine if the person has active tuberculosis. If the chest X-ray is normal, they do not have active tuberculosis. If tuberculosis is suspected, based upon a chest X-ray, the person should be isolated, and sputums collected to identify and culture the tuberculosis bacteria, if it is present.

If the PPD test is positive, and the chest X-ray is negative, then the person does not have active tuberculosis. The PPD test can also be falsely negative in persons with pulmonary tuberculosis. This can occur in persons with overwhelming tuberculosis infection, or much more commonly, in persons with severely compromised immune systems, such as that found in patients with advanced AIDS. The PPD test can also be falsely negative if it is improperly placed. All experts in the field agree that improperly placed, and improperly read, PPD tests are common.

For this reason, some experts in the field of correctional health care have argued that the best approach to screening for and identifying causes of tuberculosis among prisoners is accomplished by obtaining chest X-rays. *This is the procedure in Chicago and Los Angeles.*

Many prisoners have voiced the same religious objection to PPD testing in other states, and in these situations [the authorities] have usually agreed to have a chest X-ray. There is no risk to any who live and work in the prison if tuberculosis screening is performed by chest X-ray. In fact, the chest X-ray is a more sensitive and specific test for tuberculosis screening in prison.[27]

Others criticized the warden's decision to lock down the prison, and forcibly inject resistant prisoners in their cells, from the point of view of good prison administration.

SOCF Deputy Warden David See stated in a deposition that he had been on vacation the week before the uprising. When he heard about the plan to lock all prisoners in their cells and perform the TB injections there, See called Warden Tate:

"I told him I didn't think we should go cell to cell down in the inmate's house and do the tests in front of his peers because it gave the inmate no way out.... I felt that we should bring them one at a time up to the infirmary."[28]

During Hasan's trial, See was forbidden to testify about his successful experiences in testing prisoners for TB in the infirmary, rather than in their cells.

Mr. Otto: Deputy Warden See would have testified that in '82 and '83 he ran a series of tuberculosis tests that involved bringing people to the infirmary. It was non-confrontational. Of 120 initial refusals, there were only five people actually thrown down and tested....

[He would also have testified] that two or three days before the riot kicked off, he was on vacation; that he had a telephone conversation ... with Warden Tate, and in that conversation he described that method and suggested that this would be a more peaceful means of resolving the matter.[29]

Warden Tate replied to Hasan in a memorandum dated Thursday, April 8, as follows:

> I believe you realize that I have the utmost respect both for you personally and for your religious beliefs.
>
> Your position relative to TB testing is, however, one that is not rational nor will it be accepted by me. Your options have been explained and I expect full compliance to my orders for *all* SOCF inmates to be tested. There will be *no* deviations to this order.
>
> I trust you, as well as others who feel as you do, will comply with this policy. You are in *no* position to dictate to me how you perceive this should occur. I am certainly hoping that there will be minimal difficulties associated with this process. [30]

ON THE EVE

Narratives of uprisings and rebellions usually have a preliminary chapter with a title like "The Gathering Storm."

In fact both prisoners and guards at Lucasville appear to have sensed at the time that an explosion was coming. As April approached, prisoners were feeling "suffocated and boxed in," Keith Lamar reports. "To say that we were living in a pressure cooker is something of an understatement; it was a madhouse." [31]

On Wednesday, April 7, Major Roger Crabtree, who was chief of security, approached the warden with the information that the facility was "unusually tense." On April 9, Captain Frank Phillips told the warden that "this place isn't right—something is going to happen." [32] A gathering of Muslim prisoners on Saturday, April 10, appears to have turned into a tense discussion of TB testing. According to the Mohr Report, "Sanders, the recognized Muslim leader, and four other Muslim inmates refused to leave the chapel … resulting in the chaplain having to push Sanders out of the way in order for the chaplain to gain access to the hallway." [33]

On Good Friday, April 9, Warden Tate left the facility for the weekend without informing those left in charge there that tension among the Muslim prisoners was high. The warden knew that SOCF would have no supervisor above the rank of lieutenant for the weekend. Lieutenants William May and Wayne Taylor, in charge of the prison during the first and second shifts on April 11, were not even officially advised of the lockdown planned for April 12.[34]

Keith Lamar is convinced that Warden Tate wanted the Lucasville uprising to happen. Reflecting on the April 5 exchange between the warden and the Muslim leaders about TB testing, Lamar asks:

Why didn't Tate just lock Hasan, Taymullah and Namir up? Surely he had probable cause—and isn't it an old military theory that if you "strike the shepherd the sheep will scatter"? Why give them the opportunity not only to see your hand but to plan a counter attack? I'm telling you, Lucasville was a set up. And this whole dialogue between Tate and Hasan (et al.) brings to mind one of my favorite verses in one of Shakespeare's plays. He said:

Oftentimes to win us to our harm
the instruments of darkness tell us truths,
Win us with honest trifles
to betray us in deepest consequence.[35]

Many other prisoners share Lamar's suspicion. They speculate that Warden Tate was hoping for a controllable disturbance that would allow him to ask the state legislature for more money.

April 11 was Easter Sunday. Because of the holiday the second shift was understaffed—in fact, the complement was the lowest it had been for 30 days.[36]

Chapter 2

THE WORST OF THE WORST

THE OHIO DEPARTMENT of Rehabilitation and Correction considers the five men sentenced to death after the Lucasville uprising to be among the "worst of the worst."

During the months following the uprising, a petition and a letter addressed to the governor and members of the Ohio legislature circulated throughout southern Ohio (see Appendix 3). The petition, ultimately signed by more than twenty-six thousand people, was to be returned to "Death Penalty" at a Post Office box in Portsmouth, Ohio. Portsmouth is the capital of Scioto County, in which the Southern Ohio Correctional Facility is located. The letter demanded that the state "USE the Death Penalty!"

In this atmosphere of hatred, how could the Five communicate their side of the story and, in a larger sense, their humanity to their juries or, after trial, to the public?

One means was the "unsworn statement." A defendant, after conviction for a capital offense, is permitted to make a presentation to the jury about why he acted as he did. Although there is no cross-examination, the death penalty hangs over the prisoner's head as he tries to explain himself to a jury that has already found him guilty.

NAMIR

Namir Abdul Mateen, also known as James Were, like most of the Five grew up in very difficult circumstances (Fig. 2.1). He has been found to have an IQ of 69 and thus to be on the borderline of mental retardation. A teacher who attempted to assist him in the Adult Basic Literacy program at the Ohio State Penitentiary testified that, unlike most prisoners there, Namir faced learning difficulties that he could not overcome. [1]

2.1 Namir Abdul Mateen (also known as James Were) during surrender, April 21, 1993

"Prison is my home," Namir said to his jury. "That's where I been living most of my life, from childhood to adult, and it will be my home probably until I die." [2] In 1980, he told them,

> I got out, got off parole, got married to my wife, had two kids, times got hard, couldn't find no job, pressure was too much, no food in the house, hitting it hard, looked over, took my pistol, went out there, got me money so I could feed my kids. [3]

He tried to work, Namir insisted, and he had a job from time to time. Because of his children, Namir tried hard to stay out of trouble after his arrest and conviction for aggravated robbery. He became a Muslim and for a time served as imam, or prayer leader, of Muslim prisoners at SOCF. Namir had only two write-ups in the 10 years prior to 1993. At the time of the uprising he was within four years of going back to the Parole Board. Indeed, he had been approved to leave SOCF and go to close security at Mansfield. However, a prisoner with whom he had had a serious fight in prison was already housed at

Mansfield, so the authorities refused to send him there. Warden Tate had the opportunity to send him to another prison but refused to do it, Namir said. "Now," he told the jury, "I don't believe I will get an opportunity to make up things for my daughter and my son that I strived so hard to try to go home for."[4]

Namir has a good deal in common with certain characters of the Russian novelist Dostoevsky, at once mentally challenged and capable of extraordinary generosity. He has put his life at risk to help a fellow prisoner. Derek Cannon was indicted for being one of the "death squad" that, in the early hours of the uprising, went from cell to cell in L-6 killing supposed snitches. There is reason to believe that Cannon never entered the pod, and Namir, who was in L-6 at the time, knew this and insisted on testifying for him. Cannon protested. He pointed out that the state was seeking the death penalty for Namir, and that if Namir put himself on the stand at Cannon's trial, he might expose himself to damaging cross-examination. Namir testified regardless.[5]

JASON

In his unsworn statement, Jason Robb tried to explain to his jury why he was a member of the Aryan Brotherhood (Fig. 2.2).

Jason began by saying that he was 27 years old and had been born in Orange County, California. When he was eight or nine years old, his family moved to Dayton, Ohio. "It was explained to us kids that it was a job opportunity for my father."[6]

The Robbs lived in a Dayton neighborhood known as "little Kentucky," where young Jason was introduced to hunting rabbits and squirrels. In high school he began experimenting with marijuana, which, he claimed, people grew in their backyards. There was a lake nearby, and young people sneaked into the area at night. "They'd have bonfires. Older guys would sit around and drink with their girlfriends. We'd go swimming, smoke pot." Jason moved on from pot to

2.2 Jason Robb after capital indictment, 1994

beer, and there was a criminal trespassing incident. [7]

Jason's family sent him back to California to live with his grandparents. They were strict. Jason's older brother would take him surfing, but at the grandparents' home things became tense. Jason was returned to Ohio.

At 14 or 15, Jason was drinking heavily and using a variety of hallucinogens. He began to sell PCP to support his habit and that of his girlfriend. He bought a motorcycle and kept it at a friend's house. There was trouble at home.

At age 17, while high on PCP, methaquaaludes, valium, pot, and liquor, "all on top of each other mixed together," Jason shot and killed a man. He pled guilty to manslaughter and received a 7- to 25-year sentence. His attorney told him he would do only three years, but older prisoners explained it would be eight to nine years before Jason even saw the Parole Board. [8]

While Jason was in the detention facility before being transferred to the penitentiary, his mother and sister, who were moving back to California, visited him. He was withdrawing from drugs cold turkey and had the shakes, cramps, vomiting. At the time he couldn't hold a cup of milk without spilling it. It was painful for him that his relatives saw him in that condition.

Jason's father stayed in Ohio for a time to try to help his son. It was the first time he had seen his dad cry. He would not see his father again for approximately eight years. [9]

Jason now began "Prison 101" at the old Ohio State Reformatory in Mansfield. The shower was a giant room with a drain down the center of the floor. One hundred men would shower at the same time, each one a foot from the man next to him. The officers stayed outside the door, and Jason saw his first prison rape toward the back of the shower when it started getting steamy. After that, he stayed toward the front of the shower and usually carried a padlock, which he could buy at the commissary and which he could use to defend himself. [10]

The older cons told Jason that he and the other young prisoners were guppies in a pool of sharks. Jason was five feet five and weighed, at the time, 141 pounds. When he was coming back from the commissary with a fishnet bag over his shoulder, prisoners came up behind him, cut open the bag with a razor, and took his things. Jason fought, got a broken nose and black eyes, but stood his ground. "I learned something there. You don't back down and you don't show fear." [11]

The AB

Enter the Aryan Brotherhood (AB). "I was approached by a group of white guys ... pretty big sized guys." They had their own weight areas, they always ate together, and nobody bothered them.

"After my second fight with a black inmate in the shower area," Jason went on, "three white guys approached me and basically they told me, we like your spunk, you got heart, you won't let these guys run over on top of you, we like that."

He was suspicious. But the ABs explained to him: "Listen, man, you don't have to be by yourself no more.... Be one of us and we'll watch your back."

So Jason agreed to check them out. He found that he always had a spot on the weight bench if he wanted to work out; he always had a place to sit in the chow hall. The AB got him a good job in the prison and urged him to go to high school. "Basically I become a member of this Aryan Brotherhood at that time," he said. [12]

Luke

In 1991 Jason was sent to Lucasville. He had no conduct reports of any kind there—as would later be the case at the Ohio State Penitentiary in Youngstown.

He recalled one early experience in the day room at "Luke." The day room is a common area in a block of cells where prisoners are locked in together for an hour and can watch television. After Jason saw one prisoner chase another around the day room and stab him while officers stood outside and did nothing, he stayed away from there.

Jason became a 24-hour plumber, which was "kind of an honor-type thing" because he was allowed out of his cell at any time of day or night. He had his own toolbox. Later he transferred to spray-painting for Ohio Penal Industries, increasing his state pay from $24 a month to "$40 something."

When the uprising began on April 11, 1993, Jason Robb was 25 years old.

HASAN

Siddique Abdullah Hasan, formerly known as Carlos Sanders, was born on January 4, 1963, in Savannah, Georgia (Fig. 2.3).[13] He was the third of four children, two boys and two girls. Hasan's birth was the most difficult of the four. His mother was in labor for 12 to 15 hours. Two doctors were required to help her bring him into the world, "a world I've had to struggle in since day one."

When Hasan's mother had her first child at age 13, she didn't know whether to be happy or sad. She quit school to raise the baby. When she had her last child, she was 19. She didn't want another child at that time because of problems in her relationship with Hasan's father. "By the time my baby sister was four," Hasan says, "my parents' common-law marriage was dissolved and she was saddled with the obligation and responsibility of having to raise four children alone."

2.3 Siddique Abdullah Hasan (formerly known as Carlos Sanders) during trial, February 14, 1996.
Associated Press Photo/Al Behrman

A Family Without a Father

"My father moved to Jacksonville, Florida, after the separation and did not fulfill his verbal promise to provide financial support," Hasan recalled. His mother followed his father to Florida, seeking the money he had promised. But no money was forthcoming, so she returned to Georgia and filed a claim for child support.

The court ordered Hasan's father to pay her rent, but he refused. "Because she did not wish to see him arrested, she refused to file additional charges or even notify the authorities of his whereabouts.... She accepted menial jobs, as a cook and a housekeeper, in hostile and racist workplaces."

The family lived in a three-bedroom apartment in a low-income housing project. There was no money to hire a babysitter, so Hasan's mother bought a television. "Actually, the responsibility of raising us fell in the lap of my older sister, who is only three and a half years older than myself." Like his mother and maternal grandmother, this sister too gave birth to her first child when she was 13 years old. Hasan was practically left to care for and raise himself. He believes that both he and his brother were profoundly affected by the lack of parental supervision and the absence of a father. "To put it bluntly," Hasan says, he and his brother came "from a broken home and a dysfunctioning family, compounded by not having a male figure in our life to guide us into manhood."

Hasan was five when his father left the home and seven when his mother's mother died. Inevitably, he thinks, he developed an intense bond with his older brother, who became his role model.

Hasan's brother began to socialize with the older guys in the neighborhood. "He adopted their etiquette, thinking pattern, and criminal lifestyle." It usually took some persuasion before Hasan could be convinced to take part in delinquent activities with his brother and his brother's crowd. These consisted "of stealing, truancy from school, and sneaking in movie theaters or the Savannah Civic Center."

Hasan first aimed a gun when he was eight years old. It was aimed at his father.

I vividly recall this older white guy riding his red bike through our neighborhood, an all-black community, when my brother jumped him and seized his bike. Our father, who didn't live with us but was phoned by our mother, came to our house to discipline the perpetrator with an extension cord. The beating administered to my brother was so severe that blisters on his skin developed and burst.

Everyone witnessing the beating was deeply disturbed, including our pet dog, Penny. Penny commenced barking at our father, who instructed us, "You better come and get this dog before I kill it!"

With tears in my eyes I moved inch by inch toward my father's coat, which he had hung on a chair. He always kept his gun in a coat pocket. I grabbed it, pointed it directly at him, and yelled, "If you don't leave my brother alone, I will shoot you! Now get out of my house!"

The brothers ran out of the house. "This marked the beginning of us running away from home to avoid beatings from our father," Hasan recalls. It was also "my first vivid encounter with standing up against injustice."

Trouble with the Law

In June 1973 the Juvenile Court of Chatham County gave temporary custody of Hasan, now 10 years old, to the Department of Family and Children's Services. He was referred to the Georgia Regional Hospital at Savannah. Psychiatric examination and treatment followed. Hasan was found to have average intelligence and no serious mental illness. He was removed from the hospital and placed in a foster home.

According to the paper trail, he continues, "I developed well in my new family setting and structured environment. However, I longed to be with my natural family and frequently ran away back home to be near them. Eventually I was permitted to stay with them." This turned out to be a costly mistake.

By the summer of 1975, Hasan, his brother, and a neighborhood friend of the brother were arrested breaking into a gun store. Hasan was sentenced to four to six months at a Youth Development Center but, after running away repeatedly and getting into fights, ended up serving 18 months.

Approximately six months after his release, Hasan, his brother, and two of the brother's friends were picked up for a robbery. Hasan had not been involved but "accepted the weight instead of telling on my brother." He was tried as an adult, pleaded guilty to the robbery, and was sentenced to a "zip-six," that is, zero to six years. During this incarceration, Hasan twice took part in escape attempts. He was released in 1983.

Hasan reflects on this first long stint in an adult prison:

> I was no longer under the influence of my brother. I was becoming a leader among my peers and the convict body. I filed legal complaints to challenge the injustices and the deprivations of constitutional rights; became involved with the Islamic faith; and started taking a verbal and physical stand for weaker prisoners who were being abused by other prisoners or guards.
>
> Above all, I started striving to find a sense of purpose and structure in my life. While I will agree that prison is depressing and an evil place to be, I must also admit that it's a good place to reflect and do some serious self-reckoning and planning.
>
> However, a noticeable downside for an impressionable person

is, he can easily or gradually adopt the convict code of "survival of the fittest," and, consequently, become a no-nonsense and treacherous person when others violate his space or when push comes to shove. That is what happened to me.

After Hasan's 1983 release, his efforts to "go straight" were unsuccessful:

> Like many others who came through the prison system, I had dreams and goals I wanted to achieve once released from captivity, but the reality was: I had no realistic plans on how to achieve them. Indeed, this was a recipe for trouble. Having very little formal education, no vocational skills, and being an ex-convict were already three strikes against me when my feet hit the street and I commenced pounding the pavement. These unfortunate ingredients, coupled with my impatience, did not mix with the business establishment and, resultingly, the doors of employment and opportunities were all slammed in my face.

> I reluctantly became involved in the drug trade. My baptism into the drug trade came largely because it was a family thing, that is, everyone in my immediate family was selling marijuana. I rationalized my involvement by telling myself, "I am not stealing or forcefully taking anyone's money, but selling weed is my bread-and-butter hustle." Little did I know that such a hustle is usually accompanied with problems, such as people occasionally testing your patience, or resolvedness, when it comes time for them to pay their debts, having to defend your honor and reputation after being played or robbed, being in shootouts or far worse, and so on. Simply put, the "drug game" is a "dog-eat-dog game." And to survive in it, one has to become, figuratively speaking, a dog. That I became.

Hasan lived from day to day, making money by gambling and selling drugs. He carried a gun constantly. He was arrested again after he and a friend stole a car at gunpoint.

Regrettably, I had lost sight of my dreams and goals. Taking another fall—imprisonment—was what caused me to regain focus. By August 1984, I was back in prison—this time in the Ohio prison system—and working toward recapturing my spiritual base, that is, the guidance, stability, and purpose that Islam initially provided me.

Islam

"I was supposed to be a Muslim, but it really hadn't settled on me," Hasan says. In the Ohio prison system, his life started taking a new turn.

He earned his General Equivalency Diploma (GED) and enrolled in college classes. He read college textbooks, the dictionary, and the Koran.

Arriving at SOCF in 1988, he became a part of the Muslim community among prisoners there. By 1991, he had become the imam, the prayer leader.

At the time of the uprising, Hasan was living in the honor block at SOCF and was on the verge of being transferred out of the prison. He had only 10 months to go before meeting with the Parole Board. Questioned by the *Cincinnati Enquirer,* Officer Michael Hensley— a hostage during the uprising—said that he had never known Hasan to be in trouble.[14]

BIG GEORGE

George Skatzes (pronounced "Skates"), now in his late fifties, is the oldest of the Lucasville Five (Fig. 2.4). He is a tall, burly man, as his nickname suggests. In rural Lucasville, he stood out among African Americans and whites from the city because he shared the cultural background of the predominantly white guards. George is "country."

The best portrait of George as a child comes from affidavits by his sister, Jackie Bowers.[15]

George and Jackie had a very hard childhood, she relates. Their parents were divorced when Jackie was two and George was an infant. There were four other children: two girls from their mother's first marriage, and two boys from a second marriage. George says it was a household, not a family. "The way I see it, I was brought into this world, kicked in the ass and left to make my own way as best I could."

The Skatzes home was in perpetual disorder. The children didn't have decent clothes. They

2.4 George Skatzes with Cindy and Shane.
Courtesy of Olan Mills Portrait Studios

never invited friends to their house because they were embarrassed. George and Jackie—so Jackie recalls—never had a hug, or a simple "I love you," or praise for good schoolwork or trying to do chores around the house. George adds, "There were a lot of arguments in our home. I can't even remember a time that all of us sat together at the table to eat a meal."

George remembers himself as a "baseball fanatic" who was never good enough to make the team. Every spring he tried out for Little League but was always put on a farm team, not the "real team." One evening all the other members of the team had parents at the game, but he had no one. He has never been able to shake that sense of aloneness, George says. He has never felt accepted into the mainstream. "The feelings I had that night still haunt me."

The older sisters married, left home, and had families. The older brothers quit school and went to work at an early age. Jackie started babysitting at 13 so she could buy herself some clothes and her first pair of glasses.

George and Jackie would find pop and milk bottles to turn in at the corner grocery. George started junking. "I would walk the alleys, the railroad tracks in search for scrap metal, iron, tin, anything that would bring a penny or so at the junk yard." He hung out at an auto body job and pestered the owner for a job.

He also had a paper route. He took pride in putting the paper in a dry place in bad weather. On Sunday mornings he would always be very quiet. And every Saturday he stuffed papers all night for five dollars a shift.

Jackie and George enjoyed visits with their father. When Jackie was 14 and George was 12, their dad tried to get custody of them. It never happened. Two years later their father died, and George was very much affected. He loved his dad and needed him, Jackie says. George began to stay away from home. Jackie herself left home at 17; if she had taken George with her, she feels, he would not be in prison today.

At school George wanted to play football and put in long hours practicing shot put and discus throwing, but was unable to compete in either sport because of a heart murmur. In eighth grade he was labeled a slow reader.

In his late teens and early adult years, George was in constant trouble with the law. Breaking into parking meters and stealing cars led to time at the Juvenile Diagnostic Center and Boys' Industrial School. He enrolled in tenth grade, "got into it" with a teacher, walked out, and never went back.

Then and later, George gave a great deal of love to those around him. Once he saved five weeks' paychecks from his job at Quaker Oats to buy his mother a refrigerator and freezer. When Jackie's youngest son was killed in a car crash, he helped her through the experience.

Formation

Catholics speak of the experiences that fix the pattern of a person's character as that individual's "formation." George says that he came to know himself in prison. He grew up, he recalls, when he was 22 years old and within prison walls, surrounded by "old solid convicts."

At the time he was always defying prison authorities and being sent to "the hole." In the hole you were fed bread and water, and got a whole meal only every third day, George says. Older men like Poley and Freddie Brock told him, "You can't wear that hole out!"

The convicts who influenced the character of the young George Skatzes were both white and black. Your word is your bond, he learned. He remembers a black man who approached him and said, "I come to you because I know you'll tell me the straight of it."

After this first incarceration as an adult, George was paroled in September 1970. He completed his parole successfully and stayed out for three years. A friend would have gotten him into the carpenters' union and into a job at the mall. He chose a different lifestyle.

In December 1973 he was sent to prison again. Paroled once more in November 1975, George says, "It was my goal never to return to prison!"

Please understand that I stayed out for just shy of seven years without any trouble. I had my life pretty well together. I was married, we had a son, Shane Wesley. In my life I really never had it so good, so together![16]

Conviction for Murder

George's life came apart in the early 1980s. He worked at the local Quaker Oats plant with a man named James Rogers. The two became involved in armed robberies. Several months after George broke off their collaboration, a store owner named Arthur Smith was murdered.

In an eerie prefiguring of the Lucasville trials, Rogers turned state's evidence. In return for immunity from charges related to the murder of Arthur Smith and about 15 armed robberies, together with a favorable letter to the Parole Board, Rogers blamed Skatzes for Smith's murder. Cross-examination brought out the admission that Rogers had perjured himself on at least three previous occasions. Indeed, the following colloquy underlined his unreliability as a witness.

Q. To prevent yourself from being convicted, punished, going to prison, would you lie under oath?

A. I certainly would. I have before.[17]

Additional evidence has come to light suggesting that George was, simply, framed. Danny Stanley was a former associate of George, Rogers, and a woman named Becky Boop. At the time of George's trial, Stanley was serving 10 to 25 years for armed robbery. After Rogers turned state's evidence and George was convicted, Stanley testified at a hearing on George's motion for a new trial that George was not guilty. According to Stanley's sworn testimony:

1. Becky Boop told him that she and Jimmy Rogers were at the Arthur Smith murder and George Skatzes was not.

2. Jimmy Rogers told Stanley just before Skatzes' trial that he "was going to guarantee that George got convicted." Rogers said, Stanley continued, that "what makes it so sweet is—his exact words were—the motherfucker wasn't even there."[18]

Diane Rogers, Jimmy's wife, told investigator Linda Garrett in 1986 that Skatzes was not present at Smith's murder and that "Jimmy Rogers pulled the trigger." Sheila Lile, Arthur Smith's daughter, wrote to George in 1989, "I have never heard or saw any evidence to make me believe George Skatzes murdered my father Arthur Smith."

George was unable to afford a lawyer to handle his appeals. His conviction and sentence to life imprisonment were affirmed by the Ohio Supreme Court.

When the Lucasville uprising began on April 11, 1993, George Skatzes was in his cell, writing to the jurors who had convicted him 10 years before.[19] After the cells in L block were opened by rebelling prisoners, George like many others went out on the recreation yard. Again like many others—including Jason Robb and Keith Lamar— he made the fateful decision to go back into the occupied block.

Why did he do so? For one thing, that was where he celled, and he wanted to safeguard his legal papers. Something else weighed even more heavily, George recalls. His final appeals in the Smith case had been *pro se*. Papers had had to be filed at a time when he was in the hole and unable to do any legal work. Friends among his fellow prisoners assured him that they would make sure his appeal was filed on time even if they had to type every word themselves. On April 11, some of those same friends were inside L block. George was not about to forget their previous act of solidarity. He went back in.

KEITH

George Skatzes likes to say that he and Keith Lamar are a lot alike because they both "came up the hard way." Keith is a tall, sinewy man, nicknamed "the Boxer" (Fig. 2.5).

The Supreme Court of Ohio, in affirming Keith Lamar's conviction and death sentence, summarized the biographical evidence offered in his trial.[20]

Keith grew up in a poor neighborhood where illegal drug activity and violence were common. His aunt, Carolyn Lamar, testified that he lived with a stepfather who would beat him for minor transgressions, such as failing to take out the garbage or touching the stepfather's things.

2.5 Keith Lamar with Angela and Hassan

Although his mother tried to look out for Keith and his siblings, "she wasn't there for them because she was having her own problems." Carolyn testified that Keith and his brothers and sisters were not well fed and lived in a house that was inadequately heated.

While still a teenager, Keith quit school and moved out of the house to live with friends in an apartment. According to Charles See, a social service administrator with experience working with inner-city youth, the apartment was in one of the "most dangerous areas in the city of Cleveland."

Lamar's older brother Nelson testified that their stepfather was physically abusive and interested only in the boys' athletic talent. He beat them when they did not perform well. Nelson also testified that he introduced Keith to drug dealing.

Dr. Jeffrey Smalldon, a clinical psychologist, was the final mitigation witness. He said that Keith "used and sold marijuana when he was fourteen years old" and eventually began abusing alcohol, cocaine, crack, and PCP. According to Smalldon, Keith developed a serious crack cocaine habit that persisted until he went to prison in 1989.

In his own unsworn statement, as coldly summarized by the Supreme Court, Keith told the jurors that he was

> disappointed in their verdict but ... did not hold it against them.
> He also explained that his previous murder conviction resulted
> from a shootout in which he had also been shot. Lamar expressed
> some regret about that incident because the victim he shot "twice
> in the heart" had been a childhood friend. Lamar acknowledged
> that his background had been difficult and added that he had
> instructed his mother not to testify for him because he "didn't
> want her to feel that she had to justify, you know, or apologize for
> doing the best that she could."

Keith has his own view of these facts.[21] He is not at all comfortable about letting drug addiction stand "as the defining impetus behind my downfall." Drugs, he believes, only served to accelerate the inevitable.

> I was born into a social structure that is systematically designed to
> destroy, discourage and otherwise retard one's ambition. As a black

male born into this racist society, I learned very early that I would never amount to anything. This seed of destruction was firmly planted in my mind and cultivated way before it ever occurred to me that cocaine could supply a way out of the hopelessness, gloom and misery in which I was confined.

What the Supreme Court characterizes as "some regret" for killing his childhood friend, Keith expresses as follows: "When I shot and killed Kenyatta, my childhood friend, I simultaneously killed myself as well. I was left to live a death, to live out the remainder of my days remembering this horrible thing I'd done."

When he first came to the penitentiary, he walked around in a daze. He did not want to acknowledge the reality of what he had done. He closed down completely, distancing himself from his family, his friends, "and to a great extent from myself as well." The only thing that saved him and kept him from taking his own life, Keith says, "was the notion given to me after reading the autobiography of Malcolm X that I could redeem myself and make Kenyatta's death mean something by doing something productive with my time and energy."

The first thing Keith did was get a GED and enroll in college. But at the time he was doing more than ten years before he could go to the Parole Board, and Pell grants were available only to those with shorter sentences. He was put out of the college program.

> I then took it upon myself to educate myself, starting with Black history, moving on to the Black revolutions of the 60s and 70s, and then to what I call "true" American history. I studied philosophy, psychology, sociology, theology. As I found myself struggling with the question of God, I joined Islam, which I practiced for two whole years.

After the rebellion Lamar was charged with nine counts of aggravated murder. Writing to Mumia Abu-Jamal and myself, he explained that thereafter he adopted a new name, "feeling I would need a con-

stant reminder of what I needed to be about." His new name is Bomani
Hondo Shakur. *Bomani* is Swahili for "mighty soldier." *Shakur* means
"thankful."[22]

The Thankful Mighty Warrior also made a statement before the
court pronounced sentence.[23] He said in part: "I want the record to
reflect that I stand unbowed and unbroken by what has been allowed
to transpire inside these walls within which I sought justice....
Within the confines of prison I found myself, and I'm not willing to
sacrifice myself or belittle myself or bow down to something that
I don't believe in. I don't believe in what took place in this courtroom."

Chapter 3

WHO KILLED OFFICER VALLANDINGHAM?

THE MUSLIMS WHO BEGAN the Easter uprising at SOCF (see Chronology of the Lucasville Uprising) hoped to take officers hostage for a time, without injuring them, in order to send a message. A few years earlier, five prisoners had overpowered officers, used the telephone to tell the media what was happening, released the officers unharmed, and, so it seemed to many prisoners, for the first time caught the attention of the federal courts and received some real help from outside the walls.[1]

Similarly, some prisoners seem to have believed in 1993 that if there could be just enough disturbance to cause ODRC headquarters in Columbus to intervene, Warden Tate's intransigence about how to conduct the TB tests might be overcome.

Reginald Williams, a Muslim and a prosecution witness against Hasan and Namir, stated under oath that "we were going to basically barricade ourselves in L-6 until we can get someone from Columbus to discuss" the testing method.[2] On cross-examination, he confirmed this explanation:

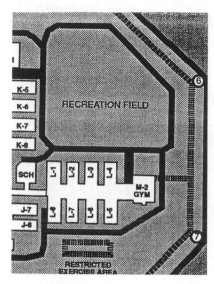

3.1 **Diagram of L block**

Q. You're saying the plan was to have a brief barricade in order to bring attention to the fact that religious beliefs were being trounced upon?
A. Exactly.[3]

Seven years later, at Namir's second trial, Williams repeated his testimony. He said that the Muslims' plan was to occupy a single living area or "pod," L-6 (Fig. 3.1), so as "to get someone from the central office to come down and address our concerns."[4]

Williams also testified that when prisoners first approached the guards in L block, there was no intention to hurt them. He described his own encounter with Officer Michael Stump.

> I put the knife to his neck, and I informed him to give me his keys and he won't get hurt.... He was saying: Don't stab me. And I was telling him: I'm not going to stab you. I just want the keys.[5]

Apparently Officer Stump reached for the knife, which broke, leaving Williams with the handle while Stump had the blade. "So at that time guys just started jumping on him, because he had the knife in his hand."[6]

CHAOS

Whatever the prisoners' initial strategy was, events almost immediately spun out of anyone's control. Too much hostility had accumulated to be channeled according to a master plan. Prisoners not only overpowered the L block guards but beat them. Some of these officers were so badly hurt that prisoners carried them out to the recreation yard and left them there to be retrieved by the authorities.

After the release of the badly injured officers, eight continued to be held as hostages. Keys were seized and used to open the pods (L-1, L-2, and so on), and in each pod prisoners took the place of guards at the consoles that opened the individual cells. Some prisoners then turned their attention to alleged "snitches," and before the day ended, six prisoners—all of them white—had been killed.[7]

The word used by almost every participant to describe these first hours of the uprising is "chaos."

The disturbance erupted just inside the door near the metal detector, where black prisoners returning from recreation on the yard assaulted guards and then moved up the hallway.[8] The first sounds to be heard were scuffling, shouts, blows, cries of "Help!" and "Man down!"

One prisoner remembers the attack on Correctional Officer George Horsley. A prisoner yelled at him, "Where are the keys? Give me the keys." Horsley yelled back that he "didn't have the keys." This witness also recalls prisoners beating on the control panel that opened the cell doors.[9]

Another participant recalls Sergeant Darrell Shepherd screaming excitedly into his radio, "Close the crash gates, close the crash gates. . . . I told you to close the fucking gates." [10]

Many witnesses heard variants of: "This ain't a black and white thing." "We're taking over." "There is an inmate police, kill the snitch."

A prisoner interviewed at an Ohio correctional facility recalls the sounds of breaking glass. He heard people shouting: "They fightin' the police, man. Open up!" "They [prisoners] runnin' out there in the hallway!" He heard the rattling of officers' keys as guards fought with prisoners and went down.

Prisoner Paul Mulryan, in his account of the first moments of the rebellion, writes:

I heard the two rollers [guards] in charge of my block.... Their voices were so full of panic and urgency that I knew something very big was jumping off. "Lock up! Lock up now, damn it!" they yelled. Someone in the cells called out, "The guards are locking themselves in the bathroom! What the hell's happening?" "They've got control of the L-Corridor! There are guys running around with masks on! They've got the keys! They've got the fucking keys!" The rumble from the corridor began to grow like a rolling thunderstorm: muffled screams, the thud of feet running through the halls, glass shattering and showering the floor, and echoes of loud ramming sounds as though heavy steel bars were battering down the walls.

At one point in this pandemonium, there was a very short pause and then the following: "Lucasville is ours! This is not racial, I repeat, not racial. It's us against the administration! We're tired of these people fucking us over. Is everybody with us? Let's hear ya." The prisoners "roared their approval."[11]

NEGOTIATIONS: PHASE ONE

"Once you start to take hostages you can't stop halfway," a prisoner reflects. By overpowering their guards, the prisoners in L block made themselves vulnerable to the most severe reprisals. The authorities began to assemble a force to storm the occupied cell block.

Within L block, the prisoners—like the workers who took over the General Motors plants in Flint, Michigan, in January 1937—began to organize a rudimentary government. An infirmary was set up (Fig. 3.2). A sign posted next to it displayed a red cross and the words: "No Weapons Allowed." Food was commandeered from the individual cells and stored centrally, for equitable distribution later on. Improvised justice was administered to prisoners who stole food from hostage guards or tried to rape other inmates. Prisoners were posted at the entrances to L block and the various pods to provide security.

3.2 Makeshift infirmary in L block

One such prisoner was a recent adherent to the Muslims, Stacey Gordon, who assumed a vaguely defined responsibility for security in L-6.

The three organized groups among the prisoners—the Muslims, the Aryan Brotherhood, and the Black Gangster Disciples—took up residence in different pods: the BGD in L-1, the AB in L-2, and the Muslims in L-6. Representatives of the three groups began to meet to deal with problems arising from the uprising and to find a strategy to end it.

This was in itself a major achievement. It demonstrated a sense of collective purpose that resembled the Attica rebellion of 1971 rather than the Santa Fe disturbance in 1980. During the Santa Fe riot, a few prisoners discussed organizing the riot as a protest against the administration, but they had little influence on the course of a bloodbath during which prisoners killed 33 other prisoners.[12]

In these early days of the SOCF uprising, the prisoners' principal demand was that the authorities provide someone with greater authority than Warden Tate—someone from the FBI or from the

Ohio State Highway Patrol or from the governor's office—with whom they could negotiate.

The prisoners also began to discuss specific demands. Not surprisingly, these demands reflected the grievances that had caused them to rebel. Early in the disturbance the authorities set up recording equipment in the tunnels under L block. Statements and conversations of all kinds were preserved in a collection of "SOCF Critical Incident Communications." Judging from these, major prisoner concerns included getting rid of Warden Tate; inadequate medical care; forced integrated celling; overcrowding; indiscriminate mixing together of prisoners with and without AIDS, TB, and mental illness, and prisoners at different levels of security; and punishment for alleged gang activity on the basis of physical appearance (dreadlocks, tattoos, etc.).

There were general demands, such as "No more oppression," and complaints about "civil rights violations," "violations of due process when a prisoner goes before the R.I.B. [Rules Infraction Board]," "religious freedom violations." There were complaints that the law library was insufficient and that in the prison work program "you sit on your ass all day." Prisoners wanted to grow their hair and beards as long as they desired. They thought the college program was "bullshit, that anyone can pass it." The offensive TB test was mentioned more than once, and one prisoner said that "the TB test could have been done by spitting." There was a demand that the administration be held to its promise to allow one five-minute phone call a year at Christmastime.

Finally, there was already concern about selective prosecution of the alleged leaders of the uprising.

The prisoners' first serious attempt to find a negotiated solution came at midday on Monday, April 12. A white man and an African American—George Skatzes and Cecil Allen—volunteered to go out on the yard and try to talk to the men in the guard towers. Skatzes had a megaphone, Allen a huge white flag. The two men feared for their lives: Skatzes' first words through the megaphone were "Don't try to cut us down."[13]

He went on to say that the prisoners sought an agreement that would preserve the lives of the hostage guards while addressing prisoner demands. As the shouted conversation continued, Skatzes became more and more frustrated by the authorities' apparent lack of interest in finding a solution. In the end he bitterly accused them of "playing games" and exclaimed, before returning to L block, "We're trying to do something positive. All you're doing is fucking us around."[14]

Skatzes' conclusion that the state was stalling was correct. Testifying in Hasan's case, Sergeant Howard Hudson confirmed:

> The basic principle in these situations ... is to buy time, to maintain the dialogue between the authorities and the hostage taker and to buy time....
>
> [T]he basic principle is to maintain a dialogue, to buy time, because the more time that goes on the greater the chances for a peaceful resolution to the situation.[15]

The state further angered the rebelling prisoners by cutting off electricity and water in L block early on the morning of Monday, April 12. There is good reason to believe that the state did this to prevent communication between the men inside L block and the media. Prisoner Anthony Lavelle, who became the key witness for the prosecution, testified:

> **A.** ... I had told Hasan that I think I could maybe hook a PA system up somehow. Him and Cummings said: Well, if you can, go ahead and try.
> **Q.** Okay. And did you do that?
> **A.** Yes....
>
>   I found a—I knew that there were plenty of tape decks in the institution, and I got one of the tape decks and I decided that

I needed speakers. So I … went down to the gym and found almost a six foot tall speaker that was bolted up into the ceiling of the gym. And I decided to take that down and use that.

Q. Okay. Were you able to actually use these materials to put together a PA system?

A. Yes.

Q. And where did you position that system?

A. I put it in L-7. . . .

Q. Which would direct out where?

A. It would direct the speaker out towards the parking lot of S.O.C.F.

Q. Okay. And what kinds of things did you play or broadcast over the PA system?

A. James Bell had made a tape . . . with a list of demands that we wanted at the time. And I started playing the tape over the system that we had rigged up.

And a helicopter started, it was either coming in or had started up and it drowned the tape out. So we stopped playing it and then we tried it again and the same result—a helicopter drowned it out. *And shortly after that, the power was turned off, so that was the end of that.*[16]

Officer Larry Dotson, who was being held hostage at the time, states that the prisoners began demanding to speak to reporter Tim Waller from WBNS-TV, Channel 10 in Columbus, whom they had seen on television offering to negotiate. As a result, Dotson continues, the warden ordered the electricity cut off to L block.[17]

The prisoners conveyed their frustration in messages to the authorities hand-lettered on sheets hung from the L block windows (Figs. 3.3–3.4): "The State Is Not Negotiating," "We Want to Speak to FBI," "This Administration Is Blocking the Press from Speaking to Us." And, later, they wrote: "We're Willing to End This Ordeal!! Must First Talk Face to Face with Our Att. Nick [sic] Schwartz."[18]

Other sheets listed demands like the following:

3.3 Message on bedsheet hung from L block window

3.4 Message on bedsheet hung from L block window

- No retaliation against any inmates.
- No selection of supposed leaders.
- Medical treatment that fits the medical guidelines, many people here are given aspirins for serious medical problems.
- Reasonable pay per work assignments.
- No petty harassment: walking in crowded groups behind yellow lines, forced to wear ill-fitting clothes, haircut standards applied at a whim of officers, arbitrary rules created to appease an officer's anger.
- No more forced integrated celling, also: Less time to be locked in a cell with an inmate you can't get along with.
- Low security inmates should not be in SOCF.
- Ban the use of unsubstantiated criminal records, dismissed RIB [Rules Infraction Board] and court cases, at parole hearing.
- Reduce the overcrowded prison conditions in Ohio.

- Food preparation and variety needs to be seriously upgraded.
- Education programs have been so diluted as to only accommodate those of a lesser security.
- Phone calls to … speak to their families other than 5 minutes at Christmas.
- Mail and visiting are arbitrarily applied.
- Complete overall review of records of all inmates for parole and transfer status.
- Inmates' committee needed for cross review with staff overseers.
- Ideal programming, outside help from statewide groups.
- If peaceful ending, cameras present when officers enter.[19]

The prisoners' attempt to communicate by means of messages written on bed sheets occasioned spokeswoman Tessa Unwin's fateful remarks at a press conference on the morning of Wednesday, April 14. Prisoners inside L block listened on battery-powered radios as reporters aggressively questioned the state's representative.

Unwin was asked about a painted message that a guard would die if the authorities ignored prisoners' demands. She responded: "They've been threatening something like this from the beginning. It's part of the language of negotiation."[20] She also characterized the prisoners' demands as self-serving and petty.[21]

All sources agree that Unwin's comments provoked a strong, hostile reaction among prisoners in L block, who interpreted them as a challenge to their credibility and manhood. Her words violated a cardinal rule of behavior behind bars: they showed a lack of respect. Anthony Lavelle testified that the gist of Unwin's statement was that prisoners' demands were "just a lot of talk." He said that her words "bruised a lot of . . . egos that, you know, we wasn't being taken serious."[22] Hostage Larry Dotson adds that negotiations deteriorated rapidly after Unwin's statement. Blindfolded as he was, he could hear a dramatic increase in verbalized tensions within L block.[23]

There is deep disagreement about what happened next.

WHO KILLED OFFICER VALLANDINGHAM?
THE STATE'S VERSION

The Morning Meeting on April 15

According to prosecutors, the four men later convicted of the aggravated murder of Officer Vallandingham—Robb, Namir, Skatzes, and Hasan—set in motion plans to kill one of the hostage guards. These plans were approved, so the juries were told, by a vote of gang leaders in attendance at a meeting between 8 and 9 a.m. on April 15.

The Ohio Supreme Court endorsed this version of events in a summary of alleged facts preceding its opinion in *State v. Robb.*

> In the early morning April 15 meeting, gang leaders agreed to demand electricity and water and issued a strict timetable for compliance or they would kill a guard. At the end of the meeting, [Stanley] Cummings asked if everybody agreed that "if [they] don't give us these things,... then we gonna kill them one." Both [Rodger] Snodgrass and Lavelle verified that defendant [Robb] voted for an officer to be killed if water and electricity were not turned on in the time demanded.[24]

Four of the Lucasville Five await execution because of this official history. The problem is that it is not true.

There is no evidence of any kind that the leadership meeting "issued a strict timetable for compliance or they would kill a guard." The FBI made a tape of the meeting from a tunnel under L block, and the only show of hands or voice vote mentioned on the tape concerns *negotiating demands* for the day.[25] (The transcript of Tunnel Tape 61 that the state used during the trials is Appendix 1 of this book: the reader can make an independent assessment.) Read in their entirety, Cummings' words envision a process: first, Skatzes was to get back on the phone and express "non-negotiable demands" for the restoration of water and electricity; second, the leaders were to "meet back after we put our non-negotiable things out." Only then would they make a final decision about killing a guard.[26]

As for Anthony Lavelle (Fig. 3.5), he testified about the April 15 meeting not only in the Robb trial, but also in the trials of Namir, Skatzes, and Hasan. In *State v. Were,* the following exchange occurred:

3.5 Anthony Lavelle, April 21, 1993

> Q. When you left the meeting, was that the understanding, that a guard was going to be killed?
>
> A. No. When I left the meeting, the understanding was we was going to meet up later on that afternoon and give them our final ultimatum. I had told them, you know, just pick a time later on this afternoon, we can all come back and take the final vote.[27]

Similarly, at the Skatzes trial, Lavelle testified that there was no need for him to voice at the morning meeting what he claimed was his own opposition to killing a guard, because "we was going to meet back up later on that afternoon" to evaluate the results of negotiations.[28]

Finally, in Hasan's trial, Lavelle for a third time affirmed that at the end of the morning meeting:

> We hadn't made a clear decision. I had told them, you know, that we should decide on what we're going to do but we need to come back after the deadline and make sure that this is what we want to do.

So I said, you know, after we give them a deadline, if they don't meet it we should come back together and decide, you know, whether we want to do this or not.[29]

At another point in *State v. Sanders*, Lavelle stated that at the morning meeting he "suggested after the deadline has been established and it's passed that we meet back up later and decide on whether this is what we want to do, be sure that this is what we want to do." The following exchange ensued:

Q. Okay. Did anybody say: No, we're not going to do that?
A. No.
Q. So then the agreement was that he would not be killed without another meeting?
A. That's correct.... I state, let's meet back up here later at another time, after we give them this 2:30, 3:30, whatever, and we decide, okay, they haven't met our demands, they had until such and such a time, they haven't met it, are we going to do it. Yes or no.
Everybody said that's a good idea.[30]

The alleged decision at the morning meeting on April 15 is the basic evidence connecting Hasan, Namir, Robb, and Skatzes to the murder of Officer Vallandingham.[31] Lavelle's testimony in the four trials, taken as a whole, was that the morning meeting discussed the murder of a guard but did not come to a final decision, and that another meeting was to happen, during the afternoon, before a guard would be killed. The testimony of the prosecution's lead witness thus suggests that when a guard was in fact killed that morning, it was not as a result of the morning meeting but because a group of prisoners, in a rogue action, took the matter into their own hands.

Thus, the participants in the meeting on the morning of April 15 did not decide to kill a guard.

The April 15 Death Squad

As for the events preceding Officer Vallandingham's murder, the Ohio Supreme Court further declared:

> That same morning, inmates from different gangs assembled to kill a guard, and defendant [Robb] told them, "They think that we're bullshitting.... [W]e have to send one up out of here." However, Vallandingham was killed before that specific group acted.[32]

3.6 Stacey Gordon, April 21, 1993

This supplementary statement of supposed facts rests wholly on the uncorroborated testimony of informant Stacey Gordon (Fig. 3.6), mentioned above as a Muslim security officer and a friend of Lavelle's. Not one of the prisoners from different gangs who allegedly "assembled to kill a guard"—besides Gordon himself, these were Robb, Leroy Elmore, Jesse Bocook, Aaron Jefferson, and Wayne Flannigan—supports Gordon's story. Moreover, that story conflicts with conceded facts about what happened between the April 15 morning meeting, which ended just before 9 a.m., and the murder of Officer Vallandingham between 10:30 and 11:00 a.m.

First, Gordon says that he saw Robb negotiating on the phone and that Robb "slammed the phone down a couple of times and called back a couple of times."[33] However, as demonstrated by the state's own timeline, introduced into evidence in *State v. Robb* as Exhibit 289-90, the only prisoner who negotiated between 9 and 11 a.m. on April 15 was George Skatzes. Gordon was apparently under the mistaken impression that Robb was the prisoners' negotiator that morning and, as Gordon testified in *State v. Skatzes*, that "me and George Skatzes, we was securing the phones."[34]

Second, there was not enough time between the end of the morning meeting and the murder of Officer Vallandingham for all the events described in Gordon's account to take place.

- Allow a minimum of 30 minutes after the meeting ended at about 9 a.m. for Robb to conduct and twice break off telephone negotiations.
- Credit Gordon's account that Robb then left L-2 for 20 to 25 minutes to consult with Hasan.[35]
- Add another period of at least 30 minutes for members of the death squad to "suit up" and assemble in L-2.
- Lastly, credit Gordon that the death squad waited between one and two hours before Skatzes informed them that they would not be needed. (In his first reported statement about this period of time, Gordon said it lasted "an hour and a half to two hours.")[36]

Thus if Gordon were to be believed, the death squad remained assembled until well after 11 a.m. before it was told about a murder that had occurred prior to that hour.

Gordon's entire narrative about a death squad is inconsistent with Lavelle's testimony that the morning meeting did not discuss which guard was to be killed, how he would be killed, or when he would be killed, because "the subject was closed until we met back up."[37]

WHO KILLED OFFICER VALLANDINGHAM?
WHAT REALLY HAPPENED

I submit that the actual history of how Officer Vallandingham came to be killed is as follows.[38]

Beginning Monday, April 12, the prisoners conducted intermittent telephone negotiations with the authorities. Their first spokesperson was a Muslim, James Bell. Bell has a speech impediment that made it difficult for him to be understood. During the afternoon of April 13, he was replaced by Skatzes.

Skatzes proposed the release of two hostages in exchange for (1) restoration of water and electricity in the occupied cell block, and (2) an opportunity to air the prisoners' demands on radio and television. He said that he was seeking a negotiated solution so that no guards would be killed. "I'd like to see those officers get out of here," Skatzes said on April 14, and David Burchett, who was negotiating for the state, replied, "I know that you'd like to see them get out of here, because you care about them too. I know you do. So, you and I can work through this." Skatzes argued that the officers' safety depended on being able to see what was going on around them; hence that restoration of electricity was in the interest of both the state and the prisoners. He asked Burchett, "Do you realize what [it] is to keep people from going off on one another and to keep peace in here and … to keep these people from going at them guards?" Responding to Burchett's concern about competition among reporters who wished to talk to the inmates, Skatzes said, "We're not worrying about hurt feelings, because somebody didn't get to be first. We're worried about lives in here."[39]

Late in the evening of April 14, after five laborious hours of negotiation, Skatzes and Burchett agreed on the release of two guards in exchange for radio and television broadcasts. The day ended for the exhausted spokesmen like an episode of *The Waltons*.

Skatzes: All right, Dave.

Burchett: All right. Thanks, George.

Skatzes: All right. Say a prayer for us.

Burchett: I sure will.

Skatzes: God bless you.

Burchett: You too.

At Skatzes' trial, the prosecutor, Daniel Hogan, conceded that Skatzes and Burchett ended April 14 "on the verge" of the release of two hostages and in "elevated spirits."[40]

But when prisoner representatives met the next morning between 8 and 9 a.m., they pointed out that Skatzes had dropped one of their key demands: restoration of water and electricity. Skatzes was alone in advocating the agreement he had negotiated the previous evening.[41] The meeting ended with a decision that Skatzes should get back on the negotiation phone and demand water and electricity.

In the meantime Anthony Lavelle, leader of the Black Gangster Disciples (BGD), had decided for himself that a guard must be killed. Lavelle told other prisoners that the Muslims and Aryan Brothers were too soft, and that he and his BGD colleagues would do what had to be done.

Accordingly, Lavelle began to recruit a death squad of his own to kill a guard. Three prisoners who were BGD members in April 1993 have stated under oath that on April 14, the day before Officer Vallandingham was murdered, Lavelle tried to enlist them in his plan to kill a guard. Brian Eskridge states that he was beaten for refusing:

> Lavelle told me that the Disciples were going to "take care of business" and he wanted me to participate, but I didn't. Lavelle had me held by other inmates because I didn't handle business. The inmates beat me because I had violated the order to take care of business—kill a guard.

Wayne Flannigan declares:

> I heard Lavelle tell Aaron Jefferson (AJ), "I've got some business for you to take care of." From my experience in prison and with Lavelle and the BGD, I knew what Lavelle meant—he told AJ to kill a guard.

And Aaron Jefferson affirms:

The first inmate to suggest killing a guard was Lavelle.... Lavelle wanted to order me to kill a guard.... I was one of the BGD who beat up Brian Eskridge. Lavelle ordered that Eskridge be beaten because he refused to participate in killing a guard.[42]

Lavelle eventually found two other prisoners who were willing to do as he directed. Next he persuaded his friend Stacey Gordon, who was in charge of security in L-6, where Officer Vallandingham was being held, to let the BGD death squad proceed. During the uprising Sean Davis slept in pod L-1, which was controlled by the BGD. Davis woke up at about 7 a.m. on April 15 and heard Lavelle tell Gordon that "he was going to take care of that business." Gordon responded, "[Y]ou go ahead, take care of it;... I will come clean it up afterward."[43]

When the leadership meeting ended at about 9 a.m. that morning, Skatzes returned to the telephone as instructed. He stated that he could not negotiate further until the inmates had water and electricity.[44] He predicted that an officer would be killed if the water and electricity were not turned back on. When prison negotiator Dirk Prise said that there was a possibility of injury because of damage to the electrical system, Skatzes responded that he knew what would happen if the electricity was *not* turned on. A fragmentary recording catches Skatzes' warning: "I stress to you,... if you turn this on, you, you think you might electrocute somebody.... If you don't turn it on, it's a guaranteed murder."[45]

Meanwhile Lavelle, carrying a weight bar and accompanied by two masked colleagues, went from L-1 to L-6 and told all but a few persons inside L-6 to leave the pod.

Prisoner Tyree Parker testified that on the morning of April 15 he had occasion to go to the door of L-6. He could see a clock as he did so. It was 10:00 a.m. or 10:05 at the latest. At the door to L-6, he met Lavelle and two other prisoners, "covered up or masked up from head to toe."[46]

Willie Johnson, another prisoner, testified in both the Robb and Were trials. He said that during the riot he celled in L-1. Around 9 a.m. on April 15 he heard Anthony Lavelle tell Johnny Long and one other prisoner that he (Lavelle) had told George (Skatzes) to tell the authorities to turn on the water and electricity by a certain time "or I'm going to send one of these honkies up out of here." He added, according to Johnson, "[T]he Muslims, they playing peacekeepers and they think that we ain't serious." Lavelle then told Long to "put on your mask," and Lavelle, Long, and the other man, who was already masked, left the pod. Lavelle was carrying a weight bar.[47]

Later the three men returned to L-1, Johnson continued. Lavelle "was like in a frenzy and he was slamming the pipe down, saying, see how they like me now, see if they think we bullshitting now. The Muslims just playing games, they ain't serious."[48]

Prisoner Eddie Moss testified that on the morning of April 15, he saw Anthony Lavelle, carrying a pipe and accompanied by two masked men, knock on the L-6 door and go into L-6. Soon after, Reggie Williams, Sherman Sims, Sterling Barnes, and Eric Girdy came out. After a few minutes, Reggie Williams said, "[T]hey should be finished," and he and the others who had earlier exited L-6 went back in. At about the same time, Lavelle and his two masked associates came out.[49]

About noon that day, as Moss was collecting water in the gym, Lavelle tried to recruit him to the BGD. Lavelle said, "We took care [of] our business.... I ain't gonna tell you, you hear about it on the radio." Lavelle went on to say, Moss reported, "Them Muslims and them Aryan Brotherhood, they want to protect these damn polices."[50]

Sterling "Death Row" Barnes likewise testified that on the morning of April 15 he saw Anthony Lavelle and two masked men come from the direction of L-1, go into L-6, and return in the direction of L-1.[51]

What makes these witness statements so persuasive is that they come from members of a variety of prison groups. Greg Durkin, a member of the Aryan Brotherhood, recalled under oath that he sat next to George Skatzes when Skatzes was on the phone with negotiators on the morning of April 15. Lavelle came in and handed George a note written on the back of a kite. George read the message out loud: "The hard-liners are taking over." Then:

> I saw Lavelle come out of L-1 with two masked inmates. They went into L-6. After Lavelle entered L-6, the Muslim inmates came out. . . . I went back to the hallway and saw Lavelle and the two masked inmates come out of L-6. Lavelle was laughing. He later said that he had taken care of business. . . . Lavelle had been mad about what the prison spokeswoman told the media about not taking the inmates seriously, and he said that showed her that he wasn't joking.[52]

Similarly, the late Roy "Buster" Donald, an unaffiliated African American, executed an affidavit stating:

> **10.** On April 15, 1993, from inside L3 I saw Anthony Lavelle and two masked inmates enter L6. Several inmates exited shortly thereafter, including Sherman Simms, Reggie Williams, Eric Girdy, and Inmate Barnes. . . . I asked Girdy what was going on and he said Lavelle and his boys put everyone out of the block.
> **11.** ... Shortly after, Lavelle and the two masked men rushed out of L6 in the direction of L1.
> **12.** Stacey Gordon next entered L6. He was in there a short time and then motioned for Kenneth Law to come inside the block. Moments later, Law, Simms, and two masked inmates drug a body wrapped in sheets out of L6 towards the gym. . . .
> **14.** Later that night, Lavelle was in L3 looking for clothes. I asked him what was going on. Lavelle told me that Gordon had given him the okay to kill a guard and that he took care of his business.[53]

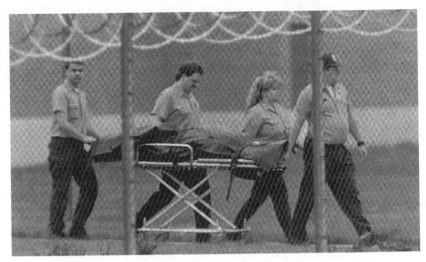

3.7 Body of Officer Robert Vallandingham being carried from the prison, April 15, 1993.
Associated Press Photo/Mark Duncan

Officer Vallandingham was killed before 11 a.m. According to the Critical Incident Communications, Skatzes was still on the telephone at 10:50 a.m., "talking about last night['s] deal." At 10:53 a.m., a "background voice said something about a dead body." Just after 11 a.m., an anguished Skatzes was heard telling Prise that he was "wasting valuable time." [54]

The murder of a correctional officer transformed the situation (Fig. 3.7). As Skatzes had warned his colleagues, the public reacted to the murder of one officer as it had not reacted (and would not react) to the killing of several prisoners. The prosecutor would later tell the jury at Hasan's trial that "there can be no doubt in your mind that the most important event in this riot was the killing of Bob Vallandingham."[55]

All of those who had come forward or would come forward as negotiators and spokesmen, whatever their individual roles had been, henceforth would have large targets on their backs. They were all perceived by the public to be cop killers, and the state would be merciless.

Chapter 4

SETTLEMENT OF A SIEGE

NEGOTIATIONS: PHASE TWO

DURING THE AFTERNOON of April 15, negotiators Skatzes and Prise resurrected the idea that the prisoners would release two hostages in exchange for access to the media. As dusk fell, Skatzes took Officer Darrold Clark out on the yard, released him, and made a radio address heard by prisoners all over Ohio. The next day, as part of the same arrangement, Muslim Stanley Cummings spoke on television after releasing Officer Anthony Demons. Demons, an African American, appeared in Muslim garb and presented himself as a convert to Islam.

In his address on the yard, speaking both to the prisoners behind him in L block and to radio listeners across Ohio, Skatzes set forth several of the prisoners' demands, including replacement of "King Arthur." He also said:[1]

> We hope there is no more violence, we hope there are no more unnecessary murders. We as a convict body send our condolences to Bobby's family. I can't pronounce his last name so I'll have to use his first. But that is something that had to happen. A lot of us didn't want it but that's, I'm sorry. That's all I can say.

And:

> I do have one more thing. A man asked me to do him a personal favor. He asked me to bring a note out here to his people. I wasn't permitted to bring a note. That's fine. I will say [Officer] Jeff Ratcliff sent his love to his momma and his papa and his people and he said that he is in there hanging in there strong. He was with [Officer] Clark all the time, he is doing good and I hope that we will have him out of here soon, too.[2]

As Skatzes spoke, prisoners listening on the radio applauded thunderously. When he returned to L block, however, he met a mixed reception. He recalls walking between two lines of prisoners holding lighted candles, almost like a returning hero. But other feelings soon surfaced. Officer Jeff Ratcliff was said to have Aryan Brotherhood tattoos and was disliked by many black prisoners. Jason Robb, although himself a member of the AB, told Skatzes that some of the men felt that he had paid more attention to Vallandingham and Ratcliff than to the prisoners' demands. The upshot was that Robb replaced Skatzes as a negotiator and spokesman.

Like the prisoners, the state had been pursuing two strategies simultaneously. While going through the motions of negotiating, the authorities continued to plan for an assault on L block (Fig. 4.1).

After the officer's death, the authorities did not immediately abandon the idea of assaulting L block. On Monday, April 19, when federal forces stormed the Branch Davidian compound in Waco, Texas, individuals at the SOCF command center are said to have commented approvingly. But this was never the dominant view among the state representatives seeking to end the standoff. As if chastened by the death of Officer Vallandingham, the state began negotiations in earnest to end the uprising.

Prison negotiator Dirk Prise proposed to Anthony Lavelle and George Skatzes, in separate telephone conversations, that the prisoners choose a leadership committee to meet with a committee of state

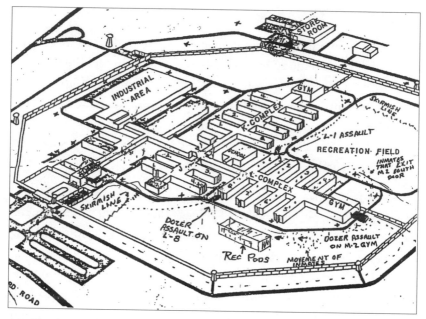

4.1 Plan for assault on L block

negotiators at a table in the yard.[3] Accordingly, the prisoners desig-
nated a negotiating team: Hasan representing the Muslims, Robb the
Aryan Brotherhood, and Lavelle (whose role in killing Officer
Vallandingham was suspected but not known for sure by other prisoners) the BGD.

The prisoners also firmed up and articulated more clearly their list
of demands (see Appendix 2). After receiving the prisoners'
demands, the state proposed a settlement agreement. This became
the instrument for ending the uprising. The subjects covered by the
so-called 21-point agreement closely followed the list of prisoners'
demands, with one critical difference: on the majority of points,
where the prisoners demanded *action* to address a problem, the state
promised to *consider* the problem or to make *efforts* to correct the
matter. The following is the text of the 21-point agreement:

1. SOCF is committed to following all administrative rules of the
Ohio Department of Rehabilitation and Correction.

2. Administrative discipline and criminal proceedings will be fairly and impartially administered without bias against individuals or groups.

3. All injured parties will receive prompt and complete medical care and follow-up.

4. The surrender will be witnessed by religious leaders and news media.

5. The Unit Management system will be reviewed with attempts to improve in areas requiring changes.

6. SOCF will contact the Federal Court for a review of the White v. Morris consent decree which requires integrated celling.

7. All close security inmates have already been transferred (on K-side) from SOCF. L-side close inmates will be evaluated.

8. Procedures will be implemented to thoroughly review inmate files pertaining to early release matters and changes will be made where warranted.

9. Over 600 inmates have already been transferred from SOCF, greatly reducing population numbers.

10. Current policies regarding inappropriate supervision will be rigidly enforced.

11. Medical staffing levels will be reviewed to ensure compliance with ACA [American Correctional Association] standards for medical care.

12. Attempts will be made to expedite current plans to install a new phone system.

13. We will work to evaluate and improve work and programmatic opportunities.

14. There will be no retaliatory actions taken toward any inmate or groups of inmates or their property.

15. A complete review of all SOCF mail and visiting policies will be undertaken.

16. Transfers from SOCF are coordinated through the Bureau of Classification. Efforts will be increased to ensure prompt transfers of those inmates who meet eligibility requirements.

17. Efforts will be undertaken to upgrade the channels of communication between employees and inmates involving "quality of life" issues.

18. The current commissary pricing system will be reviewed.

19. We will consult the Ohio Department of Health regarding any future tuberculosis testing.

20. The Federal Bureau of Investigation will monitor processing and ensure that civil rights will be upheld.

21. The Ohio Department of Rehabilitation and Correction will consider on a case by case basis inter-state transfer for any inmate, if there is reasonable basis to believe that the Department is unable to provide a secure environment for that inmate. Any inmate denied a transfer, the Federal Bureau of Prisons will review their case.

The copy of the agreement proffered to the prisoners was signed by "Arthur Tate, Jr., Warden" and had signature lines for three "inmate negotiators."

As the prospect of signing a specific document became more tangible, prisoners asked for a lawyer to assist them. The authorities recruited Niki Z. Schwartz. This part of the story is perhaps best told in Attorney Schwartz's own words, taken from his testimony as a mitigation witness in the trial of Jason Robb.[4]

Schwartz is a native of Ohio and a graduate of Ohio State University law school. On the stand, he was asked if he had experience in prison condition litigation. He answered that in 1969 he was appointed by the federal court in Toledo to represent prisoners at Marion, Ohio, in a class action. This litigation lasted until 1991. In 1978 the Council for Human Dignity asked him to file a law suit on behalf of the prisoners at the Ohio State Reformatory in Mansfield, seeking to close that institution "on the ground that it was unfit for human habitation." That case also terminated in 1991 with closure of the old Mansfield reformatory and its replacement by a new facility.[5]

On Sunday, April 18, Greg Trout, chief legal counsel for the

Department of Rehabilitation and Correction, telephoned Schwartz at his home in Cleveland and asked if he would represent the prisoners in L block. Schwartz said yes and was soon on his way to Lucasville in a Highway Patrol plane.

When he arrived, Schwartz was told that the department had already prepared an agreement in response to the inmates' demands, and that he would not be permitted to try to improve the agreement. Schwartz said that as long as he could make that limitation clear to the prisoners, he would accept it. He pointed out that once the department had the hostages back, the state would be free to repudiate the 21-point agreement on the ground that it was negotiated under duress. Did the authorities intend to honor the agreement? he asked. Yes, he was assured.[6]

Then there was a two-day delay. The state wished the prisoners to release three of the remaining five guards held hostage as a "show of good faith" before the prisoners would be allowed to meet with Schwartz. The prisoners refused. On Tuesday morning, April 20, the state withdrew this precondition, and negotiations proceeded to a successful conclusion.[7]

On Wednesday, April 21, between 3:56 and 11:20 p.m., 407 prisoners surrendered in groups of 20 and the five remaining hostages were released. Schwartz testified that it was, to his knowledge, "the only time a major prison riot has been resolved voluntarily."[8]

In the broad sweep of late twentieth-century penal history in the United States, Attica, Santa Fe, and Lucasville stand for contrasting paradigms. At the maximum security prison in Attica, New York, in 1971, armed forces of the state stormed the occupied recreation yard, killing 29 prisoners and 10 hostages. The facility in Santa Fe, New Mexico, witnessed a comparable bloodbath in 1980, except that there 33 prisoners were murdered by other prisoners. The Lucasville uprising was, tragically, not free of fatalities. But the fatalities were fewer, and the end of the uprising more peaceful, than at either Attica or Santa Fe. As they walked out of L block on the evening of April 21, unkempt and exhausted, the spokesmen and negotiators for the prisoners in rebellion could feel that they had averted a far greater catastrophe.

FROM PEACEMAKERS TO CAPITAL DEFENDANTS

What was the actual role in the rebellion of the spokesmen and nego-tiators who were later found guilty of the aggravated murder of Officer Vallandingham? Why would prisoners whose intent was to assault or kill correctional officers instead go to considerable trouble to ensure that three injured officers—Harold Fraley, John Kemper, and Robert Schroeder—were placed outside L block so that they could be retrieved by the authorities? Why would a murderer call attention to himself by going out on the yard to release a hostage, as Skatzes did on April 15 and Muslim Stanley Cummings did the next day? Why did a series of individual prisoners pick up the telephone to negotiate for the prisoners in L block and give their names, rather than seeking to hide themselves in the anonymous mass of over four hundred prisoners in rebellion?

At their trials, the attorney who represented the prisoner negotia-tors stated under oath that on the basis of what he had experienced, they deserved the title "peacemakers." There is considerable evi-dence that, each in his own way, the men subsequently convicted of the aggravated murder of Officer Vallandingham had sought to save lives during the eleven days.

Skatzes

George Skatzes volunteered to go out on the yard as a spokesman on April 12 and 15 and was the prisoners' principal telephone negotia-tor until after the death of Officer Vallandingham. He responded to requests for protection from officers held hostage. A number of pris-oners and hostage officers credited him with saving their lives.

The first person whose life Skatzes helped to save was Correc-tional Officer Harold Fraley. After the takeover, prosecution witness

Rodger Snodgrass testified, he saw Skatzes screaming to correctional officers on the other side of the gates that there was a correctional officer in L block who needed to be evacuated. Skatzes was saying: "He's hurt. He needs help. We need to get him out of here before he dies.... I am goin' to take him to the back of L-8 and I will put him there and you all better come and get him." Snodgrass saw Skatzes pick the man up and take him to the stairwell at the back of L-8.[9] State personnel retrieved Correctional Officer Fraley from the stairwell at 4:45 p.m.[10]

Prisoner Dwayne Johnson described the efforts he and Skatzes made to save the lives of other officers on the first night of the uprising. Johnson, Skatzes and other prisoners wrapped officers Kemper and Schroeder in sheets and arranged for them to be carried out to the yard, where they could be picked up. Johnson said Skatzes stayed until the last guard was released from the makeshift infirmary in the L-3 day room. This involved some personal risk because, as Johnson testified, Skatzes had to go behind the backs of other persons active in the rebellion to get the injured officers out.[11]

Skatzes did what he could to ensure the safety and well-being of the guards who remained in L block as hostages. Hostage and prosecution witness Officer Darrold Clark testified that, while under the control of Muslims in L-6, he asked Skatzes to get him out. Skatzes left, came back, said, "You are going into my block," and took Clark to L-2.[12] Clark testified that when he could not sleep he asked for George, who got a mattress and lay down between the hostage and the door—that is, between Clark and anyone who might come to harm him.[13]

When Skatzes heard that Officer Ratcliff had been beaten by prisoners, he came and got the guard and took him to L-2 as well.[14] Skatzes removed the blindfold and some tape from Ratcliff's eyes and then used water, cotton balls, and towels to clean away a red substance that was burning Ratcliff's eyes.[15] "[I]f he wouldn't have come and got me, I probably wouldn't be here," Ratcliff testified. "I would probably be dead."[16]

Negotiation tapes reveal that Skatzes made rounds to be sure that the hostage officers were safe, delivered food and water, gave medication to Officers Buffington and Dotson, and even offered Dotson his own blood pressure medication.[17]

Skatzes also saved prisoners' lives. Tim Williams, a black prisoner who testified for the prosecution, said that he was accused of being involved in a plot to kill Skatzes and a leader of the Muslims. When Williams was confronted by the Muslim leader, Skatzes said he did not think Williams had anything to do with it. Williams later told a Highway Patrol investigator that Skatzes helped to save his life.[18] When prosecution witness Robert Brookover went to Skatzes and asked whether he was going to be killed, Skatzes assured him that he would not let that happen. Brookover testified: "[N]o matter what George feels about me today, I believe in my heart he saved my life."[19]

Namir

Namir conceded in his unsworn statement to the jury that he was in L-6 at the time of Officer Vallandingham's murder. It appears that he did not interfere with the murder because, as he said in his statement, he was under the impression that Lavelle had obtained permission from Namir's Muslim superiors and that Namir could do nothing to stop it.[20]

Later on April 15, Namir talked to senior Muslims such as Hasan and Cummings, who told him that they had *not* approved the killing of a guard. Namir thereupon went to L-1 and knocked Lavelle to the floor, saying, according to the testimony of eyewitness Willie Johnson, "Lavelle, you going to be held responsibility [sic] for what you caused and you're not strong enough to make a decision like that. You ain't nothing but a little punk."[21]

Like Willie Johnson, Eddie Moss testified that on April 15 he saw Namir knock Lavelle to the floor in L-1. Namir said, according to Moss, "[Y]ou gonna be responsible for that call you just made, man. You didn't have no business making that call, man."[22]

At some point after Namir knocked Lavelle to the floor for killing an officer without a decision by the leadership of the uprising, Leroy Elmore (Taymullah Abdul Hakim) came to L-1 distributing food and water. He encountered Lavelle, in an agitated state, on the landing between the upper and lower ranges. Elmore was not permitted to testify at trial about what was said. He has declared:

13. On the evening of Wednesday, April 14, 1993, I slept in L-7. I normally got up between 10 and 11 o'clock in the morning to pass out food. When I got up, I heard a rumor that a body had been dropped off in the yard.

14. I went straight to what we called the sub-kitchen, which was a little hallway between the gymnasium and the recreation yard. That was where we prepared the food.

15. After I prepared the food, I pushed my cart to L-1 to begin to distribute it.

16. As soon as I entered the block, Anthony Lavelle approached me. He said he needed to talk to me. He seemed to be very frightened.

17. Mr. Lavelle and I spoke to each other on the landing of the stairs in L-1.

18. Other prisoners nearby when Mr. Lavelle approached me were Willie Johnson also known as "Chilly Willie," Eddie Moss, and Johnny Long.

19. Mr. Lavelle informed me that Mr. Were had knocked him down. He said he feared that Mr. Were was going to do him bodily harm.

20. I said, "What did you do?" Mr. Lavelle answered, "I had the guard killed."

21. I said, "Why?" Mr. Lavelle stated that when the female on the radio took the inmates' threats lightly, he felt compelled to teach her a lesson. I understood this to refer to a statement that a Ms. Tess[a] Unwin made on the radio on the morning of April 14.[23]

If indeed Namir had been responsible for killing Officer Vallandingham, how would one explain his anger at Lavelle?

Hasan

During the early hours of the rebellion, Hasan caused prisoners viewed as snitches to be locked in L-6 for their own safety, and on several occasions protected correctional officers from hostile prisoners.

Prosecution witness Miles Hogan testified that on April 11 two prisoners approached him with the apparent intent to rape and kill him. Believing he was close to death, Hogan started calling out Hasan's name. Hasan appeared, took Hogan to L-6, and locked him up. Hogan was asked:

> Q. Now the man seated right over here at the table, the far end of the table [Hasan], is there any doubt in your mind that that person saved your life?
> A. There's not a doubt in my mind.[24]

Prosecution witness Reginald Williams testified that when he saw another Muslim beating a prisoner named Andre Stockton on the head with a hammer, "I told him that he was out of line because Hasan didn't instruct us to do this."[25] Stockton, although badly injured, survived.

Prosecution witness Rodger Snodgrass testified about an alleged plot by prisoners Tim Williams, Doc Creager, Anthony Copeland, and "Buddy" Newell to kill George Skatzes and take control of the rebellion. Hasan directed that Creager, Copeland, and Newell should be locked up in L-6. Snodgrass testified that he wanted to kill them but didn't, because "they were kept locked up, protected by Hasan."[26]

Further, Hasan played no apparent role in the meeting on the morning of April 15 that allegedly decided to kill Officer Vallandingham. According to the state's own transcript, Hasan did not chair the meeting. In fact, not a single word was attributed to him. At Namir's second trial, Howard Hudson was asked to identify the prisoners whose voices could be heard on Tunnel Tape 61. He named Namir, Anthony Lavelle, Jason Robb, Stanley Cummings,

Rodger Snodgrass, George Skatzes, Cecil Allen, and Johnny Roper. "I believe that's everybody that is on Tunnel Tape Number 61," Hudson said.[27] He did not name Hasan.

Attorney Schwartz testified that during the negotiations leading to a settlement, Hasan expressed concern about the safety of the hostage officers.

> All three of the inmate negotiators expressed concern about the safety of the guards, indicated that in fact they had been sufficiently concerned that they gave up some of their own food to give to the guards since very little food was put out, they had worked hard to try to protect the hostages.[28]

In Schwartz's words, Hasan and the others "were peacemakers, as far as I was concerned, during the time that I was there."[29]

Robb

Schwartz described Jason Robb as the lead negotiator for the prisoners in the process that eventually produced a peaceful settlement.[30]

During the two days after Schwartz arrived but before he met with the prisoners face to face, the prisoner negotiator with whom he spoke on the telephone was Robb.[31] When a face-to-face meeting finally came about, "Jason was the one who did most of the talking." Robb's major concerns were "safety, safety of the inmates and the hostages, safety from retaliation by guards or law enforcement officials, inmate safety from each other, hostage safety from other inmates."[32]

It was Jason in particular, Schwartz went on, who

> explained this to me, that there were a lot of factions in the L block and a lot of inmates armed to the teeth with a lot of vendettas against each other and … he was fearful that if there was just everybody come out all at once, that inmates would use this last opportunity to take out their grudges against each other and inmates would be killing each other.[33]

Likewise the prisoner negotiators were concerned, and "again, this was articulated by Jason," that the prisoners be provided with flashlights because the hallway in L block was very dark and "there was a risk of inmate against inmate violence."[34]

Overall, Attorney Schwartz testified, he felt that Jason Robb

> deserved a large part of the credit for the peaceful resolution of ... the riot, that he had stuck his neck out as a lead negotiator, that he had been selfless in negotiating, not trying to ... feather his own nest, but generally negotiated on behalf of the inmates, that his concerns were legitimate ones, that he was reasonable in ... accepting things that couldn't be changed or negotiated or wouldn't be agreed to by the other side.[35]

In Schwartz's view, Colonel Thomas Rice on the side of the authorities and Jason Robb on the prisoners' side deserved the most credit for the successful settlement.[36]

TARGETING THE LEADERS OR OPEN-MINDED INVESTIGATION?

After the actions described above, how did Skatzes, Namir, Hasan, and Robb come to be charged with killing Officer Vallandingham? It seems that their guilt was assumed from the start of the investigation. If so, it could only have been because the state knew they had been spokesmen and negotiators and the state wanted to target the leaders of the rebellion.

The state denied that it targeted the visible spokesmen and negotiators. Howard Hudson, lead investigator for the Ohio State Highway Patrol, testified in Namir's second trial:

> Q. When you began your search for the evidence and the interviewing of the witnesses who were present, did you have a particular suspect or suspects in mind?

A. No, sir.

Q. At that time?

A. No, sir.

Q. What was the goal of the interview process? Was it to get evidence against a certain individual or a group of individuals or how did it go, Lieutenant?

A. No, sir. No, sir. The goal was to find the truth, as in any other investigation. We did not go in this with any preconceived ideas.[37]

If indeed this was Hudson's approach, he apparently failed to communicate it to the patrolmen he supervised. Immediately after the surrender, prosecutors and investigators from the Highway Patrol identified the spokesmen and negotiators for the prisoner body during the uprising, including Hasan, Robb, and Skatzes, as the individuals whose guilt they were trying to establish.

Johnny Fryman had almost been killed by other prisoners at the beginning of the rebellion and had no reason to wish to protect its leaders. He reports that in May 1993 he was taken to the SOCF infirmary. Two members of the Highway Patrol questioned him as follows:

> They made it clear that they wanted the leaders. They wanted to prosecute Hasan, George Skatzes, Lavelle, Jason Robb, and another Muslim whose name I don't remember. They had not yet begun their investigation but they knew they wanted those leaders. I joked with them and said, "You basically don't care what I say as long as it's against these guys." They said, "Yeah, that's it."[38]

Emanuel "Buddy" Newell, who likewise had been assaulted by prisoners and also was placed in the SOCF infirmary, implicates Hudson himself. This witness reports that on one occasion shortly after the surrender, Lieutenant Root, Sergeant Howard Hudson, Trooper Randy McGough, and Trooper Cary Sayers talked with him.

These officers said, "We want Skatzes. We want Lavelle. We want Hasan." They also said, "We know they were leaders. We want to burn their ass. We want to put them in the electric chair for murdering Officer Vallandingham."[39]

Chapter 5

THE CRIMINAL INJUSTICE SYSTEM: BEFORE TRIAL

THE PROCESS OF BRINGING A defendant to trial on a capital charge and then sentencing him (or her) to death goes through several stages:

- *Indictment.* A grand jury is convened and the prosecutor presents evidence intended to persuade the grand jury to issue an indictment (criminal charges). The defendant does not participate, either personally or through counsel.
- *Appointment of counsel.* If the defendant is unable to afford a lawyer, the court appoints one.
- *Arraignment.* After indictment, the defendant is brought into court, the indictment is read, and the defendant pleads.
- *Discovery.* Before trial, the prosecutor is required to turn over to the defendant's counsel any "exculpatory" material in the state's possession. Counsel for an indigent defendant ordinarily asks the court for funds to hire an investigator, experts, and a mitigation specialist (see below), as well as to interview potential witnesses and obtain additional documents from the state. Defense counsel in a capital case may later be found to have provided "ineffective

assistance" if counsel fails to make every reasonable effort independently and reliably to reconstruct events and circumstances—
first, those connected with a killing, and, second, those related to
the defendant's life history.

- *Motions practice.* Especially in capital cases, rights are recognized
  and implemented only to the extent that they are asserted. If a
  lawyer fails—even accidentally—to comply with a procedural
  requirement, the corresponding substantive right may be forever
  lost. Defense counsel must specifically bring to the attention of
  judge and prosecutor any circumstance that is believed to affect
  the client's position.

- *Trial: jury selection.* The jury is selected in a process known as "voir
  dire." Each side has a certain number of "peremptory" challenges
  that cause a juror to be dismissed automatically. Each side may
  also ask the judge to excuse additional potential jurors "for cause"
  if an individual's values and experience substantially impair his or
  her ability to function as an impartial juror. In capital cases, any
  potential juror opposed to the death penalty under all circumstances will almost certainly be dismissed.

- *Trial: guilt phase.* The prosecution seeks to persuade the jury that
  the defendant should be found guilty. Guilt must be established
  "beyond a reasonable doubt," and the jury must be unanimous.

- *Trial: sentencing phase.* If the defendant is found guilty in a capital
  case, a separate hearing is held before the same jury to determine
  whether the defendant should receive the death penalty. A defendant determined to be mentally retarded cannot be executed. Under
  Ohio law, the jury recommends the penalty and the judge makes
  the final decision. In order to recommend the death penalty, the
  jury must find that the "aggravating circumstances" defined by
  law—such as being a prisoner or being involved in a course of
  conduct involving more than one murder—outweigh the "mitigating circumstances." The jury's recommendation of death must
  be unanimous, and the refusal of one juror to recommend death
  requires that the defendant be sentenced to life imprisonment.

NUCLEAR WEAPONS AND SLINGSHOTS

When he testified in *State v. Robb* early in 1995, Attorney Schwartz was asked whether the State of Ohio had adhered to the 21-point agreement that ended the Lucasville uprising. Yes and no, he answered. Asked to explain, Schwartz stated that some points had been observed commendably; in other cases the results were mixed; and "one of them has been an absolute disaster."

Q. Which one is that?
A. The assurance in Point Two that criminal prosecutions would be fair.
Q. In what way do you feel that that has not been complied with?
A. I regard the prosecutions as being unfair primarily because of the resources, the allocation of resources to the two sides. To use a metaphor, the prosecution has been provided with nuclear weaponry and the defense has been provided with slingshots.

Schwartz went on to explain that special prosecutors were being paid $60 to $100 "an unlimited hour" for prosecuting these cases. "They have the total investigatory resources of the Highway Patrol with thousands of witness statements all computerized for rapid correlation and retrieval." By contrast, defendants had been appointed counsel who were paid $30 an hour out of court, $40 an hour in court, with a ceiling of $750 for noncapital cases. "Motions by defense attorneys for the appointment of an investigator have been denied and/or granted with absurdly low funding limits that really preclude any meaningful investigation by and on behalf of the defendants."

It was, he concluded, "a very unequal kind of battle."[1]

Lawyers for Robb and Hasan requested access to the voluminous discovery information in computer format used by the prosecution. The request was denied.[2]

Above the entrance to the Juvenile and Probate Courthouse of Scioto County, Ohio—the county in which Lucasville and the Southern Ohio Correctional Facility are located—appear the words,

"Tell Me Your Cause And Ye Shall Have Right."[3] It hasn't worked out that way for the Lucasville Five. The experiences of these capital defendants as they made their way through the criminal justice system are better conveyed by Dante's *Inferno*. Over the gates of Hell are inscribed the words, "Abandon hope, all ye who enter here," Dante wrote. Once within the gates, the traveler descends from one circle of Hell to the next, each more frightening than the one before.

INTERFERENCE WITH ACCESS TO COUNSEL

In his testimony on behalf of Jason Robb, Schwartz described how counsel was—and was not—appointed to represent the prisoners who had occupied L block.

When he returned to Cleveland after the surrender, Schwartz testified, he realized that the more than four hundred prisoners who had just surrendered were likely to be questioned by the authorities and "wouldn't ... necessarily know their rights" to remain silent or to have a lawyer present during interrogation. He arranged for lawyers acting on his behalf

> to go into the prison and briefly counsel each inmate as to what his rights were ... until they could get individual representation that would permit each of them to make an independent decision about whether and to what extent to cooperate and make a deal.[4]

The Office of the Ohio Public Defender supplied most of the attorneys who, at Schwartz's request, conducted the initial interviews with potential defendants to make sure that they knew their rights. Dale Baich recalls that the lawyers left Columbus at 6 a.m. on April 23. Part of the surrender agreement was a provision that prisoners who feared mistreatment by officers at SOCF would immediately be transferred to Mansfield. Accordingly, about eight lawyers went to Mansfield, and the remainder to Lucasville. Each attorney interviewed 20 prisoners. The attorneys spoke to the prisoners through the cell doors. They made it clear that they did not want to talk about the events of the riot, but only to make sure that everyone knew his rights. Each prisoner was given a two-page questionnaire. After returning to Columbus, the attorneys called prisoners' relatives to report on these visits.[5]

Attempting to ensure an effective defense for each of the more than four hundred men he represented, Schwartz encountered persistent obstruction from Special Prosecutor Mark Piepmeier. It began soon after the uprising ended, Schwartz complained to the chief justice of the Ohio Supreme Court. Schwartz had made arrangements "to convene a meeting of top State officials to consider ways and means of providing the inmates with the effective assistance of counsel." That meeting, he wrote, was aborted by the newly appointed special prosecutor. According to Schwartz, "The Prosecutor told me that he did not want the inmates to have counsel prior to indictment *because then they would not incriminate themselves*" (emphasis added).[6]

Getting the Public Defender off the Case

Organizations calling for the death penalty had been formed in Scioto County and were circulating petitions and form letters to "request and demand" that "the Death Penalty in the State of Ohio be applied as the passers intended it to be.... USE the Death Penalty!" (see Appendix 3).

In December 1993, the Public Defender filed a motion in the Court of Common Pleas for Scioto County seeking notice of the date and time the grand jury would convene so as to examine the array for possible bias. Subsequently, after the prosecutor attached the names of the potential grand jurors to a pleading, the Public Defender filed a motion to dismiss the grand jury for bias. The Public Defender named four persons who appeared to have signed the petitions, and four others whose last names suggested that they might be relatives of signers. The Public Defender also moved that grand jury proceedings be recorded.[7]

The Public Defender's pleadings were signed by assistant public defenders, describing themselves as "counsel for grand jury targets": that is, for prisoners involved in the uprising who might be indicted by the grand jury.

In response to the Public Defender's motion for notice, the prosecutor asserted that "before law enforcement could begin the interview process," the Public Defender "got into the prisons, solicited all 407 inmates involved as clients, and advised them not to speak to the police." The prosecution asked the court not only to deny the motion, but also to find that the Public Defender had "gratuitously intervened in a criminal investigation and ... made a nuisance of himself," thereby violating Rule 11 of the Ohio Rules of Civil Procedure.[8]

In later pleadings, the prosecution contended that the Public Defender was "attempting to keep its hands involved in as many cases as possible." The state's implicit theory was that the Lucasville prisoners could only be represented one by one and that any attempt to act on their behalf as a class was impermissible. No prisoner had yet been arrested, charged, or indicted, the prosecution argued. The Public Defender's clients included potential defendants, potential victims, and potential witnesses, "whose interests clearly conflict with each other.... The same firm cannot represent both sides in a lawsuit." The court should find a violation of Rule 11, and the Public Defender "should be removed from all representation of inmates involved in the S.O.C.F. riot."[9]

The Office of the Public Defender, according to Attorney Baich, recognized that it could not represent individual defendants after they were indicted. But like Attorney Schwartz, the attorneys for the Public Defender believed that all potential Lucasville defendants had certain common interests prior to indictment: to know their rights, to obtain effective counsel for their individual cases, and not to be indicted by biased grand jurors.

The prosecutor's memorandum in opposition to the Public Defender's motion for notice was filed on December 13, 1993, and mailed to the Public Defender that same day. Four days later, on December 17, *without giving the Public Defender the customary opportunity to respond*, the Scioto County court denied the motion for notice and found a violation of Rule 11.

The executive director of the Office of the Ohio Public Defender was replaced soon after. Since then, the Office of the Public Defender has only occasionally represented individual Lucasville defendants, and only in their appeals.

Henceforth publicly funded prosecutors would seek to convict Lucasville defendants while the publicly funded entity dedicated to advocacy for indigent defendants was sidelined. The state would proceed against such Lucasville defendants as it chose to indict, utilizing a single computerized data bank created by the Ohio State Highway Patrol and the prosecutors. The prisoners would no longer be represented collectively or be able to draw on the pooled legal resources of any network or organization.

Allowing Representation Only by Lawyers Who Would Plea Bargain

While the Public Defender was being ejected from Lucasville proceedings, Attorney Schwartz, with the assistance of the Ohio State Bar Association and the Ohio Association of Criminal Defense Lawyers, set about recruiting attorneys from the private bar to provide individual counsel to as many prisoners as possible. Training seminars were conducted. The expectation was that volunteer counsel would form attorney-client relationships with particular prisoners and "would be available ... to accept appointment for inmates who got indicted." But when indictments began to issue and there were motions for the appointment of the volunteer attorneys who had been recruited and trained, "the prosecutor filed objections to the appointment of the lawyers that we had recruited, and instead, a variety of Southern Ohio lawyers were appointed."[10]

According to Schwartz, "the Special Prosecutor, who had not wanted the inmates to have counsel at all, then pressured the OSBA [Ohio State Bar Association] to give assignment priority to those inmates who had indicated that they would cooperate with the prosecution if they had counsel." Schwartz wrote to Chief Justice Tom

Moyer that the special prosecutor induced Chief Judge Everett Burton of the Scioto County Common Pleas Court to tell volunteer attorneys "that if they cooperated by arranging a plea, they would be appointed to represent their client, but would not be appointed if they did not so cooperate." In connection with arraignments in February 1994, retired Judge Thomas Mitchell—later to preside over the trials of Jason Robb and George Skatzes—declared that no public defenders or volunteer attorneys would be appointed.[11]

Schwartz summarized the situation for Chief Justice Moyer as follows:

> 1. The Prosecutor, who has spent the better part of a year with a huge budget and the entire investigative resources of the Highway Patrol preparing his cases, does not want to face the highly qualified and dedicated volunteers who have attended training programs, have developed ongoing attorney-client relationships, and have acquired relevant knowledge.
> 2. The Prosecutor and the Court are manipulating the visiting judges you have assigned to preclude the most effective possible assistance of counsel.
> 3. The strenuous and laudable efforts of the Ohio State Bar Association, the Ohio Association of Criminal Defense Lawyers, and the State Public Defender Commission (to assure quality representation for indigent and despised prisoners in the highest tradition of our profession) are being thwarted.[12]

Schwartz's letter to the chief justice resulted in the appointment of some of the volunteer attorneys. But the state's interference with access to counsel continued.

Obstructing Appointment of Effective Counsel for Hasan and Namir

Attorney Niki Schwartz, and Attorney Richard Kerger of Toledo (appointed and then dismissed by the court as counsel for Hasan), have prepared detailed statements about Hasan's frustrated efforts to obtain effective counsel.[13] Hasan's habeas petition concludes, citing the record: "the overall magnitude of petitioner's case put great financial and personal strain on his appointed attorneys.... As a result from the time of Hasan's indictment until his trial, petitioner had three different sets of attorneys."[14]

The essence of this sorry story is as follows:

1. Schwartz and the public interest groups assisting him recruited "extremely competent counsel" to represent Hasan, including Kerger. The prosecutor objected to their appointment.

2. The trial court appointed the requested counsel over the prosecutor's objections but denied their motion for timely appointment of an adequately compensated investigator. Early in 1994 the court authorized $700. Ten weeks before trial, the judge authorized $25,000.

3. The lawyers were also told that there would be no "interim billings" for them: "they would have to wait until the conclusion of the case before being paid." Kerger's co-counsel was obliged to withdraw.

4. After his co-counsel withdrew, Kerger requested a continuance so that the new co-counsel (when appointed) could be brought up to speed and enabled to provide competent defense. The judge refused and, Kerger believes, determined to remove him. Kerger believes that he was removed "because he had been too aggressive in his attempt to defend his client."

5. The new lead lawyer assigned to the case resigned four months before trial because of financial stress. After a month and a half of looking, the judge appointed a lawyer who came into the case less than two months before trial. The judge denied a request for a continuance by this lawyer, who stated throughout the trial that he was not adequately prepared.

6. Hasan's two appointed lawyers feuded throughout the trial, sometimes in the presence of the jury.

7. Not until after Hasan had been convicted did his lawyers begin to prepare what would be presented to the jury in mitigation.

8. New counsel appointed to handle Hasan's appeals was utterly incompetent and ultimately had to be replaced by the Ohio Supreme Court.

When one recalls that Hasan was targeted by the prosecution as the ringleader of the rebellion, the difficulties he experienced in finding effective counsel are especially appalling.

All of the Lucasville Five had problems obtaining effective counsel with whom they could communicate. Early in 2002, the Ohio Supreme Court reversed Namir's conviction and sentence on the ground that the trial court had failed to hold a mental competency hearing despite abundant evidence that such a hearing was needed. Namir's case went back to the Hamilton County Court of Common Pleas for a new trial. Here is what happened then.

First, Judge Fred Cartolano, who had presided over Hasan's trial, was appointed to be the judge at the new trial for Namir. At Hasan's trial, Judge Cartolano had already heard much negative testimony about Namir that Namir himself, not being the defendant or even present in the courtroom, had had no opportunity to rebut.[15]

Second, Judge Cartolano appointed as defense counsel two courthouse regulars, *one of whom was married to a county prosecutor while the other had been counsel for a prosecution witness in Namir's first trial.* Namir filed a *pro se* motion asking for new counsel. I filed a friend of the court brief on behalf of the American Civil Liberties Union, supporting Namir's demand and naming the counsel he desired (the lawyer who had successfully handled the direct appeal of his first conviction). Embarrassed, the two appointed lawyers withdrew, and Namir obtained the lawyer of his choice, who vigorously—but unsuccessfully—represented him at his second trial.

CHOOSING A HOSTILE VENUE

Apart from who represented the Lucasville defendants, it mattered a great deal *where* they were tried. Hasan and Namir were both tried in Hamilton County, Ohio, which includes the city of Cincinnati.

All of the Lucasville Five were indicted in Scioto County, location of the prison. Hasan's attorneys objected that the number of local residents who worked at SOCF made a fair trial impossible. (They might also have argued that not a single African American lives in Lucasville.)[16] The case was moved to Columbus, the state capital, in central Ohio.

Then the judge assigned to try the case removed himself and was replaced by Judge Cartolano, from Hamilton County, who moved the case to Cincinnati. Attorney Kerger comments that the special prosecutors came from Hamilton County, and Judge Cartolano had himself been a Hamilton County prosecutor.

But this only begins to convey what it meant to try African American "riot leaders" in the city of Cincinnati.

Cincinnati is the death penalty capital of Ohio. As of April 2003, Hamilton County had 7.3 percent of Ohio's population but accounted for almost a quarter of the men on Ohio's Death Row (47 of 208). The Supreme Court of Ohio has rebuked Hamilton County prosecutors for prosecutorial misconduct in 14 death penalty cases over a 12-year period.[17]

Professor James Liebman of Columbia University has published a massive study of serious reversible error in capital cases. In testimony before the Criminal Justice Committee of the Ohio House of Representatives in June 2002, Professor Liebman stated that "Hamilton County (Cincinnati) has the seventh highest death-sentencing rate in the nation among relatively populous counties. Hamilton County has twice the death-sentencing rate of Cuyahoga County (Cleveland) and the state as a whole, and nearly three times the death-sentencing rate of Franklin County (Columbus)."[18]

It is not just a question of Hamilton County's lust for the death penalty; it is also a question of race. Sixty percent of the men on Death Row who were tried in Hamilton County are black. For at least 175 years the city of Cincinnati has been notorious for its racism.[19] In recent years, the killing of young black men by Cincinnati police officers prompted a Justice Department investigation; members of the African American community in Cincinnati asked performing artists and organizations seeking conference sites to boycott the city until further notice.

Attorney Kerger gives an example of how racism disadvantages black defendants in Cincinnati.

> [T]he jury pool was stacked against Hasan by the jury coordinator. When defense counsel noticed that three-fourths of the minority jurors were in the second half of the panel, a statistically unlikely event, a hearing was held. The jury coordinator explained that he, a white male, passed out written questionnaires to the jurors who would be selected to appear in court. The order in which they were to be called was the order in which they returned their questionnaires. That is to say, the ones who completed their questionnaires first went to the top of the list. He also said that he would review the questionnaires and if, in his opinion, there were any errors or incompletions, the questionnaires were returned for proper completion. This method effectively vested discretion in the jury coordinator to select Hasan's jury.[20]

Although 20 percent of the population of Hamilton County is African American, there was only one African American on Hasan's jury.

THE SEARCH FOR SNITCHES

Nowadays, public opinion in the United States is aware that DNA evidence has proven the innocence of many prisoners on Death Row.

But not all murder cases involve physical evidence that can be tested for DNA. There was no physical evidence in any of the prosecutions pursued by the State of Ohio after the Lucasville uprising. Lead investigator Howard Hudson testified that "there was no physical evidence ... linking any suspect to any weapon or any suspect to any victim."[21] The prosecutor in Hasan's case conceded in his opening statement that

> there was very little usable evidence.... [W]e're not going to bring in fingerprints. We don't have any. We're not going to bring in footprints. We don't have any. We're not going to bring you blood samples. There isn't any that we were able to match.[22]

So what evidence *did* the state have? Essentially, the statements of prisoner witnesses. More particularly, the statements of prisoner witnesses who stood to benefit from turning state's evidence (Figs. 5.1–5.4).

For a moment in recent years, a panel of the federal Court of Appeals for the Tenth Circuit suggested that testimony obtained by prosecutors in exchange for "something of value" violates the law. A deluge of amicus briefs from prosecutors around the country persuaded the circuit court *en banc* to reverse the panel decision.[23] So it remains a reality that, as in the Lucasville trials, prosecutors are in a position not to indict, to drop or reduce charges, to cause new sentences to run concurrently with older ones, and to write letters to the Parole Board, all in bargained-for exchange for testimony that will help them to obtain convictions.

In investigating the Lucasville uprising, the State of Ohio played upon prisoners' fears to secure and shape their "cooperation." Agents of the state threatened prisoners with the death penalty if they failed to cooperate. Derek Cannon stated under oath:

> After the inmate takeover, a state investigator named Howard Hudson, who worked for the Ohio State Highway Patrol,

5.1 Prisoner informant Robert Brookover   5.2 Prisoner informant Kenneth Law

approached me and asked if I knew George Skatzes. When I told him I knew George, he asked me to tell him about George's involvement in the takeover.

I told investigator Hudson that I did not see George hurt anyone during the inmate takeover.

Investigator Hudson then threatened me and said that, if I did not cooperate with the prosecution and testify against George Skatzes, they would find a way to charge me with murder. I was frightened by this threat.[24]

Hiawatha Frezzell likewise affirmed in a notarized affidavit:

I was approached by Trooper Long to act as a witness for the State of Ohio. Trooper Long informed me that if I did not testify, he would see that I was charged with a murder or murders from the incident known as the Lucasville riot and that these charges would carry the death penalty.[25]

David "Doc" Lomache, one of the prosecution witnesses against

5.3 Prisoner informant Rodger Snodgrass   5.4 Prisoner informant Tim Williams

several of the Five, wrote to prosecutor Daniel Hogan: "You want me to beg, I'll beg. You want me to crawl, I'll crawl."[26]

When the desired effect had been obtained, the investigators offered protection and security in exchange for the frightened prisoner's testimony. The following is a garden variety example of the Lucasville investigation process.

The man being interviewed celled in L-6, where six prisoners were murdered on April 11 and Officer Vallandingham was killed on April 15. These excerpts from the transcript of his interview with two patrolmen show how the state persuaded him to talk in return for vague promises of a letter to the Parole Board, lesser charges, a lesser sentence, and protection from other prisoners.

The prisoner was questioned by Ohio State Highway Patrol troopers James Brink and David Shepard.[27]

Q. [Brink]. I'm seeing who is going to be truthful with me and who I'm going to try and remain in prison for a long time. Okay.

A. But you know I was going to the Parole Board today?

Q. I knew you were having some parole difficulties.... I know you got a chance to go home. I'm going to try to keep that chance, okay? Like I said, the prosecutors are coming here today. I will sit down with the prosecutors today and discuss what [you have] to discuss.

Q. [Shepard]. What do you want us to tell them? ...

A. I, I don't know. I could say that I could clear a lot of shit up if they guarantee me a parole.

Q. Okay, how much can you clear up for us?

A. I can clear up everything.

Q. What's everything? W[h]et my appetite. Give me something to take to them....

A. If I get a written, if I get a written statement saying that I'm guaranteed a no conditional parole, I clear up everything.

Q. Okay. Understand that we don't have anything to do with the Parole Board except to say with a letter [that you have] cooperated with us in a very serious matter. I can guarantee that. I can guarantee that right now. Okay?

A. I'm saying I go to the Parole Board today.

Q. You'll still go. I'm not going to stop that. Okay? Now we may stop your release, okay? ...

A. I believe that I'm going to get some time behind this.

Q. Okay, would that be acceptable?

Q [Shepard]. What's the least you want out of this? ... What's the least that would be acceptable to you?

A. Pheew!! Parole.

Q [Shepard]. Now that's the most.... If you didn't get a parole.

Q. I'm here to help you.... You have some great information. You cleared up a lot of stuff for us. Okay? And I don't believe that deeds should go unpaid. But there is the one little problem with [naming one of the murdered prisoners]. That has to be straightened out. Okay? See what I'm saying? And that's something that I will discuss with the prosecutors today. You know I need to know what I can take to the prosecutors....

Q [Shepard]. See we got this sliding scale. If you'd said, "I ain't saying nothing." (Inaudible.) We go to (inaudible)—we're doing something like Aggravated Murder.... But now, look, you've talked to us.... Are we going to go to the prosecutor and say, "Hey, think we ought to fry this guy". I can tell you that right now—no. Okay? But we want to know what's in line with you. Do we walk in and say, "Look he was forced to do it". What do we say, murder? Okay. Without any spec[ification]s. Concurrent ... with whatever he's got right now and if the Parole Board paroles him out, we're done. Is that what I go to them and say? I mean that sounds like a pretty decent deal to me. Okay. But I'm not here to make deals but I will ... go to bat, says "Look, he's told us all this information. Good information...."

A. Pheew! I'd like to go home, I done been here 12 years, I'm tired. I want to go home.

Q. ... What can you clear up for me that I can go tell the prosecutors about that we don't already know? I've got to have something....

Q [Shepard]. You know what they're going to say though? They're going to say, "What can you tell us about Vallandingham?" They say that every single time. "What can this guy tell us about Vallandingham?" ...

A. I ain't going to have to testify or nothing like that in court or nothing.

Q. That might be part of the deal. That may be part of the prosecutor's things.

A. I'm saying how am I going to testify and be in the same camp with these guys.

Q [Shepard]. Well, you won't.

Q. You won't.

A. Why won't I?

Q. Where do you want to go? This is stuff that I have to tell them. "Hey, he'll testify if we can guarantee his protection. He'll testify if we can work something out about [the murdered prisoner] with him." ... And then of course they'll come back with their counter offer. You know how it goes. Okay. You know when attorneys sit down and talk, you know how it goes back and forth. But I have to know what you need for your testimony.

A. You, uh, talk to the prosecutor and try to work out something. I'll probably have some more for you.

Q. Well, I need to tell them what more might be.

A. I, I have some more for you. I had, I have some further.

Q. I need to w[h]et them a little bit. The more I w[h]et them, the more they're willing to deal.

A. I have something for you. I'm ready to go home. I think you know what I'm saying.

Q. Are you going to give me Vallandingham?

A. Yep.

Q. Honest to God, straight up.

A. I'm going to give you Vallandingham. Yep....

Q. No specifics. I just want to know how you know.

Q [Shepard]. Cause they're going to say, "How is he going to give us Vallandingham?"

A. I was there. I seen it.

Q. The murder?

A. Yeah.

Q. Okay, let's end it right there. Okay. And I will take that to them. Okay?

Today this prisoner is at the Ohio State Penitentiary, the supermax. He testified falsely against Namir. He believes that his testimony was coerced.

Prisoners induced in this manner to turn state's evidence were assembled at the Oakwood Correctional Facility so that they could coordinate what they would say at trial. One prisoner who was there described the process under oath.

> Sir, I was in the witness-protection program, Oakwood Correctional Facility, and there they have guys that are being witnesses for the state.... They went to trial and made a plea bargain with the Court and told the Court that they will commit to a lesser crime, you know, to save their self from going to death row and doing a lot more time.
>
> And during that time, you know, a lot of guys, you know, we all there. We talk to each other, and we show each other, you know, different things that we are doing, our statements, you know, different things like that. And guys, you know, spoke about things that they were going to say in trial. And they didn't care, they were going to help themselves. Whatever they had to do to get out of their crimes, they would do it to keep from doing more time in prison.[28]

Other prisoners dubbed Oakwood the "snitch academy."

Robert Brookover

Prosecutor Dan Hogan told the *Columbus Dispatch* how he trained prisoner informant Robert Brookover in what to say—as one would house-break a dog.

> [P]rosecutors spent hours preparing Brookover ... to testify. Their frustration boiled each time they asked a question because Brookover always began his answer: "I wouldn't lie to you."
>
> "You have to stop doing that, because when we get in the courtroom, I don't want my jury to hear 500 times, 'I'm not going to lie to you,'" said Dan Hogan, a former Franklin County prosecutor who is now a judge.
>
> Hogan rolled up a newspaper as Doug Stead, a prosecution-team attorney from Franklin County, continued asking questions.

Each time Brookover used the phrase, Hogan hit him in the face with the paper.[29]

On the witness stand in *State v. Robb*, Brookover admitted that when first questioned by the authorities, in June 1993, "I was lying."[30] He stated that at his next interrogation, in January 1994, he wasn't truthful and honest in that statement, either.[31] He lied about helping an injured prisoner (Johnny Fryman) and an injured officer, and he lied about staying in the gym throughout the 11 days, Brookover conceded.[32] Nor did he tell the investigators at that time that he had helped to murder David Sommers.[33]

As is often the case with informants, however, when he took the stand to testify against Robb, Brookover insisted that now, for the first time, he was telling the truth, the whole truth, and nothing but the truth. What Robb and his counsel did not know at the time was that even the prosecutor wondered whether Brookover was still lying.

In his direct examination at Jason Robb's trial, Brookover alleged that he had carried on certain undercover activities at the request of state officials in various Ohio prisons. Robb's counsel, Mark DeVan, began the cross-examination by asking him what he had done at Warren.

A. I infiltrated drug activity there for the major at Warren Correctional Institute [*sic*].... They wanted me to bust who was bringing drugs into their institution, and I did exactly that.

Q. Did they accuse you of having friends of yours bring drugs into the institution?

A. That's the way they started the intimidation, yes.

Q. In fact, there was a friend of yours who was found with drugs in the visiting area, correct, or trying to come in?

A. No, that's a lie. I've never had a visitor or anyone ever try to bring any contraband on to prison property or anything, so that's an error on your part, sir.

Q. Well, among the things that they accused you of was having a hollowed out bone containing residue of marijuana, correct, sir?

A. That was at London Correctional Institution....

Q. Now, while at London, were you accused of dealing in drugs.

A. At London Correctional Institute [*sic*], the same thing happened to me.... I was taken down to the Warden's office and I was questioned about drug activity.... Subsequently I was involved in some investigations to where I busted ... staff members there at that institution for bringing drugs into the institution....

Q. So you were working for the administration as an informant at London, correct?

A. Yes, sir, I was.

Before then, Brookover added, he had told the authorities "about some stuff that was going on" at the Ohio Penitentiary, and certain officers were busted.[34]

So, Attorney DeVan concluded, you were "providing information at three institutions before you ever got to Lucasville, correct, sir?" And Brookover answered, "Yes, sir."[35]

After the Robb trial, prosecutor Mark Piepmeier asked the Ohio State Highway Patrol to attempt to "validate Inmate Robert Brookover's claims of past assistance to DR&C [Department of Rehabilitation and Correction] officials." Sergeant Howard Hudson relayed Trooper Cary Sayers' findings to the prosecutor.[36]

The first incident alleged by Brookover occurred at the Ohio Penitentiary. Sayers found that the incident had occurred, "but review of the OSP [Ohio State Patrol] report finds no mention of Inmate Robert Bobby Brookover."

Brookover next claimed to have been involved in two incidents at London. Regarding one of these, the patrolman concluded "that Brookover was not involved in the incident in any form or fashion."

Finally, regarding assistance claimed by Brookover at Warren, knowledgeable officials said that information had been received from him but, in most cases, "this same information had been previously received from other inmates."

Thus the state's own investigation of one of its key witnesses— *after* Robb's trial—revealed a tendency on Brookover's part to embroider and exaggerate even as he supposedly told the truth in *State v. Robb*.

Anthony Lavelle

The most consequential snitch testimony came from Anthony Lavelle, leader of the Black Gangster Disciples and one of the three men who agreed to the surrender agreement on behalf of the prisoners. Reginald Wilkinson, director of the Ohio Department of Rehabilitation and Correction, has written that, according to Special Prosecutor Piepmeier,

> the key to winning convictions was eroding the loyalty and fear inmates felt toward their gangs. To do that, his staff targeted a few gang leaders and convinced them to accept plea bargains. Thirteen months into the investigation, a primary riot provocateur [Lavelle] agreed to talk about Officer Vallandingham's death. He later received a sentence of 7 to 25 years after pleading guilty to conspiracy to commit murder. His testimony led to death sentences for riot leaders Carlos Sanders, Jason Robb, James Were, and George Skatzes....[37]

Lavelle testified in George Skatzes' trial that he turned state's evidence because he did not want to die or spend his life in prison and he thought he would go to Death Row if he did not inform.[38] According to Prosecutor Hogan, Lavelle made his decision to cooperate with the state when Prosecutor Stead told him, you are either going to be my witness, or I'm going to try to kill you. [39]

In fact we know in detail the steps in the process that caused Lavelle to become an informant.

During the winter of 1993–94, three of the targeted leaders of the uprising—Hasan, Lavelle, and Skatzes—were housed in adjacent cells in the Chillicothe Correctional Institution. The authorities interviewed Skatzes three times, on October 13, 1993, March 31, 1994, and April 6, 1994. On each of these occasions the authorities invited him to assist them, and he responded that he could not help them.

The climactic meeting came on April 6. Skatzes was induced to leave his cell by the completely false statement that he had an "attorney visit." He was then taken to a room where, as Skatzes recalls, he was cuffed to an eye bolt in a table at the center of the room, and remained standing. Sergeant Howard Hudson, lead investigator for the Ohio State Highway Patrol, and Sergeant Randy McGough, also of the Patrol, entered the room and took up positions on either side of Skatzes. In Skatzes' words: "As I am standing there with a trooper on either side of me, they start talking to me." The following dramatization is drawn from Skatzes' description in contemporaneous letters, a letter of protest from Skatzes' attorney Jeff Kelleher to Special Prosecutor Mark Piepmeier written on April 13, 1994, and Sergeant Hudson's trial testimony.[40]

> **Hudson:** Now is the time for decision, George. We can drop Vallandingham and [Earl] Elder, but you have to stand for [David] Sommers. You will be indicted for three capital murder cases if you do not cooperate with us.
>
> **Skatzes:** I cannot help you.
>
> (The troopers leave. Three officers enter. Skatzes gets ready to go, turning in the direction of his cell. Ralph Coyle, a deputy warden, enters the room.)
>
> **Coyle:** George, I am Deputy Warden Coyle. Do you think it would be wise for you to go back to the North Hole?
>
> **Skatzes:** Yes! I have done nothing wrong. I have nothing to hide. And if I *don't* go back to the North Hole, it will make me look like a snitch.

Coyle: Maybe the other inmates in the North Hole will think of you as a snitch anyway.

Skatzes: Why should they even have such a thought in their minds? I'm not going to any lock except the North Hole. Period! (Coyle leaves. Skatzes sits down and waits. The three guards remain in the room. Nobody says much. Coyle reenters.)

Coyle: Central Office has decided that you *cannot* go back to the North Hole. The decision is *non-negotiable*.

Skatzes: You people have created a very serious situation for me. I have nothing to run and hide from. You're setting me up to look like a snitch. I went out on a visit and did not return. Anybody who knows anything about prison life will understand how inmates will take that information and run with it. When I don't come back, Lavelle and Sanders will figure I turned state's evidence. Serious damage is being done to my character. You are putting the life of my loved ones in danger. You're going to get me killed.

(The three guards form up around George, unbolt him from the table, and escort him out of the room.)

The next day, April 7, Hasan was taken to the county jail in Scioto County for indictment. Ordinarily he would have been locked up at some distance from other prisoners. On this occasion, however, he was placed with other prisoners, so that (in Skatzes' opinion) it would be easy for Hasan to spread the word that George had not returned to his cell and had apparently turned state's evidence.

But Hasan did not immediately jump to the conclusion that Skatzes had snitched. When Skatzes came back to his cell on April 8, the two men talked. Hasan wrote a note to the effect that he believed George Skatzes was telling the truth, which, according to Rodger Snodgrass, had a powerful effect on the opinions of other Muslim prisoners.[41]

It was otherwise with Anthony Lavelle. The day after Skatzes failed to return to his cell, Lavelle wrote the following to Jason Robb.[42]

Jason:

I am forced to write you and relate a few things to you that have happen down here lately.

With much sadness I will give you the raw deal. Your brother George has done a vanishing act on us. Last Friday [actually, Thursday], . . . the OSP came down to see him. Now the truth is that he was only in the room for 7–10 minutes, and as you know this is their second time coming to see him that we are aware of. So with only a short meeting I truly believed his word that he told them he was solid.

The strange thing I should have seen was what he said happened that day. He related to Hasan and me that "they said they were giving him one last chance before indictments come out to help them. He said that they claimed he would be charged with three capital murder cases." I won't put any names in the letter but I will say he acted scared.

On Wednesday, April 6, 1994, George said about 8:00 a.m. that he had a lawyer visit coming and before they were here the COs wanted to move him to the room. Now to be short and simple, he failed to return that day. Today they came and packed up his property which leads me to one conclusion that he has chosen to be a cop.

Now if I am wrong, I will do all I can to correct the problem. But JR, I am not wrong. . . . I called Niki [Schwartz] today and advised him of the situation. . . . If you don't believe my words check it for yourself, and then get back with me as soon as you can. . . .

Time to close. Hope to hear from you soon.

Lavelle

Before Skatzes was returned to his cell the next day, Lavelle had been transferred.[43]

Thereafter the state moved quickly to finalize a plea agreement with Lavelle.[44] Prisoner Antoine Odom testified in the Robb trial about Lavelle's behavior when Lavelle decided to turn state's evidence.

Q. Tell us what he said.

A. He said the prosecutor was sweating him and he had to do what he had to do—he was gonna cop out cause the prosecutor was sweating him, trying to hit him with a murder charge.

Q. Did he say ... what he meant by he was going to do what he had to do?

A. He just said he was ... gonna get a deal for his self....

Q. Uh-huh. Did he say anything about the story he was going to tell the prosecutor?

A. ... He said he was going to tell them what they wanted to hear.

Q. ... Did he say anything about the Muslims and the Aryan Brotherhood?

A. Yes, he said fuck the Muslims and the Aryan Brotherhood cause he a Gangster for life.

Q. ... Did you write it out that day, the next day, or a day later?

A. That day. The day it happened, when he was talking to me.[45]

The State of Ohio's statutory scheme purports to ensure "proportionality" in the administration of the death sentence. The Lucasville sentences and plea bargains fly in the face of that claim (See Appendixes 5 and 6). The following are only a few of the manifest inequalities:

- Anthony Lavelle plea bargained for conspiracy to murder with a sentence of 7 to 25 years to run concurrently with his previous sentence, but those members of the Five who sat in the same meeting with Lavelle on the morning of April 15 were found guilty of aggravated murder. (All were sentenced to death. Skatzes was not given the death penalty for the murder of Officer Vallandingham, apparently because of his kindness to hostage guards Clark and Ratcliff. He was given the death penalty for his alleged role in the murders of prisoners Elder and Sommers.) Lavelle was promised a transfer out of state after he finished testifying. He was to be eligible for parole in December 1999.[46]
- Rodger Snodgrass admitted participation in the killing of Earl

Elder and David Sommers. He plea bargained a sentence of 5 to 25 years for the involuntary manslaughter of Elder, to run concurrently with the 5 to 25 years he was already serving for aggravated robbery. Snodgrass was never charged in connection with Sommers' death. He also attempted to murder prisoner Newell but was never charged. Finally, during the uprising, Snodgrass "guarded" Officers Clark, Hensley, and Ratcliff, for which he could have been charged with kidnapping. He was charged with two of these kidnappings, but the charges were later dropped.[47]

- Robert Brookover testified that he had killed, or at least taken part in killing, David Sommers. He pleaded guilty to involuntary manslaughter during the commission of a felonious assault, and testified that his conviction would not add one day to the time he served.[48]

None of this concerned prosecutors in the Lucasville trials. The State of Ohio did not care whether Skatzes or Lavelle would be induced to snitch, or whether Skatzes or Lavelle would be executed. Prosecutor Hogan told the Skatzes jury in his closing argument:

Mr. Skatzes had his opportunity and he chose not to take it. Had Mr. Skatzes taken it, ... Mr. Skatzes, assuming he would tell us the truth, would be up there on the witness stand testifying and Mr. Lavelle could be sitting over there [at the defendant's table]. I make no apologies for that.[49]

Chapter 6

THE CRIMINAL INJUSTICE SYSTEM: TRIAL AND APPEAL

THE "DEATH-QUALIFIED" JURY

PICKING A JURY is the first thing that happens in a criminal trial. The process is known as "voir dire." But when the prosecution is seeking the death penalty, there is something different about the process: people opposed to the death penalty are excluded.

Roughly two-thirds of the people of the United States will tell a poll-taker that they favor the death penalty. (If the poll-taker gives them a choice between the death penalty and life imprisonment without parole, the percentage of those favoring capital punishment drops significantly.)

But a jury's recommendation of the death penalty must be unanimous. It takes only one juror in 12 to prevent a recommendation for death. Therefore, most randomly selected juries would contain at least one opponent of the death penalty, and there could be very few death sentences.

This posed a problem for prosecutors and judges who wanted defendants put to death. They have solved the problem—unless our courts become more enlightened—with the "death-qualified jury."

This doctrine is as follows. Any potential juror who states that he or she opposes the death penalty under all circumstances will almost surely be excused. A juror who indicates support for the death penalty is asked another question, namely: Would you follow the instructions of the judge about the law? If the juror answers yes, then that juror may be seated *even though* he or she favors the death penalty just as strongly as opponents of the death penalty oppose it.

The following are extracts from the voir dire at the beginning of the trial of George Skatzes. They show how the doctrine of the "death-qualified jury" works to the defendant's disadvantage.

Juror Number 1

The Court: ... I have a question I want to ask you.... [I]n a proper case where the facts warrant it and the law permits it, could you join in with others in signing a verdict form which might recommend to the Court the imposition of the death penalty?

A. No, sir.

The Court: You don't believe you could do so?

A. I don't believe so.

The Court: Under any circumstances?

A. No.

The Court: Could you tell me why?

A. I had a brother who was murdered and I found it in my heart to forgive that man. I would not have found him guilty to the extent that his life would be taken.

The Court: In other words, you feel that if you didn't do it in your brother's case, you wouldn't do it in any other case, right?

A. Right....

[Defense Attorney]: ... Do you feel that this is a teaching of your church?

A. Not so much a teaching of my church as it is an understanding of mine that I do not create life. I am not giver of life, so I feel that it's not my responsibility or within reason to expect me to take a life....

The Court: You may step down.[1]

Unidentified Woman

The Court: [I]n a proper case, where the facts warranted it and the law permitted, could you join with the rest of the jurors in signing a verdict recommending to the Court the imposition of the death penalty?

A. ... [M]y religious beliefs do not support the death penalty, but in a case where there was complete evidence and there were no circumstances that would lead me to believe elsewise ...

The Court: There could be situations, is that what you are trying to say, in which you might be willing to sign a verdict imposing the death penalty?

A. That's correct....

The Court [to prosecuting attorney]: You may inquire.

[Prosecuting Attorney]: ... Do you recall anything about the Lucasville prison riot.

A. Yes, I do.

[Prosecuting Attorney]: Tell us what you remember....

A. During that time period I was a graduate student at Ohio State University in Columbus. I was a member of the negotiation class .... [A]s part of our class work, we used this case as a case study and we had some in-depth discussion....

[Prosecuting Attorney]: ... [D]id you personally come to a feeling that the thing was handled properly, improperly?

A. Yes, I did.... I feel that some things could have been handled differently and that lives did not need to be ... lost ..., especially in the situation of a guard. My godfather is a prison guard. One of my ex-boyfriends is a prison guard. I understand what they go through every day. My heart went out to that guard and his family....

[Prosecuting Attorney]: ... Did you arrive at the opinion that the state somehow blew this thing, they screwed it up?

A. Yes, I did. I don't think they took the inmates' demands seriously. They took away water, electricity, tried to starve them out. They are prisoners, but they have human rights also. I just think it should have been handled a little differently and maybe those people would not have gotten killed.

... I don't think I can ... keep separate the riot from the murders because I think that they are all interrelated....

[Defense Attorney]: [T]he real question is regarding your ability ... to put aside that class, focus on what you hear here and make a verdict based solely on what you hear here; could you do that?

A. I find it difficult to answer that question....

The Court: This particular juror is completely unable to be the kind of objective juror which the law requires.... The Court will dismiss her.[2]

Juror Number 8

The Court: In a proper case, where the facts warrant it and the law permits it, could you join in with the other jurors in signing a verdict form which would recommend to the Court the death penalty?

A. Yes, your Honor.

[Prosecuting Attorney]: ... We brought you here because we want to discuss with you your views on capital punishment. Can you share them with us, please?

A. I strongly believe in them. I wish they were enforced more often.

[Prosecuting Attorney]: ... Do you believe the death penalty is the only appropriate penalty in all cases of an intentional killing?

A. Pretty much.

[Prosecuting Attorney]: Does that mean?

A. Yes.

[Prosecuting Attorney]: ... You can think of the wors[t] crime that comes to your mind and if you find that person guilty at the first phase, we don't go straight to death. We have the second hearing at which point you would get additional evidence to consider in making your decision as to what punishment is appropriate....

What we need to know is whether you could set aside your thoughts as to what you think the law should be and follow the law that the Judge gives you?

A. Yes.

[Prosecuting Attorney]: If you found someone guilty of a horrible, horrible crime, as bad as you can think of, would you be willing to keep an open mind and listen to that additional evidence at the second phase before making a decision as to which penalty is appropriate?

A. Yes.

[Prosecuting Attorney]: No matter how bad the crime?

A. Yes.

[Prosecuting Attorney]: ... Do you see how under Ohio law you could do the exact same crime and get a different penalty?

A. Yeah, because of the circumstances and the mitigating factors.

[Defense Attorney]: ... You mentioned in your questionnaire you have a friend ... [who] works in the sheriff's department?

A. He used to. He's a Kettering police officer now.

The Court: ... We want you back [f]or the next phase in the questioning.[3]

Juror Number 38

The Court: ... In a proper case, where the facts warrant it, and the law permits it, could you join other fellow jurors in signing a verdict that might recommend to the Court the imposition of the death penalty?

A. I don't believe that I could....

[Prosecuting Attorney]: ... Can you expand upon your feelings?...

A. My problem ... is my children.... I think in the end, I would be looking at another woman's child and I don't think that I could ever be the person to say there's no good there at all. I just don't think I could do that. I can't imagine any instance.

[Prosecuting Attorney]: ... [I]t's not a question of does he deserve death or does he deserve life. It's a question of which way does this balance come out [between aggravating circumstances and mitigating factors].

A. ... I understand what you've said, but ... I believe I would be hanging on to those mitigating things for life....

Based on my personal moral compass, I would be trying very hard to never put anyone with a death sentence because ... I would be afraid of the weight that that would give me for many years....

The Court: Under the circumstances, ma'am, I think we are going to excuse you.[4]

Juror Number 42

The Court: ... In a proper case, where the facts warrant it and the law permits it, could you sign your name with other jurors to a verdict form which might recommend to the Court the imposition of the death penalty?

A. I don't think so.

The Court: By that, do you mean under no circumstances could you do that?...

A. I don't believe in it. Is that what you are asking?

The Court: ... Under the circumstances, with the way you feel about things, we will let you off. You are dismissed.[5]

Juror Number 46

The Court: ... In a proper case, where the facts warrant it and the law permits it, could you, along with other jurors, fellow jurors, sign a verdict form which might recommend to the Court the imposition of the death penalty?

A. It's hard to say categorically, but probably not, I would say not.... I couldn't imagine circumstances in which I would sign something like that.

[Prosecuting Attorney]: ... Can you envision circumstances under which you would pick up a pen and sign your name in ink on a verdict form saying that a person should be put to death?

A. Let me answer that by saying that I spend most of my free time doing things for people, not to people, and it would be a contradiction in what I do outside of this room on a regular basis to do something like that, so the answer is I cannot imagine myself signing that....

[Prosecuting Attorney]: Challenge.

The Court: You are going to have to step down, sir.[6]

Juror Number 56

The Court: [In a] proper case, if the facts warrant it and the law permits it, would you be willing to sign a jury verdict along with other jurors which might recommend to the Judge the death penalty?

A. Yes, sir.

[Prosecuting Attorney]: ... We brought you in individually to discuss your personal views on capital punishment, you tell us how you feel.

A. I do believe in it. I think there should be more of it.

[Prosecuting Attorney]: ... Do you see how under Ohio law there is no such thing as an automatic death penalty?

A. Yes, sir.

[Prosecuting Attorney]: ... Would you be willing to keep an open mind and listen to everything before choosing among the ... penalties?

A. Yes, sir....

The Court: Come back Wednesday morning.[7]

Juror C

The Court: ... In a proper case where the facts warrant it and the law permits it, could you sign your name on a verdict form with other members of the jury which might recommend to the Court the imposition of the death penalty?

A. No, sir.

The Court: ... Is this a personal or religious belief?

A. Both.

[Prosecuting Attorney]: We're in agreement.

The Court: I will let you be dismissed.[8]

Juror Number 75

The Court: ... In a proper case where the facts warrant it and the law permits it, could you sign your name to a verdict form along with other members of the jury that might recommend to the Court the imposition of the death penalty?

A. If the evidence and the facts of the case support that, I would feel comfortable with doing that, yes, sir.

[Prosecuting Attorney]: ... Do you recall anything about the Lucasville prison riot?

A. Yes, I do. I worked close to there about a year before that happened.... I was a psychologist supervisor at Ross County

Correctional Institution and I believe ... this happened around a year, year and a half afterwards, so I did know about it and followed it somewhat in the newspapers....

The Court: Sir, we are going to have you come back tomorrow at nine.[9]

Juror Number 76

The Court: In a proper case where the facts warrant it and the law permits it, would you be able to sign the verdict form with other jurors which might recommend the imposition of the death penalty?

A. Yes, I would....

[Defense Attorney]: ... [I]f you found the defendant guilty beyond a reasonable doubt of all those murders, even though the Judge would tell you to consider ... life sentences, the truth is you really couldn't; isn't that correct?

A. Well, no, I guess I couldn't....

The Court [after prospective juror steps outside]: Is there a challenge?

[Defense Attorney]: Yes, your Honor. We challenge her.... This wom[a]n is deeply troubled by the prospect of having to vote for a life sentence with the prospect of parole, it's clear that that is foreclosed in her mind. She said she's so troubled by the prospect that this man could get out that there's no doubt she would vote for the death penalty. I think she deserves to be excused.

The Court: Motion overruled. Note your objections.

The Court [before the prospective juror]: I want you to come back at nine tomorrow.[10]

Unfair? You bet. But that is "the law" at the present time.

THE SARAN WRAP OF CONSPIRACY
AND COMPLICITY

In every one of the Lucasville capital trials, the essential charge against the defendant was the whole dreadful scenario of killings and kidnappings throughout the 11 days. Each jury was presented with photographs of gruesome murders and testimony about inexcusable acts even though the particular defendant on trial had no demonstrable connection with many of the actions shown in the pictures or described in the testimony.

The legal doctrines that allowed prosecutors to proceed in this broadbrush manner are "conspiracy" and "complicity."

To "conspire" is, according to the word's Latin roots, to "breathe together." The word itself conjures up an image of plotters huddling together over a single candle in a darkened room.

In Anglo-American criminal law, proof of conspiracy requires (1) an agreement to commit one of a long list of serious crimes, and (2) a "substantial overt act" by at least one of the conspirators to carry out the agreement.[11] Related doctrines hold that:

- Each conspirator is responsible for any criminal act within the scope and in furtherance of the agreement that is committed by any other conspirator.
- If A knows or has reason to know that B, with whom A is planning criminal action, is conspiring with C to commit the same action, A is guilty of conspiracy with C even if A does not know the identity of C.
- Conspirators are guilty even if commission of the planned action was impossible.
- Unless a conspiracy has been "abandoned," it is no defense to a charge of conspiracy that the planned criminal action was not carried out.

From an Ohio prosecutor's standpoint, there is only one problem with the concept of "conspiracy." It cannot be punished by death.

Fortunately for prosecutors and sympathetic judges, there is a sub-stitute doctrine with much the same content for which the death penalty is available: "complicity." Complicity includes conspiracy, and also includes "soliciting" another to commit a crime or "aiding and abetting" in committing a crime. One who is complicit in the commission of a crime "shall be prosecuted and punished as if he were a principal offender."[12]

Complicity casts an even broader net than conspiracy. Portraying Hasan to the jury as the sole cause of the disturbance, prosecutors also used the concept of "complicity" to connect him with everything that had happened during the 11 days.[13] The trial judge assisted them in this strategy by three times instructing the jury that they could link the defendant with the misconduct of other prisoners by means of what he called "the Saran Wrap of complicity."[14]

Finally, the concept of "course of conduct" is akin to conspiracy and complicity and is one of the specified aggravating factors that an Ohio jury is instructed to consider when deciding whether to recom-mend the death penalty. The death penalty may be imposed when "the offense at bar was part of a course of conduct involving the purposeful killing of or attempt to kill two or more persons by the offender."[15] This language may have prompted the prosecution to indict each of the Lucasville Five for two (Hasan, Namir, Robb) or more (Lamar, Skatzes) murders.[16]

What facts justified the application to these defendants of the concepts of conspiracy, complicity, and course of conduct?

Conspiratorial Agreement to Take Over the Prison?

Witnesses testified to an agreement by the Muslims, Aryan Brotherhood, and Black Gangster Disciples before the uprising to prevent petty differences between members of different organized groups from escalating into violence. There was no testimony that these discussions included planning a riot.

Witnesses testified that in the days just before the uprising, certain Muslims and certain members of the Aryan Brotherhood were seen talking together on the recreation yard, an unusual event. No one stated that he had been present at such conversations, and there was only hearsay testimony as to what had been talked about.

Reginald Williams described a discussion among Muslims on the recreation yard during the early afternoon of April 11. However, Namir testified that he was in his cell in L-1 at the time, and Hasan testified that he left the meeting, and went back into L block, before the discussion concluded. Before he could return to the yard, according to Hasan's unrebutted statement, the attack on guards in L block had begun.

At the trial of George Skatzes, Prosecutor Hogan told the jury that no one alleges that Skatzes was involved in planning the takeover of L block.[17]

One concludes that evidence of an agreement involving the Lucasville Five to take over L block is sketchy at best. Moreover, as was emphasized at the beginning of Chapter 3, the witness who testified about an agreement among Muslims to take over part of the prison (Reginald Williams) was equally clear that the plan did *not* involve harming or killing guards, nor assaulting any of the prisoners who were subsequently killed. Thus, even as to those defendants who might be thought to have entered into an agreement, it was not an agreement to murder. Any murders that happened later were not within the scope or in furtherance of the agreement.

Conspiratorial Agreement That Whites Would Kill Whites and Blacks Would Kill Blacks?

In the trial of George Skatzes, it was alleged that prisoner Earl Elder was killed after an emergency meeting of Muslims and Aryan Brothers late on April 11. The Muslims and the ABs agreed, so the prosecution claimed, that before any white was killed the ABs would be consulted and would be asked to do the dirty work themselves; likewise, the Muslims would have to agree to and take part in the killing of any blacks. According to Prosecutor Stead:

> [T]he Aryans and the Muslims had gotten together, and they had come to an agreement. They were running the show together, and there had been a lot of white people killed that first night, and to keep harmony between the groups that were in control, a decision had been made: Whites will kill whites; blacks will kill blacks.[18]

But no witness at any trial said that he was present when this supposed agreement between the Muslims and the ABs was negotiated. The character of the evidence for the alleged agreement is suggested by the testimony of Rodger Snodgrass, an AB who turned state's evidence.

At the Robb trial, Snodgrass testified to the existence of a pact between the Muslims and the ABs. This exchange followed:

Q. Were you present when that pact was made?
A. No, sir.
Q. Were you told that a pact was made?
A. Yes, I was.
Q. By whom were you told the pact was made?
A. By Paul Johnson. . . .[19]

At the Skatzes trial, Snodgrass attributed his supposed knowledge of a pact to two other persons.

A. Well, from my understanding, a pact was made with the Muslims.

Mr. Kelleher: I object.

The Court: Never mind what you understand. If you know or talked to somebody—

The Witness: Jason Robb told me a pact was made with the Muslims; therefore, when George told me that he, that no more white guys were going to be killed in that riot, without sanctions from the AB, you know, that if they were to be killed, they were goin' to be killed by their own kind or at least given that opportunity, you know, that's basically what was said.

Q. Mr. Skatzes said that?

A. I can't be positive about that neither, but I believe it was.

Mr. Kelleher: Object. Move to strike.

The Court: No, it's his best estimate, best opinion. Overruled.

Q. If it was not Skatzes, who was it that said it?

A. If it wouldn't have been Skatzes, it would probably have been Robb.[20]

This evidence is worse than "sketchy." It is unadulterated hearsay, it is internally contradictory, and it is so vague that a reviewing court should consider it unconscionable to use such evidence in sentencing a man to death.

Conspiratorial Agreement to Kill an Officer?

Of course, the heart of the theory of group guilt—whether labeled conspiracy or complicity—concerned the murder of Officer Vallandingham. The prosecution argued that at a meeting of leaders of the three organized groups on the morning of April 15, there was a *decision* to kill an officer. Therefore each person present was guilty of murder even if he had nothing to do with the hands-on killing.

The transcript of the meeting between 8 and 9 a.m. reports discussion of killing a guard but no decision (see Chapter 3). The only show of hands or voice vote mentioned on the tape of that meeting concerns negotiating demands for the day. The transcript indicates that if the state did not promptly restore electricity and water, there was to be another meeting of the leaders before a guard was killed.

The key witness used by the prosecution to supplement the transcript, Anthony Lavelle, testified in three trials that the meeting did *not* come to a final decision to kill a guard. Lavelle said in Namir's trial: "When I left the meeting, the understanding was we was going to meet up later on that afternoon and give them our final ultimatum."[21] He said in Skatzes' trial that "we was going to meet back up later that afternoon" to evaluate the results of negotiations.[22] Finally, in Hasan's trial, Lavelle for a third time affirmed that at the end of the morning meeting, "We hadn't made a clear decision" to kill a guard. Rather, the group decided that they would "meet back up later and decide on whether this is what we want to do, be sure that this is what we want to do."[23]

To repeat what was concluded earlier: if we consider Lavelle's testimony in the trials as a whole, he stated that the morning meeting discussed the murder of a guard but did not come to a final decision, and that another meeting was to happen, during the afternoon, before any guard would be killed. Thus, the testimony of the prosecution's lead witness suggests that the killing of the guard that morning was not a result of the morning meeting, but a rogue action by a group of prisoners.

In summary, there is very little evidence for conspiracy, complicity, or a planned course of conduct in the murders that occurred between April 11 and 21.

- Muslims may have planned to take over L-6, but Namir was not at the meeting, Hasan appears to have left before the discussion ended, and Skatzes was not a part of any agreement. Moreover, it does not seem to have been the intention of any of the Five to harm the guards, let alone kill them.

- Once L block was occupied, there is no solid evidence of a group decision to kill any prisoner or any guard. As we have seen, the evidence is overwhelming that Lavelle himself independently initiated a rogue action to kill Officer Vallandingham.

RESULT-ORIENTED JURISPRUDENCE

It would be unfair to point the finger of blame only at Hamilton County prosecutors and the Ohio State Highway Patrol. The state courts of Ohio have thus far been grievously at fault in their rulings in the Lucasville cases.

What is ultimately disturbing about these opinions is that they are result-oriented: that is, that as in Alice's adventures in Wonderland, the verdict comes first and the judicial rationale later.

Professor James Liebman of Columbia University, author of a massive study of reversible error in death penalty appeals, states that Ohio "has one of the largest and slowest moving capital systems in the nation." (For example, George Skatzes' direct appeal from the verdicts in the Court of Common Pleas to a decision by the Court of Appeals took seven years: from January 1996 to January 2003.) Because of these delays, Professor Liebman continues, Ohio had no "track record of federal court outcomes" during the period of his study. He observes, however, that the Ohio Supreme Court has developed the habit of passing serious problems to the federal courts.

> [A]lthough the Ohio Supreme Court very frequently *finds* error in capital cases, it also very frequently goes on to *approve* the capital verdict on the ground that the error—and even patterns of error in particular counties [such as Hamilton County]—are not serious enough to warrant reversal. As the experiences of Georgia, California, and Pennsylvania suggest, the Ohio Supreme Court's forgiving approach to identified error is a recipe for high rates of reversal years later, once Ohio cases reach the federal courts.[24]

Here are a few examples of the state courts' result-oriented jurisprudence.

Misstating the Facts

A pattern of carelessness pervades the presentation of facts by Ohio appellate courts in these cases.

Jason Robb's case is the furthest advanced of the death-penalty cases arising from the Lucasville rebellion. The following misstatements are drawn from the opinions of the trial court, the Court of Appeals, and the Ohio Supreme Court in *State v. Robb*.

The trial court stated in its opinion that "nine inmates were killed during the early days of the riot."[25] In fact, seven prisoners were killed at that time.

The trial court also declared that "around the 5th of April, apparently by lottery, a victim, [Officer] Robert Vallandingham, was selected."[26] The disturbance lasted from April 11 to 21, a period that did not include the fifth of April. The evidence concerning the April 15 meeting says nothing about a lottery.

The Court of Appeals stated that at a meeting on the morning of April 15, leaders of the three gangs represented in the rebellion chose a "set time" to kill a guard.[27] This may have been the origin of the previously quoted statement by the Ohio Supreme Court that the meeting "issued a strict timetable for compliance."[28] But Tunnel Tape 61 contains no reference to any particular set time or timetable for compliance, nor did any witness who took part in the meeting allege that a set time or strict timetable had been established there.

The trial court said that Robb was "the main leader of the White [sic] Aryan Brotherhood."[29] The Court of Appeals opined that "the Aryan Brotherhood … were led by defendant [Robb] and George Skatzes during the riot."[30] The Supreme Court found that "Defendant [Robb], along with Freddy Snyder, led some twenty to thirty Aryans in L section."[31] Seemingly, as long as defendant Robb was said to have been a leader, it didn't matter who else was named. Moreover, Freddy Snyder was not in L block at any time during the uprising.

With regard to the death of prisoner David Sommers, the trial court stated: "On the last day of the riot … Carlos Sanders and Robb ordered the killing of David Sommers, an inmate, because he knew too much."[32] But no witness testified to any such order on the last day of the riot. And in its opinion in *Robb*, the Supreme Court offered a completely different scenario: "While the surrender was underway, the Aryans decided to kill inmate Sommers."[33]

And that is not all that is wrong with the Supreme Court's narrative about Robb's alleged participation in Sommers' death. Its complete statement is as follows:

While the surrender was underway, the Aryans decided to kill inmate Sommers because he knew too much about what had happened in L-2, the Aryan stronghold. In fact, even earlier, defendant had talked with Hasan about killing Sommers or putting his eye out with a cigar. While defendant, Bocook, Skatzes, and a recent Aryan recruit, Robert Brookover, were together in L-7, they talked about killing different inmates. At one point, defendant left, returned, and announced, "We still got one." Bocook then said, "Go get the bitch David Sommers." Defendant left, then came back in running with Sommers running right behind him. [As other Aryans stabbed, choked, and beat Sommers, Robb] stood by and watched from a distance on a walkway.[34]

Consider these asserted facts in chronological order.

The only witness to an earlier conversation about killing Sommers is the unreliable Stacey Gordon. Gordon was unable to say on what day and at what time this purported conversation occurred. Moreover, he said that it took place after one of a series of meetings between only three persons: Anthony Lavelle, Robb, and Hasan, whom he refers to as Carlos Sanders.

> Q. Mr. Gordon, I believe you indicated you stood guard outside of a number of meetings that took place in the L2 unit offices; is that correct?
>
> A. Yes, it is.
>
> Q. Who were the people who would routinely come to those meetings?
>
> A. Anthony Lavelle, Carlos Sanders, and Jason Robb.
>
> Q. Now, would other people be involved in the meetings or be present when the meetings took place?
>
> A. No.[35]

But no other witness, in any trial, ever testified that there had been such meetings. The state's own tunnel tapes, like Tunnel Tape 61, without exception reported the presence of many more than three persons at all leadership meetings.

Supposing for the moment that Robb did say, "We still got one," he was not referring to David Sommers. The testimony at trial was that a number of Aryans went to L-7 with the intent of doing harm to fellow prisoners Creager, Copeland, and Newell, who were thought to have planned to kill Hasan and/or Skatzes earlier in the riot. Creager and Copeland were found to have converted to Islam, and the Muslim prisoners would not release them to the AB. If anybody said, "We still got one," the words referred not to Sommers but to Emanuel "Buddy" Newell, who, indeed, was later assaulted by Rodger Snodgrass and Aaron Jefferson.

According to the trial testimony, Sommers was *not* mentioned in any conversation among Aryan prisoners before Bocook blurted out, "Go get the bitch David Sommers." There was no decision by the Aryans to kill Sommers.

Above all, the Ohio Supreme Court does not explain why (still assuming that the trial testimony was truthful) Robb returned to L-7 "running with Sommers running right behind him," and if this was so, how it constitutes evidence of aggravated murder. On its face it would seem to be evidence that Sommers intended to assault Robb. But if so, Robb did *not* respond violently but turned aside, or retreated, to a walkway.

How are these narratives created? Juries do not make findings of fact in capital murder cases. They only render verdicts. The facts set forth in the opinions of trial judges in these cases are cursory and, as we have seen, unreliable. Yet at the outset of appellate decisions, detailed histories blossom forth. Do the judges of these courts wish us to believe that they have read the 4,000-, 5,000-, or 6,000-page transcripts of the cases before them? If not, were law clerks or other court personnel asked to prepare factual summaries? And if this is so, how did they know which witnesses the trial juries found to be credible? Or did they, without the opportunity to assess witness demeanor, substitute their own impressions of the evidence? Or—in the worst-case scenario—did they merely replicate the factual summaries in prosecutors' briefs? In the decisions of the Ohio Supreme Court in *State v. Robb* and *State v. Sanders*, there is not a single citation to the record to support the facts asserted in their preliminary factual narratives.

One is left with the impression that for these decision makers the facts are of secondary importance. If this impression is correct, we confront both bad history and grave legal error.

Withholding Exculpatory Evidence

In *Brady v. Maryland*, a 1963 decision of the United States Supreme Court, prosecutors were ordered to provide the defense prior to trial any "exculpatory" evidence in their possession. In the trial of Keith Lamar, the prosecution produced summaries of witness statements, and a list of witnesses, but refused to say which witness had made which statement. The prosecution did provide complete statements—the same material the defense requested in Lamar's case—in the trials of two other SOCF prisoners accused of some of the same crimes. Moreover, after trial Lamar's defense identified six additional witnesses whose potentially exculpatory statements had not been turned over.[36]

The Ohio Supreme Court held that there was no *Brady* violation because all of the witness statements at issue either identified Lamar as one of the assailants or "did not exculpate Lamar because each victim had been attacked by multiple assailants." However, prisoner Aaron Jefferson (whose statement was made available to the Lamar defense) confessed to the Highway Patrol that he *and he alone* had killed one of the men Lamar was accused of murdering, Darrell Depina.

Q. Were you alone?
A. Yeah. By myself....
Q. You were the only one in there?
A. Yeah I was the only one....
Q. Okay, did someone tell you to go in there and get Depina?
A. No....
Q. And you done this on your own?

A. Done this on my own accord.

Q. Nobody told you to do it?

A. Nope.[37]

Lamar's defense counsel should have been given all the potentially exculpatory statements.

Judicial Overreaching

In Namir's second trial, his counsel protested the admission into evidence of the state's transcript of Tunnel Tape 61 because the prosecution could not produce the person who had transcribed it. The trial judge thereupon directed the court reporter to transcribe the tape over the weekend. She reported on Monday that it appeared there would be significant differences between her transcript and the one that the state wished to put in the record. At that point Judge Cartolano said he had been thinking about it all weekend, and he was going to let the state use its transcript, after all.[38]

Similar judicial overreaching was evident in Robb's trial. In *State v. Robb*, the Court of Appeals decided that the "tunnel tapes" had been recorded in violation of Ohio wiretap law as it was in 1993, so that the tapes and their transcripts should not have been used at trial. The violation of the statute was apparent. Yet the Ohio Supreme Court reversed the Court of Appeals, stating in pertinent part:

> [W]e cannot reasonably interpret former R.C. 2933.51 *et seq.* as granting a statutory right to privacy in communications between rioting inmates. The General Assembly could not have envisioned creating such a right in a state prison under siege. Granting privacy rights in these circumstances makes no sense in view of the state's interest in operating a prison and, in this case, restoring order, saving the lives of hostages and nonrioting prisoners, and protecting state property.... The idea that rioting prisoners are entitled to privacy in plotting the deaths of guards and other prisoners is absurd. [39]

In other words, if the court were to do what the law required, the prisoner might win—which would be "absurd."

Overriding a Juror's Reservations

Even more troubling is the Supreme Court's endorsement of the treatment of *Robb* juror Katrina Fehr. During the third day of penalty deliberations, because of Fehr's refusal to recommend death, the jury foreman sent out a note that said, "We have become deadlocked." The trial judge then suspended jury deliberations and questioned each juror separately. Thereafter, the judge asked the jury, "Can you continue to deliberate or are you unalterably deadlocked?" The jury foreman answered, "We cannot agree unanimously on either verdict [that is, death or life imprisonment]." The judge told the jury to continue deliberating. After further deliberation, the jury asked if the judge could impose a life sentence even if the jury recommended death. The judge said yes. The jury then unanimously recommended death, and the judge accepted their recommendation, to the consternation of juror Fehr, who had thought that the judge would override the jury's recommendation.[40]

Ohio law is clear that if one juror declines to recommend the death penalty, the trial judge must impose a life sentence. But the Ohio Supreme Court affirmed what the trial judge had done in *Robb*.

Jason himself summed up the situation as follows, writing in 2003 at the Ohio State Penitentiary:

> The system is flawed. Look at the Lucasville prosecutions. In this book you read of five examples of the injustice system but that is only five out of 47 people who either pled guilty to reduced charges or went to trial and were found guilty. Their struggle is not being heard and they remain victims to this injustice. It's bigger than just five people's journey in chaos and torture. Who will take up the torch for them? Or do they just gather dust and remain forgotten?[41]

Chapter 7

OVERCOMING RACISM: THE LUCASVILLE REDEMPTION

Attica lived on in the Lucasville uprising in many ways. One of them had to do with race.

Tom Wicker's memorable book on the Attica rebellion drew on the experience of a prisoner named Roger Champen.

> "You're *always* going to have a problem" with black-white relations, Champen believed. But in D-yard, "as days went by, food got scarce and the water began to be scarce, [blacks and whites] became more friendly. The issue about race became minimal.... Nothing means anything except the issue at hand." When he had made his first D-yard speech, Champ saw that "the whites had backed off and had a little, like, semi-circle off to the left." He told them that the revolt was not a "racial thing," that they had "one common enemy, the wall. The wall surrounds us all. So if you don't like me, don't like me after, but in the meantime, let's work together." That advice had prevailed.[1]

Pondering the totality of his own immersion in what happened on the Attica rec yard,

Wicker thought again that there was little evidence of black-white antagonisms in D-yard in what the observers could see and hear. When black orators like Florence spoke of unity in the yard but coupled this with blasts against "The Man" or "Whitey," white inmates seemed to be cheering with the rest. Similarly, Florence, Champ [Roger Champen], Brother Herb, and Brother Richard all seemed to accept white inmates as legitimately a part of the oppressed class.

Could he be seeing in D-yard, Wicker wondered, that class interest might overcome racial animosities? Was it possible that the dregs of the earth, in a citadel of the damned, somehow in the desperation of human need had cast aside all the ancient and encumbering trappings of racism to find in degradation the humanity they knew at last they shared?[2]

This vision contrasts sharply with some historians' view that white workers in the United States are incurably racist. These historians ask us to recognize the racism of white workers as an aspect of their "class formation" and to a significant degree the product of their own "agency"—that is, their own will and desire. The making of the American working class, it is proposed, has been in part a process whereby immigrants from Ireland and Eastern Europe learned to "become white" so as to appropriate the "wages of whiteness," both economic and psychological.[3]

These historians accurately describe a good deal of observed behavior. One may nonetheless argue that racist behavior, when and where it has occurred, is not an essential aspect of white workers but rather the product of specific historical circumstances, such as the following:

- Whites were a majority in the workplace and in the local union, if there was one.
- The number of persons seeking work exceeded the number of available jobs, or the number of jobs was decreasing.

- Employers, usually white males, deliberately pursued hiring policies that separated black and white workers and set them at each
  other's throats.

Perhaps if the circumstances were different, whites (and blacks, who
have often become strikebreakers) might behave differently. What if
we could change the context? What if we could vary the variables?
We might then have a method of analysis that could account both for
racist behavior and for behavior that overcomes racism. It could
account for the comradeship of Red and Andy in *The Shawshank
Redemption* and for the love between a black man, Othello, and his
white wife, Desdemona, as well as for the acceptance of that love by
Shakespeare's original audience, who watched the play at the Globe
Theater at almost the same time that the first permanent English
colony, Jamestown, was established in what became the United States.

Suppose many decision makers were black, competition between
the races was not objectively demanded, and people of color and
whites were approximately equal in number. The U.S. military has
moved in that direction since World War II. Prison sometimes goes
even further.

LUCASVILLE

African Americans were 57 percent of the prison population at
SOCF before the uprising.[4] Thus the Lucasville Five, three blacks
and two whites, mirror the make-up of the prisoner body at the time.
No one—administrators, guards, white prisoners, or black prisoners—had ever experienced this degree of numerical racial equality
outside prison walls.

Both white and black prisoners found confinement at SOCF to be
racially discriminatory. Whites emphasized the high percentage of
African American prisoners, and the fact that the warden, a deputy
warden, and the director of the Ohio Department of Rehabilitation
and Correction were all black.

But black prisoners could make an even stronger case for racial discrimination. As the Cleveland *Plain Dealer* commented at the time of the uprising, 85 percent of the guards at SOCF were white and the town of Lucasville had no black residents. For these reasons, it stated, "the Southern Ohio Correctional Facility should not have been built in Lucasville."[5] The Mohr Report found that:

> A review of use of force incidents at SOCF from January 1992 to the time of the disturbance not only reflects a very high rate but also indicates a disparity in use of force against black inmates. Specifically, 74% of all reported use of force cases involved black inmates compared to their percentage of the SOCF population being 57%.[6]

And although prisoners of both races were *beaten* by the guards, it appears that the only SOCF prisoners *killed* by guards in the years preceding the uprising were black.

How did interracial celling affect these dynamics? The Mohr Report says that interracial celling increased beginning in 1991 after the decision in a federal court case, *White v. Morris*. But there is reason to believe that what prisoners—black and white—most resented was *forced* celling with another prisoner, whether that prisoner was of the same race or not. "Little Rock" Reed asserts:

> Structurally, the Lucasville prison cells were built to accommodate one man per cell.... However, due to overcrowding, most of the cells had two men in them the entire time I was at Lucasville (from 1984 through 1992). In order to reduce the potential violence resulting from forced double-celling, Arthur Tate's predecessors at Lucasville had always maintained the practice of allowing prisoners to cell with each other if they requested to do so.
>
> ... The entire time I was in Lucasville prior to Tate's administration, at least 33 percent of the prison cells were racially integrated on a volunteer basis.... However, with "Operation Shakedown" came a policy of prohibiting prisoners from celling with each other

if they requested it. Tate intended to fill his quota with blacks and whites who hated each other. His oppressive policies and practices were bound to cause an explosion sooner or later, and he wanted the explosion to be between the whites and blacks, rather than the prisoners and his administration.[7]

During the uprising, black and white prisoners alike demanded that the policy of *forced* integrated celling should be rescinded. At George Skatzes' trial, the state's principal investigator testified that "many" SOCF prisoners objected to racially integrated celling. "Black and white?" he was asked. "Yes, sir," he answered.[8]

Consider what happened to a black prisoner, as narrated by "Little Rock" Reed.

> [A]n 18-year-old black kid, William, who weighed no more than 125 pounds,... arrived at Lucasville. He was ordered into the cell of a confirmed member of the Aryan Brotherhood who had expressed to Tate's administration that if they dared place a "nigger" in his cell, he would kill him. The little black guy, William, was terrified. He was brand new to the prison system and didn't know what to do when the white man stepped out of the cell and loudly proclaimed: "If you step into my cell, nigger, you're gonna die!"
>
> William stopped in his tracks, turned to face the guards who were escorting him, and pleaded for help. The white guards made it very clear to William, and to the several dozen witnesses including me, that William was going to have to fight for his life on that day.... William hesitatingly walked into the white man's cell when it was clear he had no choice.
>
> Before William got his second leg into the cell, he was hammered in the face with a padlock that the white man concealed inside a sock. William instantly turned[,] running down the cell block calling out for help. He was ultimately placed in the hole and charged with the offense of failure to obey a direct order because he ran from the cell.[9]

When William returned to the cell block, he agreed to let "Little Rock" file a suit on his behalf. Reed included affidavits from dozens of prisoners asking for a restraining order or injunction forbidding forced integrated celling because

> it was creating violence and would result in a riot if we didn't obtain the injunction.... Unfortunately, the court ignored our plea..., as did the governor, the prison director, the chief inspector of the prison system, and everyone else with the authority to intervene.[10]

FORMING A CONVICT RACE

Once the uprising began, the overriding problem for the prisoners in rebellion was the possibility that what had begun as a protest against the authorities might turn into a race riot among prisoners. *All* of the prisoners killed during the first hours of the Lucasville uprising were white, and *all but one* of the guards taken hostage were white. A war of race against race in L block could easily have erupted. Toward the end of that first afternoon, many of the insurgent prisoners gathered in the L block gym, whites in the bleachers, blacks on the other side. The atmosphere was tense.

According to an eyewitness, two black men—one of them named Cecil Allen—approached George Skatzes.

> [They] said, Big George. Would you please be a spokesman? This thing has gotten out of hand, and we need some help.
> ... [Skatzes] was a little reluctant at first because he didn't know what was happening.... But then, as he looked around, he said sure. If I can help in some way, I will do that....
> Mr. Allen ... said, tell them that this is not a race thing. This is not a race war. It is a war against the administration, against Arthur Tate.[11]

Another African American previously unknown to Skatzes, Little Willie, said, "George, come over to the gym. The whites are all on one side, the blacks on the other."

As Skatzes remembers it, he went to the gym and stood facing his fellow whites in the bleachers, with Little Willie beside him. He had never been a public speaker, Skatzes recalls, but a kind of power came into him at this moment. He put his arm around Little Willie's shoulders and said words to this effect:

This is against the administration. We are all in this together. They are against every one in here who's blue [the color of the prisoners' uniforms].... Don't be paranoid. Mix it up.... This is no time for you to be calling me "honky" or me to be calling you "nigger." If they come in here, they're going to kill all of us. They're going to kill this man and me, no matter what color we are.... Is everybody in agreement?[12]

Skatzes remembers that one of the Aryan leaders in the bleachers was visibly uncomfortable with his remarks.

The prospect of a race war abated. Several later incidents required mediation. But when Skatzes went out on the yard as a spokesman for the prisoners on April 15, he announced:

We are oppressed people, we have come together as one. We are brothers.... We are a unit here, they try to make this a racial issue. It is not a racial issue. Black and white alike have joined hands in SOCF and become one strong unit.[13]

After the prisoners surrendered and the Ohio State Highway Patrol entered L block, the authorities found graffiti on the walls. Some expressed the ideology of the various groups involved in the takeover: a crescent moon, which the authorities understood to represent the Islamic community; a six-pointed star, said to be associated with the Black Gangster Disciples; and swastikas and lightning bolts together with the words "Honor," "Aryan Brotherhood Forever," and "Supreme White Power."[14]

But a greater number of graffiti testified in substantially similar words to something quite different (Figs. 7.1–7.2). Sergeant Hudson identified a photograph taken in the L corridor.

Q. On the wall on the right there appears to be something written?

A. Says, "Black and White Together."

Q. Did you find that or similar slogans in many places in L block?

A. Yes, we did, throughout the corridor, in the L block.

Q. Including banners that the inmates produced?

A. Yes, sir.[15]

7.1 Graffiti in L block: Black and White Together 11 Days

7.2 Graffiti in L block: Convict Race

Further:

> **Q.** [What is photograph] 260?
>
> **A.** 260, the words, "Convict unity," written on the wall of L corridor.
>
> **Q.** Did you find the message of unity throughout L block?
>
> **A.** Yes....
>
> **Q.** Next photo?
>
> **A.** 261 is another photograph in L corridor that depicts the words, "Convict race."[16]

Evidently the cultural creation of racial identity can work in more than one way. At Lucasville, the process operated not to separate the races, but to overcome racism.

EXPLANATIONS

So what explains the Lucasville Redemption? The lives of the two white Aryan leaders—Skatzes and Robb—and Hasan, the Sunni Muslim imam, offer clues.

George

In Marion, Ohio, where George Skatzes grew up, neighbors regarded the Skatzes family as "white trash."[17] George found the black side of town more welcoming than the people next door. One of his best friends was the child of an interracial couple.

According to George, he has never felt racial superiority. "You won't find anyone at Lucasville I judged because of the color of his skin," he insists. Black prisoners, whether testifying for the prosecution or the defense at trial or in private conversation, agree.

George nonetheless joined the Aryan Brotherhood because he perceived whites at SOCF as a minority who needed to band together for self-protection.

Jason

Jason Robb is no doubt more typical.

There was a lot of racial tension in the penitentiary system, Jason told his jury in his unsworn statement. He had grown up in predominantly white neighborhoods. He had had little contact with blacks. Now he was in a prison community where—at least in his perception—"it was basically two, three blacks to every white." And what Jason called his first "real contact" with blacks was "not positive."

Jason didn't have to cell with blacks because he had a "separation tag." But at SOCF he worked with blacks and "got to talking" with them. Working as a plumber, he came in contact with a black electrician: "This guy's showing me how to do electric work and I'm showing him how to do things and basically we're teaching each other how to do work."

The electrician was a pretty militant black guy, Jason recalled. Black prisoners had "their own little cliques." Their thing was Black Power.

But we talked and it surprised me that me and him could talk. And he explained to me his beliefs. And that kind of surprised me that he would be open with me like that. So I explained to him how I felt. And we built a respect between us.

Thereafter, Jason says, he was a separatist but not a racist. "A racist is a person filled with hate who'll cause trouble between the races. You don't do that in a penitentiary. It don't work like that. You live together." What then is separatism?

> They stay on their side. I stay on my side. They do their thing, I do my thing. They have different beliefs, I have different beliefs. Their culture's different, my culture's different. Their music's different, my music's different. Can't be in a cell and play country music and he wants to play rap. They just don't mix in a cell. There would be a conflict there.

Summing up, Jason said: "I gave them respect, they give me respect. We just stay separate."[18]

At my request, Jason Robb has described what it means to him to be an Aryan Brother.

> A big part of who I am is shaped around my belief in Asatru and following the Norse traditions. My beliefs in Asatru and in the Aryan brothers are not one and the same but distinct in themselves.
>
> In Asatru, one does not surrender his belief to a god, or pray to a god. Basically it's a combination of a pantheistic notion that holds nature sacred with a polytheistic view of a plurality of gods and goddesses, allowing a closer bond between gods and man.

Asatru, Jason continues, "is the ethnic religion of Northern Europeans. It is a tribal religion that studies as well as encourages European traditions, history, art and culture." Nowadays, he says, this attitude is considered politically incorrect: we are taught to be ashamed of our ancestors' warrior nature.

Jason believes that without reason or the ability to think, we remain in a state of limbo, thus making it much easier for the powers-that-be to subjugate and control us. He was blind to this until he read *The Prince* by Machiavelli. "Then it was like a door into my inner consciousness opened wide," he writes. "In the prison system everyone is stripped of their identities coming in the door. They give you the same clothes and hair cut. All personal property is taken. You become a number as in George Orwell's book *1984*."

The administration uses hate to control and manipulate prisoners. "I choose," says Jason, "not to be a puppet to that manipulation, and to separate myself from that thought process and brainwashing tactic." In this prison system, whites, blacks, and Hispanics all strive to educate themselves about their culture and history. In the process they become politically conscious as well.

He goes on: "In prison all we have is our word, our honor. Without that you become only a number." He believes "that only a white man can speak for a white man's point of view and vice versa for blacks and Hispanics, because the truth is we are all treated differently. That's a fact. We experience life by shades of color and belief."

When he came to prison, Jason explains, "I became for the first time in my life a minority!... Because of this I could truly see what it meant to be in the minority, and how important it was to keep in touch with my heritage and culture by all means, and not to become assimilated." It's also true for blacks in prison, he believes.

I've witnessed blacks who came up in bi-racial families and lived in white neighborhoods become victimized in prison by other blacks for being too white. The same [is true] for whites who came up in ghettoes and black communities and become targets for other whites because they act black, not white.

Those who are proud of their skin color, heritage, and culture become identified as a threat to the safety and security of the prison system. Labeled gang members and racists, they are isolated and punished by the prison administration, "be you white or black."

Jason Robb states that he tries to live his life according to the "Noble Values"—courage, truth, honor, fidelity, discipline, hospitality, self-reliance, industriousness, and perseverance—and

The Nine Charges

1. To maintain candor and fidelity in love and devotion to the tried friend: Though he strike me I will do him no scathe.

2. Never to make wrong-some oath: For great and grim is the reward for the breaking of plighted troth.

3. To deal not hardly with the humble and the lowly.

4. To remember the respect that is due to great age.

5. To suffer no evil to go un-remedied and to fight against the enemies of faith, folk, and family: My foes I will fight in the field, nor will I stay to be burnt in my house.

6. To succor the friendless but to put no faith in the pledged word of a stranger people.

7. If I hear the fool's word of a drunken man I will strive not: For many a grief and the very death groweth from out such things.

8. To give kind heed to dead men: straw dead, sea dead, or sword dead.

9. To abide by the enactments of lawful authority and to bear with courage the decrees of the norns.

"What you do in life comes back around to you in the circle of life," Jason believes. He does what he does "for my brothers' advancement in knowledge, treatment, etc., and if others benefit because of it, so be it."

Finally, Jason writes, he wishes to define the word "Aryan" not as it came to be defined in propaganda after World War II, but as defined in *Webster's Illustrated New Standard Dictionary*, published by Albert Whitman & Company in 1935: "Aryan, belonging to the Indo-European family of language, supposed to have existed in Central Asia in prehistoric times, and from which Hindu, Persian, Greek, Latin, Slavonic, Teutonic and Celtic descended. The original language of the Aryans."

I am, adds Jason, Greek and Irish in ancestral lineage.

Most people mistakenly identify the word "Aryan" with Hitler's philosophy of the Aryan *Übermensch* and the Third Reich, according to Jason. The true definition refers to the Europeans who conquered India and Iran and is taken from the Sanskrit *arya*, meaning "noble" as well as "lord and ruler." Jason says, "I strive to be noble and hope my life will reflect that fact when I have moved on to Valhalla."

At the Ohio State Penitentiary, Jason Robb served as one of two spokesmen for the class of prisoner plaintiffs in the law suit that sought to improve conditions there. The other spokesperson was black, and when he was transferred, Jason urged the lawyers to recruit another black man. "The blacks need to be represented," he said.

Hasan

SOCF, Hasan says,[19] was similar to the ghettoes outside prison in some ways, different in others. The vices were the same, from "alcohol, drugs, hatred, violence, cheating, gambling, killing, lying, pimping, stealing to idleness, illiteracy, lack of educational and vocational pursuits, lewd sexual behavior and appetites, lack of respect for self and others, profanity and provocative epithets for women." To that extent most black prisoners felt right at home.

On the other hand, there were no poor whites or pockets of Asians, Arabs, or Hispanics in the segregated communities of Bayview and Yamacraw Village, where Hasan was raised: "Except for one white family who temporarily lived in Yamacraw Village, but moved when their children were being physically harassed by other residents, I cannot recall any whites ever living in my neighborhoods."

Residential segregation was the rule in virtually all the lower-income housing projects and ghettoes—Fellwood, Katon Homes, Fraizer Homes, Garden Homes, Hitch Village, Fred Wessal and Frances Bartow—in which he socialized. While there were white ghettoes in Savannah, and their inhabitants "most likely experienced the same problems as blacks living in ghettoes," according to Hasan, he made it his business never to socialize in places where he was not welcomed and wanted.

"Before becoming a Muslim in 1981, I had basically seen everything in either black or white," he writes. However, "Islam has instilled
in me the belief that we do not live in a bipolar world, but in a mul-
tiracial society, and should *recognize one another's differences* and right
to exist and worship the Creator." He cites texts from the Koran:

> O mankind! Verily, We have created you from a male and a
> female, and We have made you into nations and tribes that you
> may recognize one another. Verily, the noblest of you by Allah are
> your most pious. Verily, Allah has knowledge (of everything) and
> is fully aware. (Chapter 49, verse 13)

> Mankind was one community. (Chapter 2, verse 213)

"Islam negates racism and sees it for what it's worth," Hasan continues, "a disease of the heart that instills bigotry. If any man thinks
that he's better than or superior to another person because of the pig-
mentation of his skin, then he's actually living an illusion about his
own worth and humanity, and he needs to immediately wake up and
smell the coffee."

ON DEATH ROW

The solidarity of the Lucasville prisoners condemned to death continued after their trials.

Keith Lamar recalls how he was befriended by George Skatzes.
"I've never seen George as a racist," Keith recalls.

> In fact, he was the first one out of the so-called Lucasville Five
> who embraced me and let me know that we were all in this
> together, and that, I think, is what cemented our bond. Being the
> only one who didn't stay inside the whole eleven days, and the
> only one not affiliated with any group, I felt like an outsider, like
> I was in this all by myself. George saw that and moved to assure
> me that that was not the case.[20]

Of course it has been a struggle to create and maintain solidarity. George recalls the time when he, Hasan, and Anthony Lavelle were confined in adjacent cells in the North Hole at Chillicothe. Lavelle was forever throwing out antiwhite barbs, George recalls. According to George, Lavelle wrote on the shower wall the words, "Die, nigger scum, die," hoping to make Hasan believe that George had written them.

Yet both Hasan and Lavelle shared with George the extra food that they received during the Muslim holy month of Ramadan. At the time Lavelle was a Muslim, George says, and "Muslims are not supposed to let a neighbor go to bed hungry."

The moment of truth for George and Hasan came when George, having been removed from his cell on April 6, 1994, was allowed to return on April 8. George says he immediately went up to the bars that separated his cell from Hasan's. Grasping the bars he said, "You don't know me, I don't know you. I didn't tell them anything." Hasan believed him, and as described in Chapter 5, volunteered to write a note saying so to other black prisoners.

Confined together under harsh conditions, the five Lucasville prisoners have launched several hunger strikes. An early reference to the group as "the Lucasville Five" appears in a statement in which George Skatzes explains the reasons for a 1996 hunger strike. "I'm sure," he wrote, "that we—'the Lucasville Five'—have been placed ... under these conditions ... so as you may continue to maintain a safe prison environment." How do we defuse this situation? he asked. "Very simple—place the 'Lucasville Five' on their proper level, which is B level." Concluding, he wrote: "Let me state a fact—you have not had any problems from any of the 'Lucasville Five.' All we want is what we have coming to us—and that is being placed on our proper level."[21]

During another hunger strike by the Five the next year, Keith Lamar drafted their demands. The first was better medical care for a white man. "At the forefront of our list of concerns," he wrote, "we are asking that George Skatzes receive immediate medical attention for what is, as yet, an undiagnosed problem he's been having with his stomach. With respect to this," Keith continued,

> he has repeatedly tried, to no avail, to have the Doctor order some
> tests in order to determine what the problem is. Surely, he is enti-
> tled to the same attention that is accorded to everyone else and
> we're asking that he be given the attention capable of addressing
> these concerns and preventing his problem from becoming any
> worse, than what it already is.[22]

When the Five were transferred to the Ohio State Penitentiary in
Youngstown in May 1998, George and Hasan undertook yet another
hunger strike. After a week, a savvy member of the prison administration approached each, stating, "Look, we know we have problems.
Just start eating again so we can work on them together." And each
responded, "Let me talk with the other guy. When he's ready to eat,
I will think about it."

The following morning all of Hasan's complaints were resolved,
but not George's. When the prison officials brought Hasan his meal,
he refused to eat until George's issues were also settled or until he
received word from George that they would be resolved. After talking to the prison authorities about his complaints and receiving a sat-
isfactory answer, George sent a message to Hasan to resume eating.
Hasan explained in a letter:

> Since these people always come to me and try to discuss and work
> out any problem, I chose to stay on the fast to let them know that
> I was down with George's struggle too and I would not sit quiet
> and allow the system to mess over him. As anticipated, they got
> the message and know that we are one and will keep on pushing
> until we reach our destiny, i.e. equal protection under the laws as
> other general population inmates.[23]

BLACK AND WHITE TOGETHER?

In prison, it seems, the rewards for interracial solidarity may be more
substantial than the wages of whiteness. A young white prisoner
from the South describes how his attitudes changed while he was

imprisoned at the Ohio State Penitentiary:

> I have to say that I came to O.S.P. a stone cold racist. I wasn't
> racist when I was first imprisoned, but prison quickly turned me
> into one because of who was picking on me....

Note that the young man's experience in this respect parallels that of
Jason Robb. He continues:

> Three years at O.S.P. has changed that 100%. It's the WHITE
> police, administrators and nurses who treat me like a "nigger";
> treat all of us like that. It is *so frustrating* to live under such an
> intense, voiceless oppression; to be picked on just because I'm an
> inmate; to be pushed and harassed, physically, while I'm in full
> restraints, and to be antagonized non-stop.

Then we come to the ideological consequences of the oppression
shared by white and black prisoners.

> I used to be proud of white historical domination, the way whites just
> crushed and conquered all who stood in their path historically.
> But now when I watch documentaries on PBS like "Conquistadors"
> or "The West" it makes me mad because in those conquests and
> legal genocides I now see the arrogance of Lt.—or the administrators
> at O.S.P., with the blind assumption of superiority by all the fron-
> tiersmen/conquistadors/correctional officers. It's the same mental-
> ity really. Nothing on this planet has equalled the juggernaut force
> of white violence, ingenuity, conquest and superiority-through-
> numbers moving in coordination, but in that there was an *igno-
> rance* that led to the death of millions and the extinction of entire
> cultures and animal species. And this continues still today.

And he concludes:

> I guess living under this O.S.P. stuff has sapped my view of white
> nobility and made me realize just how impossible it is to fight the
> entrenched administration (on all levels of life) of an established
> majority. It makes me respect the Indians who fought to the death

when the white man just wrote up a document (manifest destiny) which made it perfectly legal to annihilate the Indians; or the Incan/Aztec natives who stood up to the conquistadors (and were mauled as a society); or the slaves who found the courage to revolt, knowing that there was no real win to be had except self satisfaction.

That's not to say I'm a bleeding heart liberal now, but I have a new perspective now when I see black ignorance because I see "the machine" that maintains that level of ignorance and oppression on others; I see how the foot is on the necks of second class citizens; how the whole set-up is impossible to defeat until the entire administration of all levels (president, judges, police, etc.) has been renewed by several generations. Sadly, I fear that whites will have a tough time once that overhaul takes place.[24]

CONCLUSION: RACE IN PRISON

Thinking of all the complex facts set forth in this chapter, I offer the following observations:

1. Many young whites who are imprisoned have had relatively little experience with blacks on the street.

2. In prison, the young white man finds himself in a situation where whites do not outnumber blacks eight to one (as in the United States as a whole); instead, as in the Ohio prison system, blacks and whites are approximately equal in number. Moreover, in the prison system blacks may occupy more important administrative posts, relative to whites, than they would be likely to hold outside the walls.

3. This combination of circumstances may cause such young white men, when they experience harassment from black prisoners, to become more racist than they were before incarceration and to join a whites-only group for protection.

4. From the point of view of the black prisoner, in contrast, the white oppression that existed before he went to prison continues behind the walls.

5. In the long run, the common oppression experienced by black and white prisoners may cause them to join together in resisting the authorities.

6. It can be a step toward such a common front for white and black groups to enter into agreements to settle disputes without violence, to make joint demands on the prison system, and the like. At this point, the ideology of both groups will likely be: you respect our autonomy, we will respect yours. Thus at Lucasville both blacks and whites opposed forced interracial celling.

7. Ultimately, prisoners stand together against dehumanizing treatment not as blacks or whites, but as human beings. The qualities all prisoners respect are courage; the ability to "maintain," to "stay strong"; respect for oneself and for others; refusal to snitch. Not all prisoners display these qualities, and those who do are not all of one skin color.

8. As the process unfolds, black and white prisoners, like the young man who wrote the letter quoted above, will begin to feel solidarity not only with each other, but also with people outside prison who are struggling against the same oppressive system: for example, rank-and-file workers; Third World farmers displaced from their land; Puerto Ricans struggling for self-determination; young people protesting economic inequality as promoted by the World Bank, the International Monetary Fund, and the World Trade Organization; and the victims of military occupation in Palestine and Iraq.

The process I have described—this "Lucasville Redemption"—contains a message for organizers outside prison.

Toward the end of the 1960s, black organizers in the civil rights movement said to their white colleagues, in effect: "Look, for a time we are going to organize Black Power in the black community. We suggest you do parallel work among working-class whites. Then, after a few years, we will bring the two movements together in an interracial movement of the poor that can change this society." In the labor movement, too, African Americans frustrated by the hostility of white fellow workers have organized their own all-black enclaves of power or, at least, organized separately within their plants and unions to seek equality.[25]

The problem is that the separate currents of struggle, black and white, have not been brought back together. The prisoners described in this book therefore have something to teach us all. Like blacks and whites on the outside, they first organized as Muslims and as Aryan Brothers. Then, under the hammer of common oppression, these groups joined to wage a struggle against an oppression shared by all.

To be sure, not every prisoner did so. There were informants in every group, such as Muslim Stacey Gordon, BGD leader Anthony Lavelle, and ABs like Rodger Snodgrass. And, of course, as in any human enterprise under difficult conditions, cooperation was ragged and uneven. Still, on the whole, Lucasville offers an extraordinary instance of blacks and whites overcoming their differences in common struggle.

We may yet be able to bring to birth a new world from the ashes of the old. Another world is possible.

Chapter 8

ATTICA AND AMNESTY

They came for the communists, and I did not speak up because I was not a communist; They came for the socialists, and I did not speak up because I was not a socialist; They came for the union leaders, and I did not speak up because I wasn't a union leader; They came for the Jews, and I did not speak up because I wasn't a Jew. Then they came for me, and there was no one left to speak up for me.

Martin Niemoeller

T HERE IS A PATTERN. It is a pattern of responding to violence with ever more repression and violence. Rather than addressing the causes of discontent and rebellion, the perpetrators of the pattern respond with greater and greater violence of their own.

The pattern has been described as a "culture of control." More specifically, it is

a highly efficient and technically controlled system of crime management directed almost exclusively at protecting crime's potential victims instead of coping with its causes. Its principal instru-ments [are] swift arrest, tough sentencing, and extensive incarcer-ation. Penal welfare and rehabilitation got lost in the process.[1]

There are four times as many persons in prison in the United States as there were 30 years ago, and our incarceration rate is between four and 10 times that of other industrialized countries. Yet all the time the overall rate of crime has held steady; in fact, after 1992 the rate of violent crime actually decreased.[2]

The experience of the Lucasville Five illustrates this pattern of official behavior. As a young man George Skatzes was imprisoned at the old Ohio Penitentiary in Columbus, where a rebellion occurred in the late 1960s. The State of Ohio responded to the rebellion by building its first maximum security prison, the Southern Ohio Correctional Facility in Lucasville. When Beverly Taylor was killed by a prisoner at SOCF in 1990, the system reacted by sending in Warden Arthur Tate and instituting Operation Shakedown. All the activities that might have encouraged prisoners to pursue alternatives to violence—educational programs, the opportunity for social inter-action, access to the law library—were curtailed. Not surprisingly, the uprising that is the subject of this book erupted three years later.

In the aftermath of the Lucasville uprising, all arms of Ohio gov-ernment—the Department of Rehabilitation and Correction, state court judges, the Ohio State Highway Patrol, and the special prose-cutor—pursued a policy of vengeance rather than rehabilitation.

ODRC'S FALSE SOLUTIONS

After the Lucasville uprising, ODRC director Reginald Wilkinson took three steps intended to show that there would never be another Lucasville. All exemplified the pattern: instead of going to the root of the problem, he built on top of it an unstable scaffolding of sup-pression and control.

First, Wilkinson promulgated a new rule that no Ohio prisoner classified maximum security (and, later, high maximum security as well) could be paroled until reduced to "close" security, now Level 3.[3] This rule did not directly affect the Lucasville Five, since they are sentenced to death, but it penalized many of the other participants in the 1993 uprising, who were reclassified high maximum security and transferred to the Youngstown "supermax." The new rule sent a message to all high security prisoners: no matter how many years you have served beyond the "guidelines" for your particular offense, and no matter how exemplary your conduct while in maximum or high maximum security, the Parole Board is denied discretion to release you.

Second, Wilkinson institutionalized new regional Special Tactics and Response (STAR) teams and Special Response Teams (SRT) at each prison. The teams' first major outing was directed at a group of three dozen men on Death Row who took over one of the living units, DR-4, on September 5, 1997. The Lucasville Five were all housed in DR-4. The prisoners who began this action overpowered and then released the three officers on duty. When the STAR and SRT teams stormed the block, almost all prisoners in DR-4 were in their cells, including George Skatzes, who never left his cell at any time. As the officers entered the block they could be heard shouting, "Where's Robb?" Robb, although he offered no resistance, was beaten so severely that his skull was fractured. When dragged from his cell, he was covered with blood, and a prison official who knew him well could recognize him only by his tattoos (Fig. 8.1).[4]

A Use of Force Committee entirely made up of department employees was appointed to investigate the incident. The Committee concluded, among other things:

- "The Assault Teams ... were all dressed in black and wore gas masks. Therefore the ability of the Committee to pursue investigation of specific personal identification of any employee or inmate was severely compromised."

- "The use of gas, mace, and distraction control devices was excessive."
- "A general loss of control existed in the manner in which inmates were controlled, restrained, and escorted from the cell block. The failure of supervisory staff to provide videotaping was instrumental in providing an environment for this to take place."[5]

Finally, Director Wilkinson caused to be constructed the new "supermax" prison in Youngstown, the Ohio State Penitentiary (OSP). The Lucasville Five were among the first prisoners to be transferred to OSP when it opened in May 1998. Indeed, one can plausibly suggest that OSP was built for them: that is, this expensive new prison is intended to send the message that the State of Ohio is *doing something* to prevent another Lucasville uprising. Unlike most supermax prisons, OSP was constructed with no outdoor recreation facilities of any kind. At a deposition conducted by the author, Director Wilkinson was asked why. this was so. He answered that the Lucasville uprising of 1993 began on the rec yard. Federal Judge James S. Gwin has concluded that OSP was "[c]onstructed in reaction to the April 1993 riot at the Southern Ohio Correctional Facility at Lucasville."[6]

Judge Gwin also noted that evidence presented at trial suggests that Ohio does not need a high maximum security prison, or, at least, does not need one with the capacity of OSP:

> Peter Davis, a member of the Ohio Parole Board and former executive director of the Correctional Institution Inspection Committee of the Ohio General Assembly, testified about the Department of Rehabilitation and Correction's use of the J-1 cellblock at the Southern Ohio Correctional Facility. The Southern Ohio Correctional Facility is Ohio's only maximum security prison, the security level immediately below the OSP's high maximum security level.... The J-1 cellblock is the most restrictive cellblock within the Southern Ohio Correctional Facility....

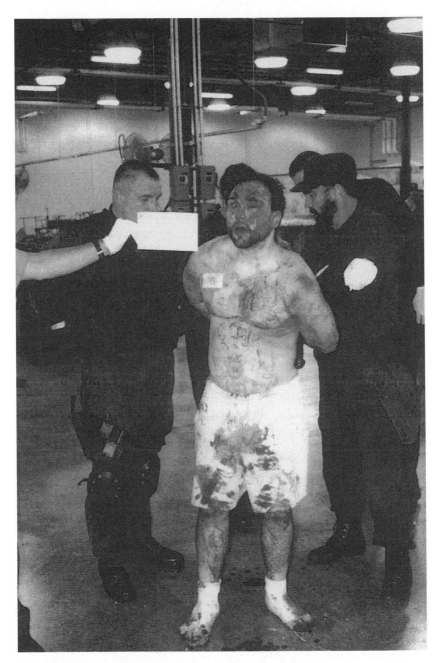

8.1 Jason Robb after uprising on Death Row, September 5, 1997

Suggestive that Ohio never needed the 504-inmate capacity of the OSP, before the OSP was built Ohio did not fill the J-1 cells at the Southern Ohio Correctional Facility. Instead, Ohio … did not have a sufficient number of maximum security cells.

Judge Gwin concluded: "After the huge investment in the OSP, Ohio risks having a 'because we have built it, they will come' mind set."[7]

In OSP's first four months of operation, more than a hundred prisoners were transferred to OSP without notice or hearing of any kind. The former director of the Correctional Institution Inspection Committee testified that there were no criteria explaining why some prisoners were sent to the supermax and others, who had committed similar offenses, remained in other facilities. Several prisoners were sent to OSP although they had been acquitted by juries of the alleged offenses that were used to justify their transfer. One prisoner was transferred to OSP after being hit over the head in the chow line by another inmate. A second prisoner was kept at OSP because the way he made the capital letter "B" was viewed by authorities as an expression of disrespect by the Crips toward the Bloods. On the witness stand, this man turned to the judge and said that he had made his "B"s that way since third grade. Approximately sixty prisoners were transferred to the supermax for placement offenses that involved nothing more than conspiracy to convey, or possession of, small quantities of drugs.

Once at OSP, prisoners face conditions that Judge Gwin found to constitute "atypical and significant hardship as compared to the ordinary incidents of prison life." OSP prisoners typically spend years there, alone for a minimum of 23 hours a day in a cell about the size of a small bathroom or the parking space for a compact car. Cell doors are solid metal, not bars as at SOCF. The OSP Warden had metal strips welded to the sides and bottom of the cell doors, further hindering communication between prisoners. There are no contact visits. Although separated from visitors by a solid sheet of plexiglass, prisoners are shackled and subjected to humiliating strip searches coming and going between cell and visiting booth.

Getting out of the Ohio supermax is as problematic as getting in. These administrative detentions are reviewed once a year by a committee of prison officials. But even when the committee determines that the prisoner is ready for release, a higher official—sometimes the man who sent the prisoner to OSP in the first place—can veto the recommendation.

The four members of the Lucasville Five who are still at OSP[8] have been informed, in writing, that they should expect their placement there to be permanent. Along with three other supermax prisoners who are accused of killing prison staff, Hasan, Lamar, Robb, and Namir were told in August 2003:

> You were admitted to the OSP in May of 1998. We are of the opinion that your placement offense is so severe that you should remain at the OSP permanently or for many years regardless of your behavior while confined at the OSP.[9]

The indefinite solitary confinement of these men does not allow for the possibility of change. The prisoner is locked up with his past and can do nothing about it. "Solitary" without end takes away hope and meaning in life: it is slow-motion death, inch by inch, moment by moment. As the Supreme Court of the United States concluded 125 years ago:

> A considerable number of the prisoners fell, even after a short confinement, into a semi-fatuous condition, from which it was next to impossible to arouse them, and others became violently insane; others still, committed suicide; while those who stood the ordeal better were not generally reformed, and in most cases did not recover sufficient mental activity to be of any subsequent service to the community.[10]

Austin v. Wilkinson, the class action on behalf of OSP prisoners, was filed after three prisoners committed suicide.

"THIS IS A MURDER CASE"

Like the Department of Rehabilitation and Correction, the state
courts of Ohio have been interested only in punishing the Lucasville
offenders, not in understanding why they rebelled. Disregard for the
causes of their discontent continued in court proceedings after the
surrender.

Anyone trying to respond to a conflict between other human
beings is likely to begin by saying, "Tell me how this got started."
Once the origin of irritation, anger, and violence has been discerned,
it is possible to make amends and change future conduct. Similarly,
one might reasonably have hoped that somewhere in the more than
twenty-five thousand pages of trial transcripts related to the five
Lucasville prisoners sentenced to death there would be some indica-
tion of an effort to find out why the uprising occurred. Even in a
homicide arising from a barroom brawl, a criminal defendant is
allowed to present evidence of provocation. The Lucasville Five,
however, were not allowed to call witnesses or enter documents into
the record that might have helped their juries to understand why the
uprising happened.

The most determined effort to introduce such evidence came in
the trial of the alleged leader of the disturbance, Hasan. In *State v.
Sanders*, the trial judge permitted the prosecution to dwell at length
on the state's one-sided and highly prejudicial "history" of how the
riot came about, but prevented defense counsel from presenting evidence in rebuttal.

Prosecutor Gerald Krumpelbeck began his opening statement to
the jury in *State v. Sanders* as follows:

> Ladies and gentlemen, let me introduce you to the riot at the
> Southern Ohio Correctional Facility of Easter Day, April 11, 1993.
>
> The evidence will show, to begin with, that this riot is mis-
> named. This riot was the idea of one man. This riot was planned
> by one man. This riot was organized by one man.[11]

Co-prosecutor Richard Gibson sounded the same theme at the beginning of his closing argument:

> Now before I get into talking about the specific offenses with which Carlos Sanders is charged, there's one issue that I think is very important to you that you, as a jury, really need to decide in deciding what he's guilty of, and that is this question: Whose riot was this?... Who called for this riot?... Ladies and gentlemen, first and foremost, without question this was his riot.[12]

To counter this broadbrush prosecution strategy, Hasan's counsel first tried to cross-examine prosecution witness Warden Arthur Tate about prison conditions that caused the riot. The prosecutor objected, and the court barred the question, ruling that the riot was "only incidental.... This is a murder case. It has nothing to do with the riot, except that it happened in a prison at the time of the riot."[13]

Then, in presenting its own case, the defense tried to call witnesses to testify about the riot's causes.

First, Hasan's defense team called Frederick Crowder. Crowder was a Muslim prisoner who would have testified that in 1992-93, while housed at Mansfield Correctional Institution (ManCI), he and other Sunni Muslims expressed their objections to the form of tuberculosis testing proposed at ManCI and were able to resolve the issue peacefully with the administration there. The judge refused to let Crowder testify, explaining:

> This case is not a case concerning the riot. The riot occurred incidentally, as far as I'm concerned. We're concerned with a number of charges that Mr. Sanders or Mr. Hasan is charged with—two aggravated murders, some kidnapping, some felonious assaults. They happen to have occurred in an institution.
>
> The justification or the necessity or the right or wrongness of the riot is irrelevant. The TB testing, whether or not they were justified to riot because they were going to be subjected to it, is irrelevant to me.

This is a murder case, a felonious assault case, a kidnapping case. I don't care what they did in Mansfield concerning a TB testing. It is irrelevant. There was no murder in this courtroom in Mansfield, Ohio.[14]

When the exclusion of this testimony came before the Ohio Supreme Court on appeal, the court opined:

Sanders ... argues essentially that, if the state was permitted to show that he was responsible for the riot, then the defense had a right to show that the prison administration also bore some responsibility for it....

Evidence that Sanders instigated and led the riot was not introduced for the purpose of showing that Sanders, as opposed to the prison administration, was "responsible" for the riot. Instead, it was introduced to show that he was an inmate leader whose orders were obeyed—a fact that was directly related to his culpability for Vallandingham's murder.[15]

This retrospective rationale for the prosecution's strategy is not supported by the record. The prosecution went far beyond seeking to prove Hasan's alleged authority over other prisoners. The prosecutors presented him to the jury as the sole malevolent force behind everything that happened during the riot, including the death of Officer Robert Vallandingham.

Finally, in the sentencing phase of the trial after Hasan was found guilty, the defense called as its first witness Joseph R. Rowan, an authority on prisons who has testified as an expert in about three hundred fifty lawsuits.[16] The judge asked the witness what he was going to say. Rowan said he would testify about "the impact of administration and the total system at Southern Ohio Correctional Facility which led to this riot ... which could have been easily prevented." "Is there anything else?" the judge inquired. Yes, Rowan responded: "[t]hat David See, if his advice was followed—and there are other good approaches—it is highly likely this riot could have been prevented. But the warden refused to follow it."[17]

The judge excluded Rowan's testimony, explaining:

> He's just going to criticize the administrator of prisons, and riots
> are not created by the prison. Riots are created by the inmates.
>
> Now I said before in this trial, it is not going to be a trial of a
> riot. What this is is a murder that happened to happen in a prison
> during a riot.[18]

On appeal, the Ohio Supreme Court said that Rowan should have
been permitted to testify. But, the court added, the exclusion of his
evidence was harmless error.

> This error does not require a new sentencing hearing.... We have
> held that, when independently reviewing a death sentence..., we
> may "consider proffered evidence that the jury was erroneously
> not allowed to consider." ... [W]e find that it deserves no
> weight.... [W]hatever mistakes prison administrators may have
> made, Sanders need not have ordered Vallandingham's murder.[19]

THE ATTICA EXAMPLE

More than ten years after the negotiated surrender, the Ohio State
Highway Patrol and the Office of the Special Prosecutor implacably
seek to add five more premeditated deaths to the 10 deaths tragically
experienced in April 1993. Now that the trials are over and the appeals
are not yet concluded, public opinion has a further—and final—
opportunity to put a stop to the pattern of ever-escalating violence.

Attica offers an instructive alternative. At Attica, armed forces of
the state assaulted the occupied recreation yard on the last day of the
riot, killing 29 prisoners and 10 hostage guards. But if one sets to one
side the dreadful events of that last day, there are parallels between
what happened at Attica in 1971 and what happened, 22 years later,
at SOCF. At both institutions an officer was killed. At both, alleged

prisoner "snitches" were killed: three in four days at Attica; nine in 11 days at Lucasville. Moreover, there were seven additional prisoners at Attica who kept to themselves in a tent near the handball court. One of them put a white cloth on a stick on top of the tent. The seven were thereupon accused of being "traitors," and the committee that sought to coordinate the uprising repeatedly debated their fate, some prisoners favoring their execution. Charges against these seven prisoners were similar to the accusations against the three who were killed, suggesting that at least some of the seven might well have been killed had the disturbance lasted longer. Indeed, on the final morning, the young man who hoisted the white flag and one other were blindfolded, bound, and left in an exposed position to await the state's assault.[20]

Thus the allegations against prisoners at Attica and Lucasville were similar, and so were the initial judicial proceedings. At Attica a special prosecutor was appointed and grand juries were convened. Three prisoner leaders were charged with felony murder resulting from the kidnapping of two of the supposed snitches. Two other prisoners were charged with actually killing them, and two more were charged with the murder of Officer Quinn. In all, 62 prisoners were charged with more than a thousand counts of criminal activity.[21] Similarly, after the surrender at Lucasville, 152 indictments were brought, charging 50 prisoners with much the same kinds of crimes.[22]

The difference lies in what happened next. At Lucasville, prosecution was pursued. There were 50 trials in 10 counties, 47 guilty verdicts or plea bargains, and five death sentences.[23]

Judicial proceedings after Attica had an altogether different conclusion. According to Bert Useem and Peter Kimball:

> Scandal broke out in 1975, when a chief assistant to the special Attica prosecutor went public with charges that his investigation of reprisals and reckless use of firearms by guards and police was being stifled from above. In the clamor over his disclosures, *a general amnesty was declared.* All outstanding indictments of inmates

were dropped. Seven inmates who had pleaded guilty to reduced charges were pardoned by Governor Hugh Carey. The sentence of John Hill (Dacajaweiah), convicted of killing Quinn, was commuted, and he was paroled in March of 1979.[24]

The unraveling of the Attica prosecutions began in January 1975, when Charles Crowley, a former prisoner, testified in a pretrial hearing that he had lied to the grand jury because he was beaten and coerced by guards. In April Assistant Prosecutor Malcolm Bell resigned and charged the chief prosecutor, Anthony Simonetti, with covering up possible crimes by law enforcement officers. In February 1976, Special Prosecutor Alfred Scotti requested that all but one of the remaining indictments should be dismissed "in the interest of justice."[25]

The end came in a dramatic statement by New York Governor Carey on December 31, 1976. Explaining that "we now confront the real possibility that the law itself may well fall into disrespect" and that "equal justice by way of further prosecutions is no longer possible," Governor Carey vacated the plea agreements of seven former Attica prisoners, commuted the sentence of the prisoner convicted of killing Officer Quinn, and barred disciplinary action against 20 state troopers and correctional officers. He went on to say:

I am moved to recognize that Attica has been a tragedy of immeasurable proportions, unalterably affecting countless lives. Too many families have grieved, too many have suffered deprivations, too many have lived their lives in uncertainty waiting for the long nightmare to end. For over five years and with hundreds of thousands of dollars and countless man-hours we have followed the path of investigation and accusation. We have succeeded in dividing and polarizing the people of the state without satisfying the quest for justice in this tragedy. To continue in this course, I believe, would be merely to prolong the agony with no better hope of a just and abiding conclusion.

The governor concluded by saying that his actions should not be understood to imply "a lack of culpability for the conduct at issue." Rather, "these actions are in recognition that there does exist a larger wrong which transcends the wrongful acts of individuals."[26]

ATTICA APPLIED

As I have sought to show in this book, the prosecutorial misconduct that triggered a general amnesty in New York had its counterpart in Ohio. Indeed, prosecutors in both states displayed the same "arbitrary, reckless, and some would say malicious, pursuit of the death penalty" as prosecutors in Texas, Illinois, and other states across the nation.[27]

The Ohio special prosecutor must be assumed to be familiar with the overwhelming evidence pointing to Anthony Lavelle as the actual killer of Officer Vallandingham. The very first prisoner from L block to be questioned by the Ohio State Highway Patrol, at 11:48 p.m. on the night of the surrender, was Emanuel "Buddy" Newell. He told two troopers:

> That head guy of the disciples, the leader, I heard him one day, you know, talking … about executing police he said and I want to execute some more police. Those were his words. He said I want to execute some more police but the Aryans don't want me to do it.[28]

Moreover, Lavelle himself, in a videotaped interview with Trooper Shepard in May 1994, told a story wholly at variance with the testimony he later offered to convict Robb, Namir, Skatzes, and Hasan.

Lavelle confessed to Shepard that he "was there" when Officer Vallandingham was strangled. He had recognized the officer who was murdered by his bandaged shoulder. He was three or four cells away from the cell or shower in which Officer Vallandingham was killed.

"When they brought his body out, I was standing at the top of the range," Lavelle concluded.[29]

Yet in trial after trial, Lavelle was permitted to tell unsuspecting juries that he was nowhere near L-6 at the time Officer Vallandingham was murdered.

Kenneth Law, a key witness against Hasan and Namir, was likewise permitted to present perjured testimony. Law has since executed a series of affidavits in which he states that: (1) He, Sherman Sims, and Stacey Gordon made up a story about the Vallandingham murder, which they knew "was the key to the door [out of prison]." (2) The state did not believe his story and tried him for the kidnapping and aggravated murder of Vallandingham. He was found guilty of kidnapping, but the jury hung on the murder charge. (3) The state then told him that he would be retried for aggravated murder unless he agreed to testify against Hasan and Namir. "I was interviewed several times before both trials and was told what to say," Law now states in his affidavits. "They told me if I did anything but what they told me ... I [would] be recharged."[30]

Law has also stated under oath that he knew, and had informed the state, that Lavelle killed Officer Vallandingham.

> On the morning of April 15, 1993, I was in L-1 and heard Anthony Lavelle, Aaron Jefferson, and Tim Williams talking about killing a guard. Lavelle left L-1, along with two others whom I recognized to be Gangster Disciples, despite their masks.
>
> A few minutes later, I also left L-1 and went toward L-6. As I approached the door of L-6, the two masked Disciples came out. I entered L-6 and saw Lavelle inside. I looked into the shower and saw Officer Vallandingham dead. It was very clear to me what had just happened: Lavelle and his associates had killed the guard.

During his interrogation, Law went on,

> prosecutors, including Brower, and troopers, including McGough, placed tremendous pressure on me, saying that they would convict

and execute me for killing Vallandingham, which I had nothing to do with, unless I said that Hasan had commanded the killing. At one point, I revealed to them that Anthony Lavelle had killed Vallandingham. *The prosecutor told me that my story would have to change, because Lavelle was a State witness.*[31]

Alvin Jones, also known as Mosi Paki, was also accused of helping to kill Officer Vallandingham. Jones was tried, not in court, but by an administrative body known as a Rules Infraction Board (RIB). One of the witnesses was Sergeant Howard Hudson of the Ohio State Highway Patrol, the state's chief investigator in the Lucasville cases. Hudson testified in part: "Law failed polygraph. Law took himself out of act [of killing Officer Vallandingham] and replaced himself with inmate Darnell Alexander."[32] Nonetheless, after Jones's RIB proceeding, the state called Law as a witness in the subsequent trial of Hasan and permitted him to testify under oath to the narrative the state knew to be false.

If the convictions of Hasan, Robb, Skatzes, and Namir for the murder of Officer Vallandingham are fatally flawed, what is left of the other aggravated murders for which members of the Lucasville Five have been convicted?

Hasan and Namir

Hasan and Namir were each found by a jury to be not guilty of the only other murder with which each was charged, the killing of prisoner Bruce Harris on April 21. Therefore, if their convictions for Officer Vallandingham's death are vacated, neither should remain on Death Row.

Robb and Skatzes

Jason Robb was convicted of the aggravated murder of prisoner David Sommers, and George Skatzes of the aggravated murder of prisoners Sommers and Earl Elder. It is impossible within the scope of this book to examine each of these murders in detail. At least two eyewitnesses, one of whom has confessed to taking part in killing Elder, state that Skatzes was nowhere in the vicinity and had nothing to do with that murder. Prisoner Aaron Jefferson was found guilty of killing Sommers with a massive blow to the head with a baseball bat, the very crime for which Skatzes had previously been found guilty and sentenced to death.[33]

But it is not necessary to descend to this level of detail to see why the death sentences of Robb and Skatzes for the Elder and Sommers killings should be vacated. In their trials, prosecutors insisted—over the objections of defense counsel in each case—on trying the defendant in one proceeding for a single "course of conduct" that included all the crimes with which he was charged. The evidence in support of these alleged additional crimes was shaky and might well have resulted in findings of not guilty had each crime been tried separately. The charge of killing Officer Vallandingham was obviously the one most likely to influence their juries. By trying the additional charges as part of a single course of conduct together with the false charge of murdering Officer Vallandingham, the prosecution inevitably caused the Robb and Skatzes juries to be prejudiced against defendants and to be more likely to convict for the murders of Elder and Sommers.

The lengths to which prosecutors went to implicate defendants in the murder of Officer Vallandingham, because of its predictable effect on juries, is most dramatically illustrated by the case of Derek Cannon. Cannon was indicted for the murder of prisoner Darrell Depina on April 11. However, during Cannon's trial the prosecution called Dwayne Buckley, an inmate at the Hamilton County jail, where Cannon was being held for his trial. Buckley testified that Cannon told him that Cannon and some of his friends had "taken" a guard (who could only have been Officer Vallandingham) and tortured the officer before they killed him. According to Cannon's defense lawyer, the judge commented after the trial that it was this witness who "impressed a lot of the jury as to what kind of person"

Cannon was. There was only one difficulty: on April 15, when Officer Vallandingham was killed, Cannon was not in L block. The state has certified that Cannon was transported from SOCF to Lebanon Correctional Institution on April 16. Since no prisoner entered or left L block between April 11 and April 21, he could only have been *outside* L block on the day Officer Vallandingham was murdered there.[34]

The prosecution having insisted that the charges against Robb and Skatzes for murdering Vallandingham should be tried together with the other charges against them, and the Vallandingham charge having been shown to be unfounded, the Elder and Sommers convictions should also be vacated.[35]

Lamar

It was shown above that Aaron Jefferson confessed to killing *by himself* one of the prisoners (Depina) whom Keith Lamar was convicted of murdering. The witnesses to the other murders for which Lamar was convicted were in many instances the same men who testified, apparently untruthfully, to his responsibility for killing Depina. Moreover Lamar was tried in rural Lawrence County in southeastern Ohio, where there was not a single African American on his jury and only two blacks in the "pool" from which the jury was selected.[36]

A Case for Amnesty

Thus at Lucasville, as at Attica, there is a strong case for vacating all convictions and sentences. Amnesty should also extend to administrative proceedings that found other Lucasville prisoners guilty of crimes. For example, the Rules Infraction Board that found that Alvin Jones had helped to murder Officer Vallandingham relied on testimony by a witness who said he had seen Jones standing on a weight bar and rocking back and forth on it so as to crush the guard's neck as the officer lay prone on the ground. But the evidence of the coroner, not considered by the RIB, was that Vallandingham was killed by strangulation. The coroner found no evidence of the use of a rigid object like a weight bar, and also found that the larynx was not crushed.[37]

It may be objected that a general amnesty for all crimes charged against all Lucasville defendants is "impossible." This is precisely what was said at Attica. Negotiations during that uprising collapsed when the state refused to offer amnesty to the prisoners in rebellion, and 39 human beings, including 10 hostage correctional officers, died as a result. Later, as described above, amnesty was provided. Ohio can and should do the same.

In the words of Professor Michael Nagler, an authority on non-violence: "We don't need to find out who is to blame for all the violence; we just need to find out how to make it stop."[38]

"TREAT US LIKE HUMAN BEINGS"

The most difficult and challenging concept of Mahatma Gandhi is *satyagraha*. The literal meaning of the word is "clinging to the truth." Gandhi said that *satyagraha* defined what he believed in, and he entitled his autobiography *The Story of My Experiments with Truth*.

What sort of definition of nonviolence is this supposed to be? What can Gandhi mean when he says that the opposite of violence is truth?

Prisoners have their own ideas about the judicial system, about incarceration for long indefinite sentences, and about the death penalty. Underlying any specific solutions they may propose is a widely held value that prisoners articulate with the word "respect."

The word "respect" derives from the Latin verb "to see." It might be paraphrased in Gandhian terms as *seeing* the truth or reality of another person. To respect someone is *not to overlook* him: it is to recognize who he is. Or as Mumia Abu-Jamal puts the same idea, "[T]he greatest love we can show our children is the attention we pay them, the time we take for them. Maybe we serve children best simply by noticing them."[39]

Thus Keith Lamar relates that he grew up without caring about his own feelings, and so he did not care about the feelings of others. When he began to care about his own feelings, Keith believes, he could begin to care about others, too.[40]

There is an interesting resonance between "respect" in the sense of "really seeing me" and the judicial concept of habeas corpus. The ancient writ of habeas corpus—the foundation of the Anglo-American system of criminal justice—requires the state to produce a prisoner in open court so that friends and relatives can *see* the prisoner, and can *confirm with their own eyes and ears* that the government has informed the prisoner of the specific crimes with which he or she is charged.

There were three suicides at the Ohio State Penitentiary during its first two years of operation. After a second suicide at OSP in July 1998, an assistant to the warden asked Alice and Staughton Lynd what OSP could do to make life there more worth living. Attorney Alice Lynd sent a form letter to prisoners at OSP in which she asked them what they would answer if someone asked them that question. More than a hundred prisoners replied. The following are quotations from these letters. Think of them as graffiti written on the walls of the supermax cells, supplements to the affirmations found on the walls of L block after the Lucasville uprising.

"I ask for the respect I give to the staff to be given back to me. Let me do my time in peace."

"It doesn't matter if you gave me all the television and commissary in the world. None of those [things] will make a difference if the willingness isn't there to treat me like a human being."

"If you hate me it's only natural I hate back."

"Nothing is done to help me cope or prepare me to re-enter general population or society."

8.2 A Prisoner Behind Bars

Drawing by Jason Robb

"[We want to go outside for recreation] in rec cages like at Lucasville. We feel like rats in a tube who need air."

"There will be more suicides here. It's sad because the conditions and staff contribute to it. I see it every day. I'm living it!"

"I've heard Correctional Officers and Lieutenants say to inmates on suicide watch, 'you ain't dead yet' (while kicking the door). Then as they depart, 'We'll come back when you're dead'."

"The overall problem [is that] people don't care if we live or die."

"Treat us like humans."

Jason Robb, himself an artist with pen and ink (Fig. 8.2), has brought to my attention the fact that Bomani (also known as Keith Lamar) is a poet. A poem by Bomani can serve as a last reflection.[41]

Stop the Violence

God is alive and
resides inside of us.
All we have to do is trust
and have faith,
stop the madness and give thanks
for the blessings that shape
our lives. . . .
We have to look ahead instead
of always looking back at the past,
slow down instead of moving so fast,
and laugh, reach deep and have
the courage to dream
about beautiful days
and different ways
to give, with love . . . in peace.

CHRONOLOGY

The following account is drawn primarily from the testimony of Sergeant Howard Hudson of the Ohio State Highway Patrol, chief investigator of the Lucasville events for the State of Ohio, in *State v. Skatzes*.

Sunday, April 11, 1993

3:00 p.m. As prisoners returned from the yard at the end of the recreation period, the disturbance began.

4:45 p.m. Officer Harold Fraley was released through the end of L-8 stairwell with severe head injuries.

6:46 p.m. Johnny Fryman, white inmate, was put on the yard, severely beaten.

8:05 p.m. Officer John Kemper was placed on the yard, severely beaten.

9:17, 9:27 p.m. The bodies of white inmates William Svette, Bruce Vitale, Franklin Farrell, Albert Staiano, and Darrold Depina were placed on the yard. "Itchy" Walker and Andre Stockton, black inmates, were placed on the yard with severe injuries.

11:02 p.m. Officer Robert Schroeder was placed on the yard with severe injuries.

[First night, time unknown] Earl Elder, white inmate, died of stab wounds in L-6-60.

Monday, April 12

1:30–3:21 a.m. Inmates on the yard surrendered and were locked 10 to a cell in K complex.

[Date unknown] Dennis Weaver, black inmate, was strangled in a cell in K-2.

8:05 a.m. L complex water and electricity were turned off.

10:15 a.m. Earl Elder's body was placed on the yard.

Tuesday, April 13

5:56 a.m. Recording of negotiations by the authorities began.

Wednesday, April 14

10:45 a.m. Tessa Unwin, ODRC public information officer, stated that threats against officers were part of negotiations. Inmates interpreted her remarks as a sign that the state was not taking them seriously.

3:30–3:40 p.m. First delivery of food and water, and of medications for officers, was made.

Thursday, April 15

11:05–11:10 a.m. Officer Robert Vallandingham's body was placed on the yard by four inmates.

7:30 p.m. Officer Darrold Clark was released in exchange for a live radio broadcast by George Skatzes.

Friday, April 16

1:35 p.m. Officer Anthony Demons was released in exchange for a live television broadcast by Stanley Cummings.

Saturday, April 17

Robb took Skatzes' place as negotiator.

4:55 p.m. Second delivery of food and water occurred.

Sunday, April 18

Warden Arthur Tate signed a 21-point agreement proposed by the state.

Monday, April 19

Negotiations continued.

Tuesday, April 20

11:59 a.m. Attorney Niki Schwartz met with inmates Anthony Lavelle (Black Gangster Disciples), Jason Robb (Aryan Brotherhood), and Hasan (Muslims).

7:08 p.m. Third delivery of food and water occurred.

Wednesday, April 21

11:00 a.m.–12:37 p.m. Schwartz met with Hasan, Lavelle, and Robb.

3:56 p.m. Inmates began to surrender in groups of 20; 129 inmates were immediately transported to Mansfield Correctional Institution. The remaining inmates were locked on K-side.

10:40 p.m. The five remaining hostages were released.

11:20 p.m. The last inmate surrendered.

Thursday, April 22

The body of white inmate David Sommers was found by the Highway Patrol in L-7-41. The body of black inmate Bruce Harris was found in cell L-6-31.

APPENDIX 1

TRANSCRIPT OF TUNNEL TAPE 61

Using sensitive recording equipment in the tunnels under L block, the authorities recorded meetings of the leaders of the Lucasville uprising. Everyone agrees that these recordings are imperfect: parts of the conversations are inaudible, and background noise sometimes drowns out the words.

The most important of the so-called tunnel tapes is Tunnel Tape 61, which purports to record a meeting held between 8:07 and 8:52 a.m. on Thursday, April 15. Officer Vallandingham was killed later that morning.

There are a number of different transcripts of Tunnel Tape 61. What follows is the transcript prepared by the state with the assistance of prisoner informants and offered by the state at the Robb, Namir, and Skatzes trials to "assist" juries listening to the tape recording.

Tunnel Tape #61
4/15/93
0807–0852 Hours
Location L-2

James Were: The only thing I care about is dying right ... the other ... right now ... you, you guys ... everyone's in on it ... this is what we got to come together for ... Now if we come together, come together, and be real strong brothers sustained ... we can achieve something.

Part of the thing is bodies is bodies ...

In so many day, in so many days what have we achieved... Everybody in the world is looking at this. What have we achieved. They don't know what's happened ...

Unknown: The first thing we want to discuss is the people in the med unit ...

Anthony Lavelle: Me and my brothers, I am the only one to make decisions for ... what I say to the man ...

Be solid be together be solid they are not principled ... if we all stay together ...

I'm the one ... George

[phone rings, train whistle]

Jason Robb: As far as, ahh George coming down ... coming down ...

James Were: ... If we all be together

Just like he ... came in and told them ...

Tell them cut that fan off right now. What did they do, what did they do they ... cut it off. That's because they fear ... They have more fear than we do ...

They know when they come in here they got to bring artillery artillery

Cummings: ... when I said that I would ask for a show of hands, I want to hear a voice. When we leave up out of here this morning, let's have this established. All three things. Going to the phone. All that what we talked about in the past concessions ...

[phone rings]

Let's this be the format ... We might have to sit a day or two to do that. Stall to them. Tighten our own belts like they been doing us. Let the first business be our first format for the day. Let us tell them. Water, electricity, turn it back on ... People up underneath this basement out from down there. Let this be our first format before we even talk about. You know we won't be losing. You understand what I'm saying.

This is as it should be these things, for the officers

Do this as good faith for the well being of your officers. Cut the lights, water and get your police out from underneath these tunnels.

[many talking]

Jason Robb: We only flush one flush and it stops. We got to get buckets and get that water?

Cummings: Some cells, I think, some cells still have ... and should be the only one allowed to use it ... Everybody understand what I said ...

We ain't asking for nothing else today but for the water, lights, and power, and the people down there get out from in there. This is what negotiations is now. You can do this as good faith for all your officer in here. They suffering just like we suffering. Okay. We ain't going to mention the news media if at all possible, we ain't going to mention that, okay. First of all we want what we had when we started plain and simple. Now we can talk and say deliberate on that for a half hour with them. That's all, that's all we going to talk on. Then, they say well, I got to get with such and such. Well, when you come up with a decision you call me back and then we going on about our business planning ahead what we gonna do next. If we get this here we're not talking about you know ahh, the news media. Okay, we gonna move these hostages out or we gonna pay enough now ... we already got the fans out we already did that

If you don't comply with this here however long the heads sit here figuring like they should have the appropriate time to adhere to this here then we will, ahh, we will resort to drastic measures and we will let them see. This is whats gonna happen because you are bullshitting with us. Excuse my expression. I want to know if we all in accord that when we go out here on this phone, whoever does this, I got no problems with George talking on the phone or somebody else can talk on the phone or myself use the phone, but I want to know is this the format here. We ain't talking about the media we ain't talking about high ranking FBI official now. We want what we started with lights, water, people out from in that tunnel out from down there.

Snodgrass: I had a question.

Cummings: I want a show of hands on the force, after you say, what you say. This is what we going out with today. Let that stand for negotiating. Ain't nothing else to talk about.

Snodgrass: We already understand that once we give our demands ... they're not going to meet those demands before they try and throw a diversion or give us something else that we did not demand. We already seen that. Okay. So if, in the event that they say, well, we're going to send you in this do you want it, that should be we shouldn't even have to confirm that. We should say no we don't we told what we want, we don't want your charity, we don't want no, we don't want nothing but what we was owed. Please give us back its gonna be, it's ours, it's ...

Cummings: We don't want no news media until you cut the lights,

James Were: I think ...

I think ... expect us, expect us to choose by ... negotiating on that phone

Give us back respect that you had ...

Give us back what we had or the hardliners ... that way if you put it like that, and everything still have respect ... see what's I'm saying

Skatzes: Let me say this ...

That's exactly the way I left it with them. . .

That's exactly what we're saying right now. He's talking on this here tape stuff ... that was my, that was my conversation. They wanted hostages ... not giving you nothing for this electricity and this water and your gonna ...

Now the way I left it ... We want, the ... we want the ...

Unknown: We want water back on, now hold on hold on ...

James Were: ... we have control up to the gate when they come over this side past that gate they violated our rights. We have a home this side of that gate ... This is our area. This is our home. They violating our home. . . I don't give a damn what they allow or do not allow, it's what we allow if we allow them to decide ... we will get control back ... right now

Anthony Lavelle: ... just shut the fuck up we don't want that. We want what we said, the media we'll would hold off on that. The FBI will hold off on that we want the lights and the power, that's it ...

Skatzes: ... The way I left it the other night ... that is exactly the way I left it. I told that man that we want power, the t.v. and water back on and if he doesn't agree with that then ... we have nothing more to say and I put down ... the conversation ... if you are not going to give us this stuff we have nothing to say to you and hang up the phone that all I told him I said. If you want to talk to me turn on these lights. When I left out of here somebody else begin negotiating with FBI or something ....

James Were: George you get on there say that there. Say from this point we, turn it over to the hardliners. There will be no more conversation.

Until we have everything that they took from us from day one you understand? That must be said.

Don't worry about ... don't worry about ... Don't worry about that no more. Their lives are in your hands and everyone lives are in Allah's hands. See what I'm saying.

Unknown: We got that part but what kind of timeframe ... say like ...

James Were: At what point ... At what point ... If they refuse to give us ...

Anthony Lavelle: What should our next step be ...

Cummings: Hold up Nameer. You said ... You're talking about our original plans. . . we got to show everybody ...

How long do we wait? ...

Jason Robb: Well, we want some daylight left so we can talk you ... Know what I'm saying. So it's got to be a ... you know what I'm saying ...

... told them yesterday ... on the bullhorn, telling these people we gonna off this motherfucker ... you know what I'm saying ...

Hey man, this motherfucker is going to take us serious. I mean they're jacking us off I I I believe this the only way they gonna take us serious ... because as soon as I made them announcements with that bullhorn like that that's when all that movement started happening ...

James Were: ... this is what, this is what's happening ...

Unknown: Make it very clear, very clear ...

[heavy equipment noise covering conversation]

Unknown: We identify the degree of force ...

James Were: I agree I want it back on ...

Unknown: I feel ... Should have been done a couple of days ago ...

It's gonna be after this ... if we ... water ... then we kill one of them ... of the water ... that's the end of it ...

If they give us water ... we say it right then

Then we kill another that day. The same thing. That's where I'm ... the rest of it. That's what I'm saying. That's not righteous but that's what we had coming into this ...

Unknown: We want our lights and ... then we're talking killing ...

Jason Robb: ... So that's what I'm saying.

James Were: ... water ... turn it back on we ask them to turn it off. If we want it off we ask them to turn it off or we turn it off ourselves

What we're saying you understand after we get what we supposed to, after we get what he supposed to have that they took from us in this situation, then we start ... The point is your questioning you under-

stand ... after he says we want our lights turned back on. He didn't ...
  ... talking ... something ...

We give a certain time a certain time. If it's not on in a certain
time that's when a body goes out ... Part of the body going out
because it better be ...

[many talking at same time]

Anthony Lavelle: ... I'm just using this as a time frame. We give
them until 2 o'clock to make their decision. Hang up the phone.
Don't answer the phone until 2:00. If they say, well, we gonna give
you ... tell them NO. You got one minute to decide whether you
gonna give it all to us or we send somebody out ...

Unknown: ... 1:30 ...
  Hold on, hold on.

[many talking]

Anthony Lavelle: ... hypothetical time ... And then you tell them
you got one minute to decide. What you gonna do? You've had an
hour to decide. Alright you count your one minute is up. What are
you going to do. They say we'll give you water. Hey alright, well
you're going to get a body. Hang up the phone. All of us get together. We've already said we're going to do this. We send them a body
part up out of here.
Unknown: But but let's stress the fact that we sending it because
you did not meet all of our demands, not because the water or electricity because you didn't send nothing in here.
Cecil Allen: Uh ... unconditional ... They said five unconditionals,
five unconditionals you understand. These are the main things.
Anthony Lavelle: You must tell them through whoever is talking on
the phone, must tell them there is, you know, you been on this thing,
it looks like it could be a good day for all of us, there is a possibility
that we could end this as soon as possible.
Unknown: Give them an ultimatum alright.

Anthony Lavelle: ... have to put an end it. You can't keep it up. The media is tearing your ass apart and you know it. You can't keep this shit up this way.

Unknown: ....

Anthony Lavelle: What can you do to us. We, you already took everything. We want it back. We want what we asked for from the very fucking beginning ...

Jason Robb: ... problems ... they ain't going to get this guy until after our shits broadcast ...

Skatzes: Live.

Jason Robb: ....

Skatzes: Get it live.

Unknown: ... live on t.v.

Skatzes: ... We are running into a lot of problems here ... we right now are at the point where we can go over there. We can have ... we can go over and we can have ... this live, live news media tape ...

Tell these people you got the water cut off let them start putting pressure on them to turn that shit back on. Exactly, it's exactly the way I left them guys last night. Turn the fucking shit on or we are not talking no more

Cummings: Okay. Hold it, hold it, can I say something ...

I hear what you are saying and I heard what you said also

You said quote unquote get the media in here now ... We will give two hostages right. Now get the media in here and give us all that back that we had and ahh, ahh, officially that we want then we give a hostage ... one hostage, ONE HOSTAGE.

Skatzes: Now we're stepping backwards ...

[many talking]

Cummings: Okay. Let me finish ... hold on hold on, let me finish ... Okay ... I'm gonna go on and get this out. We all men I'm gonna say this right now because I'm not the type person that like to pull punches because we all men ... You negotiated two. You never conferred with me, I think Jason was there ... he already looked at me because ... because he and I, he looked at me and I look at him. First you was talking about let's take 'em all over there. I'm like, you know, I said I don't know if ... on the phone ... so called ... but you negotiated two. Ain't none of us in here that ever said nothing about two, I mean you was on the phone talking, well ahh, I'll stand up for it and I think Jason or even your brother over here ... if we do anything to get the media to get these people to give back what you took we will give you *one* hostage. We not giving you no *two* or no *three* ...

Skatzes: Night before last everyone was in agreement with the two

Unknown: No no never never ... just one

Jason Robb: Ratcliff ... We can't give them ... we gave them too much already ... We already them too much they ain't giving us ...

They can only have one man because that's cutting us down. They got below the numbers. They been set down so far so many hostages, we got to think of that

We don't know how many that is ...

Unknown: ... we got eight ... five ...

[many talking]

Anthony Lavelle: ... and one of these five hostages gonna have to be sacrificed if we have to ...

Even if they kill these motherfuckers everybody has heard of Attica and all these other places where they rioted the OP. If they come in here, if they can get one of these guards one of them, if they do what we said ... they fucking around ... they still be alive. So everyone of us. They going to hype this shit up saying we the one that ... We're the ones stab them. We gonna take this shot or whatever. We're the ones that did this to them. They the only ones to be had.

If one guy is still alive all the rest of them already dead

[many talking]

Plus we have to consider once we get this live, we see it live. What is our next step, I me myself I see if we get the live coverage plus what we already said, the water the lights, are non-negotiable, and the people in the tunnel, it's non-negotiable. We got their book. And the things they say is non-negotiable. I think we ought to do is get that book and read to them. Okay. You said weapons and transportation are non-negotiable. This is what your rules and regulations say. We got it here so don't play fucking games with us about what you can and can't negotiate. We know!

This is what we're going to negotiate with you we want light, we want power back on we want the guards out of the tunnel, these are our non-negotiables. Point blank. Here is what you gonna get. You get that for us. Now we are going to negotiate upon good faith you bring us the media we will take a guy out, we'll take a guard out of here. Once we get this live media. We can start closing this, this show down.

You can do whatever you want to as rebuttal to our comments, or whatever. We can't stop you but you do not have, and as far as the rights over those tapes, you do not have the state Supreme Court to commandeer them tapes or hold it as evidence and keep them locked away. Or the feds can lock them away. You must make it clear that the media is to maintain possession it has to. You have to tell them you want the cameras. The cameras will be property of the media. You want the film to be the property of the media.

Unknown: ....

Anthony Lavelle: That way copyright laws and everything will be observed so they can't say, well, wait a minute it was the federal government's cameras it was the state this, it's not theirs, it's ours. You must make clear to them ... they have it

We get out there and air our views, by the time we air our views, we should be able to close this shit down

Cummings: We give them one hostage

Jason Robb: Did I tell you all what they said about that t.v., now that they was supposed to give us last night ... set up already and we can play it straight ...

[everybody talking]

Unknown: We want our power. We got our own t.v.'s.

Jason Robb: They didn't want to give us that that's what I figured … batteries …

Anthony Lavelle: We can, we can rig a t.v. from batteries

Roper: Okay. This is a closing thing … I talk with all these guys. Okay, your guys and your guys. I talk with everybody in the joint man. And I had conversation with guys that they have been supportive with us from the word go. But when we made statements like we gonna do this and do this. And we didn't fulfill these statements. When we make serious statements. A lot of the guys morale are down because they don't have the confidence that they had when we first come up in it. Because we ain't made no progress. See what I'm saying. They also, they also conveyed to me, that, ahh, well ahh, I had to explain to them the Muslims did this … or the Aryan Brotherhood did this. We might have a different reason, but everybody needs this shit that we did because everybody's getting stepped on. We getting stepped on our way, you getting stepped on your way, your getting stepped on your way. We all should have the same basic needs. And that's to win and, and, and to get out from under oppression. But like I say, they're real supportive, but their morale is going down. Because you guys, they told me yesterday, you guys was gonna do this two days ago and we ain't did nothing. Any they go you know ahh so we need to make progress to ahh, because you can't ask guys tho to ahh, keep supporting us if we ain't making no change … no progress … we have to make progress …

Cecil Allen: … Top priority … they gotta go to that and these guys …

    … some got in they have their head cracked … they saying something about killing a guard, killing a guard … We use them

Anthony Lavelle: ….

Roper: We use them.

Anthony Lavelle: For what we're doing

Roper: We use, that's right, we using them

Anthony Lavelle: They wouldn't be here so

Roper: I'm gonna tell you. I know for a fact ... I've been talking about it for a long time. I have accepted the reality that we need to ... but the thing is like we using people to help us benefit. If you go out in the hallway ... these people, they out there they talkin' they don't want to be part of it, don't be ... We should be able to get everybody integrated. We shouldn't be using ... we need everybody's support. Not just in here but everybody that's a part ... those guys come to use and they ...

Jason Robb: Whatever.

[heavy equipment]

Cummings: Say, ahh, can we move to close this up. An we put it out there I ain't got no can we close this up ... you'll before ... put it out there.

I ain't got no additional comments. The phone call ... listen up. Lights, water, peoples out from in the tunnel.

[heavy equipment]

Jason Robb: ....

Cummings: ... Jason made a good statement like that.

If we're not talking about water and lights, don't be tricked now about the media ... on the phone ...

Okay. You come right back with your live media but we still want the lights and water turned back on before we bring your hostage out of here ...

Jason Robb: ... this is priority ... this is priority.

Cummings: The priority is you've got to get the light and water back on and the peoples out from in the tunnel.

Jason Robb: That's non-negotiable.

Cummings: That's non-negotiable.

Jason Robb: Okay. So the media and etc. is negotiable.

Cummings: Yeah. You see, that's the point. After we get over the non-negotiables ...

Jason Robb: ... get ...

Cummings: Right.

Let that be our agenda for the day ... we going to give them a time element for this here to give us what is non-negotiable. I mean, I want us to leave out of here with an understanding that the non-negotiable things is all that we talking on. Even if he ask you when you if you happen to be on the phone.

... but what about the ... talking to your ... and, ahh,... something about movement progress with the hostages.

First and foremost this is what's happening now. The hardliners like he used that word ... the hardliners are came in effect now.

We want back what you took. Once you do that then we going to the next phase.

James Were: After you say the hardliners are in place then we say ... the hardliners ...

Anthony Lavelle: He should be the first one to talk to them ... as a matter of fact, he would be the first one to talk. Let him talk once then said okay, when you get back to me cuz when he gets back to him we know that when they first get back they gonna say well we can't do this. Okay. I have nothing else to do with it.

Snodgrass: Hold on ...

Anthony Lavelle: The hardliners gonna take care of the situation now.

James Were: When you have talked to them ... From this point on we're turning it over to the hardliners ...

Cummings: You understand they held you in great esteem they held you in great esteem, that you ahh, you two guys working with the understandings ...

I really tried, ahh, I really tried to work with you to ahh, George, we know you're a good guy but like the guy said you losing control over things and we try to work with you. And you said but I need you to work with me. And the talking about but I need you to give me something. Tell them the non-negotiable things. This is what is happening now, and the hardliners are coming and I don't know where I'm at.

James Were: you should try to work with them ... trying to work with you ... and the hardliners appear to be ... control of this ... after you got off the phone with me talking about being ...

All that stuff ... they're asking about coffee on the phone, about we give you some toilet paper you know all of this goofy stuff ...

Cummings: Total disrespect.

[everybody talking]

Hardliners ...

Cummings: I am ready to go ... we can do that and have somebody sit by the phone.

Roper: What you need to do is don't forget that negotiable and non-negotiable things and what they got.

Unknown: Now look, look when we send this guy up out of here, if we don't get no demands. I said ...

Unknown: ... ...

Cummings: Okay, we can but we can sit down and come back in and we put the non-negotiable things up then we came back with the time element that we give them to do it. Hey Jason, ahh, Hassaan, why don't we put the non-negotiable things up, George, go back in. Talking about the the hardliners came up with non-negotiable things. Then we going to set down and go over the time element, if they don't do these things ... if you don't give us these things, the non-negotiable things we going with the time element, then we gonna kill them one. Then we open up negotiations again. I mean, is everybody in agreement on that?

Bell: ....

Jason Robb: Yeah, at nine o'clock ...

[everybody talking]

Anthony Lavelle: Why don't we all meet at 10:15 … Why don't we all meet in unit 2 at 2:30.

James Were (?): Better yet, better yet, because because I'm gonna be staying here,… we say at such and such a time we meet … security will come and get you all and we all meet at a certain place …

Unknown: Okay … that way we got … right here.

Snodgrass: Could I make one more point? Yesterday we all agreed that all day long we were saying …

Jason Robb: Well, we really ain't up for that right now.

Anthony Lavelle: Okay. wait a minute if you didn't' tell none of us until 3 days later fuck it … yeah … fun and games …

I would suggest that if we find these guys going around here trying to rape these guys. I already told my brothers if they catch somebody trying to rape somebody in our block … which I know I don't have to do hopefully I know it ain't no Muslims …

Jason Robb: In this town, rape is death it's as simple as that.

Anthony Lavelle: … and the Aryans … if I catch anybody in that block trying to rape anybody I am going to fuck 'em up.

Jason Robb: Rape is death.

Anthony Lavelle: I'm not going to kill them but I'm gonna fuck em up and then if one of y'all brothers was raping then and you'll do what you have to do.

[everybody talking]

Cummings: Ahh … Hold up … Jason another thing … ahh … between ahh … Hassaan okay,

Me and him gonna get on the phone, okay? I'm gonna send somebody down to get …

… see we meet back after we put our non-negotiable things out …

[many talking]

Cummings: First you going to let me tell them this on the phone. George tell them this on the phone. Before we go down there.

[many talking]

James Were: Hold on. Just like, just like we had agreed when we said that had enough time to move out before we start …

Cummings: But it might be

Anthony Lavelle: Okay. They gonna know, they gonna know, they know that we know that they're there

Cummings: If they know that we getting ready to go down there …

Jason Robb: I want security on that spot, whatever we decide … I want it tight man I want it 24 hours a day, that's the schedule, man, 24 hours a day man …

Cummings: When we, ahh, when we mention on the phone about people getting out from in the tunnel.

Unknown: ….

Cummings: When George, when George mention to them about getting out from in the tunnel would it be prudent, would it be prudent to let them know we gonna give you enough time to get out from in the tunnel just like you did when you brought the food and back up because a one of our people, some of my people go into it and let them think if one of them go down and get harmed. One of your officers is going to get harmed. So this will really assure that they get up out of the tunnel.

How does that sound? Will you tell them that?

Get your people out of that tunnel. We gonna give them enough time like you did when you got off the yard out there. Then one of our people is going down there in the tunnels, you know, but if something happens to one of our peoples …

[End of Tape]

APPENDIX 2

DEMANDS OF THE PRISONERS IN L BLOCK

The following list is drawn from Lucasville Telephone Negotiations (inmate tapes), Tape X. Similar lists are found in Lucasville Telephone Negotiations (inmate tapes), Tape IV, pp. 26–31, 33, and the state's Negotiation Tape # 11, pp. 9–15, 17.

1. There must not be any impositions, reprisals, repercussions against any inmate as a result of this that the administration refers to as a riot. Reprisals means beating by staff members, starved, locked in strip cells with no clothes for a long period of time other than what ARs [Administrative Regulations] state.

2. There must not be any singling out or selection of any inmate or group of inmates as supposed leaders in this alleged riot.

3. We want adequate medical treatment for inmates that have been injured, will provide list of names.

4. We want religious leaders present as well as the media when any statement is made concerning the inmates' surrender. When we surrender we want some type of media present to record this live. That one is non-negotiable.

5. The system commonly known as unit management must be revised or abolished. This shall include the system commonly known as the point system where convicts are judged by arbitrary process by the unit management to determine one's security status, supervision level and possible transfers.

6. Rescind policies that force integrated celling. We should not be forced to integrate racially or religiously.

7. SOCF is a maximum security facility. Inmates that are classified as close or medium security must be transferred to an appropriate facility. We are tired of having to give up certain things to close or medium security. L-8 should be set up for inmates that have proved themselves to be responsible and should have certain privileges as max inmates.

8. The procedures for determining early release on parole must be reviewed and revised or abolished. Currently criminal and institutional records used in determining the possibility of parole are not accurate; institutional file[s] contain notations or conduct reports that are in whole or in part lies by the reporting officer, and in the subsequent appeals process and/or grievance procedure, all SOCF employees stand by one another. We want to have guarantees that counselors, sergeants, unit managers, or anyone else who has authority to go in inmates' files and place documents in there, that all files, all police records, everything is double-checked before it is taken to the parole board for consideration, because a lot of inmates here find things in their files that they knew nothing about. They are supposed to be allowed to review their files and they're not allowed that.

9. Reduce overcrowding conditions at SOCF and all of the institutions in the State of Ohio. Most of the cells have two men. Overcrowding is a problem as far as the [day] room, rec periods, and library are concerned.

10. Create and enforce policy to stop prison officials, especially officers and unit managers, from harassing inmates using the power of their positions in prejudicial or discriminatory manners, including speaking to inmates in a demeaning manner.

11. Review and impose guidelines for the infirmary to properly treat medical problems. We are given Tylenol ... for just about everything. If guys have a severe problem we want it looked at and addressed. We want guys to receive adequate medical attention within set guidelines and a set time span. Some guys have been waiting for months to go to OSU or Frazier.

12. Implement a phone call program as promised years ago. Currently we get one five minute call on Christmas. We were promised when new construction began that telephones will be placed in all these blocks. We haven't seen them yet.

13. Reduce the amount of idle time inmates spend in their cells. Implement progressive rehabilitation programs. We want college and voc school opened up for max 4s. The majority of population here are max 4s, longtimers. Guys that have just got out of AC [Administrative Control] and have more than five years to parole board, these guys cannot participate in any of these programs. We feel that is an unfair practice set up by this institution.

14. Do not damage or destroy any inmate's personal property as a result of this incident. A lot of guys have TVs and radios and stuff, they cannot get another one, and they may be here for years. We want a guarantee that the inmates' property will not be destroyed.

15. Review and amend the policy for imposing visiting restrictions. Some guys that receive mail or money or a contraband item, the person is taken off the visiting list and the guy doesn't know anything about it. There is no formal investigation by the mail and visiting supervisor to ascertain the problems and find an equitable solution for the inmate and the institution.

16. Order exhaustive and complete review of all inmate security supervision status, review in-for-transfer. Some close security and medium 3s have been here for the longest time waiting to be ridden out of here and no one has taken an initiative to have these inmates transferred. Some are in max 3 blocks.

17. Create and establish an inmate advisory committee to work in cooperation with an appointed institution employee that will have reasonable say-so in various matters that affect inmate life. We want something like the review board that you use for reviewing inmates' cases, whether they are to go parole board at their half times. Only we want to set up to review certain guidelines with inmate groups. The institution select inmates to perform on this committee.

18. Review and implement new and/or revised regulations. Increase in inmate pay. Commissary prices on everything continuously increase but our pay remains the same. Some guys make $16–17 a month, but the way that the prices keep increasing in the commissary these guys couldn't even afford to buy hygiene [articles] for the money. They only receive state pay. The prices keep increasing, inmate work increases, but their pay remains the same. We want that looked into.

APPENDIX 3

DOCUMENTS CIRCULATED BY ADVOCATES OF THE DEATH PENALTY FOR LUCASVILLE RIOTERS

The following documents were prepared by a citizens' committee that sought, during the spring of 1993, to ensure that whoever was condemned to death after the Lucasville uprising would be executed as rapidly as possible.

The first document is a petition addressed to Governor George Voinovich, to the President of the Ohio Senate, and to the Speaker of the Ohio House. Signed petitions were to be returned to "Death Penalty, P.O. Box 1761, Portsmouth, Ohio 45662." Portsmouth is the county seat of Scioto County, in which SOCF is located.

The Office of the Public Defender identified four persons who signed the petition and whose names also appeared on the "array" from which a grand jury would be chosen to indict Lucasville defendants. The arrow at the left-hand side of the petition points to the name of one of the four.

The second document, also circulated for signatures, calls on Governor Voinovich to "USE the Death Penalty!"

Petitions and letters were signed by an estimated twenty-six thousand persons.

The Honorable George V. Voinovich, Governor, State of Ohio
The Honorable Stanley Arnoff, President, Ohio Senate
The Honorable Vernal G. Riffe, Speaker, Ohio House

We the undersigned request and demand that the present stature of the Death Penalty in the State of Ohio be applied as the passers intended it to be.

We feel that Governor George V. Voinovich, President of the Senate Stanley Arnoff, and Speaker of the House Vernal G. Riffe must accept their responsibility to carry out the wishes of the Voters of the State of Ohio. Two appeals are enough.

Request for petitions or to return, write: Death Penalty, P.O. Box 1761, Portsmouth, Ohio 45662.

Residents of the State of Ohio from high school age and up may sign this petition.

Name	Address	Name	Address
Margaret Ruggles	1409 7th St. W.P.	Lori Diaks	307-A Clayton Ct. W.P
	227 Columz W.P		
	1364-1528 Col.P.O	Lori Alcita	1239 11th St. W. Ports PA
	227 Col. I W Po		Rt 5 Bx 502½ W.
	902 W. Rehland Park	Karla Coleman	1525 Wash Blvd
	108 Washington W. Ports.	Carl A. Scott	Wash Blvd
Horton Moron	1453 Washington Blvd W.Port		330 21 W.
Brett Horton	1430 10th West Ports. Oh.		1515 4th St U. W. Port
Teri Tolliver	1346 Country Run W.P Port	Sally	1431 Wash Blvd
Carol Shy	2214 Roseau. W. Ports.	Johnny	Rt 5 Box 573
Melissa Kent	3555 Globe Hollow	Brian McNab	310 Lincoln St
Judy	129 City View W. Ports		Star Rt Box 301c.
		Sandy Taylor	W. Ports Oh
		Melia	Rt 5
Jenny Cullum			1537
Bumper	1511 7th W. Ports.		1578
	1902 Fah W. Ports	Esther	1344 5th
	1410 Custer Street W Ports		
Herman	9th St W. Ports O		1902½
Betty	20110 th W. Ports O		408
	1257 8th W. Ports		P.O. 435 Ports
	2130		Rt 14
Aaron	507 Colm W. Ports		Rt 6 Box 94 Lucasville
Pamela			1351 Col W.P
	2021 Rescue Ave		R18 2nd St
	1022½ Lincoln St		478 Front Street
	W High St. W. P		
	1431 Washington Blvd	Walter	319 City View
	2409 20th Ports	Donna	2126 Ports OH
Pat Coleman	1562 14th St W.P		1350 13th St W. Port Oh

Ohio

[To] Governor George Voinovich
[and] Members of the Ohio State Legislature

Your worst nightmare: You arrive for work prepared for the usual rounds of meetings and correspondence. Instead, you are handed a stick and ushered into an area where you are surrounded by hardened, violent criminals. Your assignment is to ensure that the criminals— *who are free to wander around, work out in a gymnasium, entertain visitors, browse through a law library, and pursue a free college education—* obey the rules and do not harm one another, their visitors, or their teachers. You are warned that the criminals may taunt you, throw excrement in your face, seriously injure you, hold you hostage, or even kill you; but, should you be "proven" to have been "unnecessarily rough" trying to restrain them, you will be suspended, possibly fired, probably sued, and maybe even imprisoned. You shudder at the prospect of your day on the job. Then you awaken, greatly relieved that this has been just a horrible dream.

Unfortunately for the Correctional Officers at the Southern Ohio Correctional Facility, this nightmare is their everyday reality. The state must wake up and eliminate the extremely dangerous working conditions for SOCF Officers and the expensive, unnecessary privileges being dished out to the inmates:

- Make SOCF a real maximum security prison with complete lockdown of prisoners.
- Stop trying to rehabilitate the hardened, end-of-the-line criminals housed at SOCF, and stop giving them privileges denied the Correctional Officers and other law-abiding citizens:
  - Take away *free* higher education priviliges for prisoners.
  - Stop allowing prisoners to wile away their hours in their free gymnasium, building their bodies into more potent killing machines.
  - Stop allowing prisoners to spend their days in the law library becoming legal experts on the side of crime.

- Institute *severe* punishment for prisoners who throw urine and feces on Correctional Officers.
- Pass legislation that prevents prisoners from filing law suits; or, in the event that is not possible, ensure that all monies collected go directly to the Ohio Victims Fund.
- *USE* the Death Penalty!

SOCF is supposed to be a *maximum security* prison, not an educational/recreational center for criminals. As a taxpayer, I strongly object to paying for inmate privileges denied to the law-abiding population. As a citizen of a nation that is preoccupied with safety and health, I am outraged that the SOCF Correctional Officers are subjected to such nightmarishly unsafe working conditions.

Please immediately introduce and support legislation or take other actions needed to bring about the reforms cited above.

Very respectfully,

APPENDIX 4

PETITION ON BEHALF OF THE LUCASVILLE FIVE
AND IN SUPPORT OF A MORATORIUM ON ALL
EXECUTIONS IN OHIO

The Lucasville Five support both an amnesty for all prisoners sentenced in court or administrative proceedings after the uprising, as at Attica, and a moratorium on the execution of any of the more than two hundred persons on Death Row in Ohio.

Copies of this petition may be sent to the Lucasville Five Support Project (P.O. Box 1591, Marion OH 43301-1591). Persons preferring to sign this petition by e-mail may use the following address: peachtub@msn.com.

Readers who wish to correspond with the Five can do so at the following addresses. (Be sure to put the prisoner's number together with his name on the face of the envelope. Addresses are subject to change.)

S. A. Hasan #R130-559
    878 Coitsville-Hubbard Road, Youngstown OH 44505-4635
Keith Lamar #317-117
    878 Coitsville-Hubbard Road, Youngstown OH 44505-4635
Jason Robb #308-919
    878 Coitsville-Hubbard Road, Youngstown OH 44505-4635
James Were #173-245
    878 Coitsville-Hubbard Road, Youngstown OH 44505-4635
George Skatzes #173-501
    PO Box 788, Mansfield OH 44901-0788

PETITION FOR JUSTICE AND A MORATORIUM ON ALL EXECUTIONS IN OHIO

Five men known as the "Lucasville Five"—Siddique Abdullah Hasan, Keith Lamar, Namir Abdul-Mateen a/k/a James Were, Jason Robb and George W. Skatzes—have been condemned to death for their alleged roles during the disturbance at the Southern Ohio Correctional Facility in Lucasville, Ohio on April 11–21, 1993.

1. There is no physical evidence linking any of these defendants with the crimes charged. All were convicted on the basis of testimony from other prisoners who were promised protection, letters to the parole board, reduced charges and sentences, dismissal of charges, or other benefits.

2. The State of Ohio interfered with attorneys' efforts to counsel defendants during the investigation phase prior to indictments. This occurred at a time when, according to law, they should have been presumed innocent.

3. The prosecution had access to resources far greater than the resources available to the defense, e.g., the prosecution had virtually unlimited funds at their disposal while the defense were not given adequate funds. Attorney Niki Schwartz testified that it was as if the prosecution had been provided with nuclear weaponry and the defense had been provided with slingshots.

4. With regard to several of the defendants, they were prosecuted because of the roles they played as spokespersons and negotiators for the prisoners.

5. Although the indictments did not mention conspiracy, the prosecution based several of the convictions on an alleged conspiracy among rival gangs.

6. The State of Ohio engaged in repeated unscrupulous trial tactics, such as putting on perjured testimony, and withholding exculpatory evidence and information.

7. Counsel appointed for defendants provided ineffective assistance in numerous instances.

We, the undersigned, ask that 1) justice be assured with respect to the fate of these five men and that they receive new trials for the reasons enumerated hereunder, and 2) for a moratorium on all executions in Ohio.

PHONE	NAME	ADDRESS	ZIP CODE	I WANT TO HELP ORGANIZE (CHECK)

PHONE	NAME	ADDRESS	ZIP CODE	I WANT TO HELP ORGANIZE (CHECK)

If possible, make additional copies of this petition and share them with other concerned persons and death penalty opponents in your school, workplace or place of worship.

Finally, when the petition has been completed with signatures, please forward the petition to the below address:

The Lucasville Five Support Project
P.O. Box 1591
Marion, Ohio 43301-1591

APPENDIX 5

SELECTIVE PROSECUTION OF LEADERS OF
THE REBELLION COMPARED WITH INFORMANTS WHO
CONCEDEDLY COMMITTED THE SAME ACTS

Prisoners whose names are followed by an asterisk (*) became witnesses for the state.

DEFENDANT	ALLEGED ACTION	ULTIMATE DISPOSITION
Hasan (Carlos Sanders)	Allegedly planned aggravated murder of Officer Vallandingham	Death
Namir (James Were)	Allegedly planned aggravated murder of Officer Vallandingham	Death
Jason Robb	Allegedly planned aggravated murder of Officer Vallandingham	Death
George Skatzes	Allegedly planned aggravated murder of Officer Vallandingham	Life Imprisonment
Anthony Lavelle*	Allegedly planned aggravated murder of Officer Vallandingham	7–25 years concurrent with previous sentence; eligible for parole in 1999

DEFENDANT	ALLEGED ACTION	ULTIMATE DISPOSITION
George Skatzes	Allegedly planned aggravated murder of prisoner Earl Elder	Death
Johnny Roper	Allegedly took part in killing Earl Elder	Indictment dropped
Rodger Snodgrass*	Allegedly took part in killing Earl Elder	5–25 years consecutive to previous sentence; eligible for parole in 1998
Tim Williams*	Implicated by other prisoners in murder of Earl Elder	Paroled in 1998
Jason Robb	Allegedly took part in killing David Sommers	Death
George Skatzes	Allegedly took part in killing David Sommers	Death
Robert Brookover*	Allegedly took part in killing David Sommers	5–25 years concurrent with previous sentence; no additional time
Rodger Snodgrass*	Allegedly took part in killing David Sommers	Not indicted
Hasan (Carlos Sanders)	Allegedly took part in killing Bruce Harris	Not guilty
Namir (James Were)	Allegedly took part in killing Bruce Harris	Not guilty
Stacey Gordon*	Allegedly took part in killing Bruce Harris	Not indicted
Reginald Williams*	Allegedly took part in killing Bruce Harris	Not indicted

APPENDIX 6

SELECTIVE PROSECUTION BASED ON
IDENTITY OF VICTIM

Exhibits A and B in their original form were attached to a motion filed by defense counsel for George Skatzes. The exhibits indicate that, except for Keith Lamar, the state sought the death penalty only for prisoners alleged to have been involved in the murder of Officer Vallandingham.

Exhibit A: Inmates Indicted Without Death Penalty Specifications

DEFENDANT	VICTIM	CHARGE
Rodger Snodgrass	Elder	Aggravated murder
Johnny Roper	Elder	Aggravated murder
Thomas Taylor	Staiano	Murder
Timothy Grinnell	Depina	Aggravated murder
Eric Girdy	Farrell, Svette	Aggravated murder
Gregory Curry	Vitale, Svette	Aggravated murder
Derek Cannon	Depina	Aggravated murder
Rasheem Matthew	Vitale, Depina	Aggravated murder
Stanley Cummings	Vallandingham	Conspiracy to commit aggravated murder
Eric Scales	Vitale	Aggravated murder
Michael Childers	Weaver	Murder

William Bowling	Weaver	Murder
Ricky Rutherford	Weaver	Murder
Frederick Frakes	Svette	Aggravated murder
Jesse Bocook	Sommers	Aggravated murder
Anthony Lavelle	Vallandingham	Conspiracy to commit aggravated murder
Robert Brookover	Sommers	Involuntary manslaughter
Aaron Jefferson	Vallandingham	Conspiracy to commit aggravated murder
	Sommers	Aggravated murder

Exhibit B: Inmates Indicted with Death Penalty Specifications

DEFENDANT	VICTIM	CHARGE
Keith Lamar	Depina, Svette, Staiano, Vitale, Weaver	Aggravated murder
Hasan (Carlos Sanders)	Vallandingham, Harris	Aggravated murder
Jason Robb	Vallandingham, Sommers	Aggravated murder
George Skatzes	Vallandingham, Elder, Sommers	Aggravated murder
Kenneth Law	Vallandingham	Aggravated murder
Namir (James Were)	Vallandingham, Harris	Aggravated murder

NOTES

INTRODUCTION

1. E.g., Reply Brief to Brief of Amicus Curiae, American Civil Liberties Union of Ohio Foundation, *State v. Skatzes* (Ct. App. Montgomery Cty.), Case No. 15848, p. 8. Similarly, hostage Officer Larry Dotson's memoir (as told to ODRC Training Officer Gary Williams) repeatedly refers to the Lucasville events as "the longest and third most bloody prison riot in U.S. history." Gary Williams, *Siege in Lucasville: The 11 Day Saga of Hostage Larry Dotson* (Bloomington: 1st Books Library, 2003), pp. viii, xiii, xv, 1, etc.

2. Reginald A. Wilkinson and Thomas J. Stickrath, "After the Storm: Anatomy of a Riot's Aftermath," *Corrections Management Quarterly* (1997), p. 16. The Lucasville uprising lasted from about 3 p.m. on April 11 to about 11:20 p.m. on April 21, a total of approximately 248 hours (see Chronology). Cuban detainees at the United States Penitentiary in Atlanta seized the facility in November 1987 and appear to have held it, without fatalities, for over 260 hours. Bert Useem, Camille Graham Camp, George M. Camp, and Renie Dugan, "Resolution of Prison Riots," National Institute of Justice Research in Brief (Washington, D.C.: U.S. Department of Justice, Oct. 1995), p. 1; Reid H. Montgomery, Jr., and Gordon A. Crews, *A History of Correctional Violence: An Examination of Reported Causes of Riots and Disturbances* (Lanham, Md.: American Correctional Association, 1998), pp. 77–78.

3. Williams, *Siege in Lucasville*, p. 5.

4. Bruce Porter, "The Lucasville Follies: A Prison Riot Brings Out the Worst in the Press," *Columbia Journalism Review* (May/June 1994), p. 2.

5. These examples from Porter's article (ibid.) are highlighted in Joe Hallett, "Pack journalism added to the confusion during the '93 Lucasville riot," *Columbus Dispatch*, Apr. 13, 2003.

6. Kevin Mayhood to Siddique Hasan, Feb. 19, 2003. Hasan reports that the Ohio Department of Rehabilitation and Correction has denied access to him by reporters Tim Clifford and Malka Margolies of *48 Hours*; reporter Bruce Porter of the *New York Times*; reporter Greg Donaldson for *Vibe* magazine; and author Maryhard Horowitz, who wanted to write a book about the investigation of the Lucasville rebellion. S. A. Hasan to Staughton Lynd, Jan. 6, 2004.

7. *Morris, et al. v. Voinovich, et al.*, Civ. No. C-1-93-436 (S.D.Ohio 1994).

8. Williams, *Siege in Lucasville*, pp. 218–19.

9. Opinion, *State v. Sanders* (2001), 92 Ohio St.3d 245, 260.

CHAPTER 1

1. This anecdote may be apocryphal. It seems to have first appeared in Jared Sparks's edition of Franklin's *Works* about 1840 and then in Sparks's *Life* of Franklin (Boston: Whittemore, Niles, and Hall, 1856), p. 408. See Carl Van Doren, *Benjamin Franklin* (New York: Viking Press, 1938), pp. 551–52.

2. Jack A. Goldstone and Bert Useem, "Prison Riots as Microrevolutions: An Extension of State-Centered Theories of Revolution," *American Journal of Sociology*, v. 104, no. 4 (Jan. 1999), p. 986.

3. John Perotti, "Lucasville: A Brief History," *Prison Legal News* (Dec. 1993), pp. 7–9. Much of Perotti's narrative is corroborated by the findings of fact of federal courts in the following cases: *Haynes v. Marshall*, 704 F.Supp. 788, 790 (S.D.Ohio 1988), aff'd in part and rev'd in part, 887 F.2d 700, 701–2 (6th Cir. 1989) (guards beat Haynes after he was shackled and restrained, and continued to beat him while dragging him to a strip cell and "as he lay in a subdued condition in the strip cell. It was while in the strip cell that another officer allegedly placed his foot on Haynes' neck, applied his body weight, and inflicted the blow that led to his death"); *Wolfel v. Morris*, 972 F.2d 712, 717–18 (6th Cir. 1992) (punishment for circulating petitions to Amnesty International must be rescinded because prison permitted other petitions to be circulated). Officer Larry Dotson says that between SOCF's opening and April 10, 1993, 38 prisoners and five staff members were murdered there. Gary Williams, *Siege in Lucasville: The 11 Day Saga of Hostage Larry Dotson* (Bloomington: 1st Books Library, 2003), p. 29.

4. Excerpt of proceedings, *State v. Cannon* (Ct. Com. Pl. Hamilton Cty.), Appeal No. C-950710, Case No. B-957633, p. 7.

5. Lucasville prisoner Bill Martin says of Lincoln Carter that "he was not beaten to death. After he touched the nurse's hand, he knew he was going to be severely beaten and took a handful of pills to dull the pain. After he was beaten, Carter died of a drug overdose." Bill Martin to Staughton Lynd, Dec. 10, 2003.

6. In his Dec. 10, 1993, letter to Staughton Lynd, Martin described the "Lucasville 14" who sought to be released to various countries in Eastern Europe.

> Not everybody wanted to go to the Soviet Union. I was born in Augsburg, Germany, so I wanted to emigrate to East Germany. The legal authority we were using was the Helsinki Accords of Human Rights and the Universal Declaration of Human Rights.
>
> The guys who cut off their fingers were Richard Armstrong, August Cassano, and David Cattano. (Cattano actually cut off *two* fingers.) The self-mutilation caused such a stir that the Tass news agency tried to get permission from the State Department to interview all of us. We knew this from a Freedom of Information Act request we made.
>
> The law governing someone renouncing their citizenship required them to travel to a foreign country and renounce their citizenship at a U.S. embassy. To get around this, three of us gave power of attorney to a well-known human rights activist in the Netherlands and she went to the U.S. embassy at the Hague and attempted to renounce our citizenship.

Armstrong's attempt to renounce his citizenship is described in Aaron Caleb with Douglas Slaton, *Subpoena George Bush: The Anatomy of a Cover-Up* (Trotwood, Ohio: Cedar Mills Publishing, 1993), p. 8. Cassano states: "In the late 70s I cut off my left pinky finger and sent it to President Carter. He never received it, but it went out from the super max part of Lucasville which was call[ed] J block. I did this 'cause I renounced my U.S. citizenship, 'cause the conditions were so bad in lockup." August Cassano to Staughton Lynd, Dec. 27, 2003, p. 5.

7. Shirley Pope, Senior Research Associate, CIIC, to Terry Morris, Warden, SOCF, Nov. 30, 1989, re: "Concerns Pertaining to Unit Management and Snitch Games," pp. 1–2.

8. Ibid., pp. 5–6 (emphasis added).

9. "Little Rock" is quoted in an article by his New Mexico attorney Steven Douglas Looney, "Little Rock Reed: America's Most Wanted 'Fugitive from Justice,'" *Journal of Prisoners on Prisons*, v. 9, no. 1 (1998), pp. 57–58.

10. Keith Lamar to Staughton Lynd, Jan. 2003.

11. Chrystof Knecht, "Letters from Lucasville Prison," *Race Traitor* (Spring 1994), p. 2; William Martin, letter to Attorney Richard Kerger, Feb. 20, 1995.

12. CIIC, "Concerns Pertaining to Unit Management and Snitch Games," p. 5.

13. Keith Lamar to Staughton Lynd, Jan. 2003; Taymullah Abdul Hakim (Leroy Elmore), "Lucasville—an inside view," *Prison News Service* (Jan.–Feb. 1994), p. 5.

14. William Martin to Richard Kerger, Feb. 20, 1995.

15. "Disturbance Cause Committee Findings," Executive Summary, pp. 1–3.

16. "Disturbance Cause Committee Findings," p. 5.

17. Ibid., Executive Summary, p. 2; Keith Lamar to Staughton Lynd, Jan. 2003.

18. "Disturbance Cause Committee Findings," Executive Summary, p. 3.

19. Interview with George Skatzes, Jan. 14, 2003.

20. "Disturbance Cause Committee Findings," p. 13. Hasan explains: "Except for a death in one's family or some other major emergency, prisoners were not privileged to any other phone calls. I was briefly in the honor block prior to the uprising and we were allowed one phone call per week. Since there was no double-celling in the honor block, only about 80 prisoners were privileged to the one weekly call. The one five-minute call per year was only given to those in general population, not those in any of the lock-up blocks." S. A. Hasan to Staughton Lynd, Jan. 20, 2003. However, general population prisoners at ManCI were permitted one 20-minute telephone call daily. "Disturbance Cause Committee Findings," p. 13.

21. CIIC, "Concerns Pertaining to Unit Management and Snitch Games," p. 6; "Quarterly Report of the Correctional Institution Inspection Committee, January 31, 1991 thru March 31, 1991," pp. 107, 111.

22. "The Prison's Attitude," enclosed in a letter from S. A. Hasan to Staughton Lynd, Jan. 20, 2003.

23. Taymullah Abdul Hakim, "Lucasville—an inside view"; S. A. Hasan, "Synopsis," contained in a letter to Staughton Lynd, Oct. 5, 1998.

24. Major Roger Crabtree, in charge of security at SOCF, was also present.

25. Warden Tate testified at Hasan's trial that Hasan said: "You do what you have to do and we'll do what we have to do." Testimony of Arthur Tate, Transcript, *State v. Sanders*, pp. 1277–78. However, in a deposition in a civil case arising from the uprising, Warden Tate said that Elmore "very well may have said" that if someone were to force him to submit to a test, he would resist. Ibid., pp. 1304–5. Hasan emphasizes that what Taymullah meant was not "we will create a riot," but rather "we will refuse to take the test." Interestingly, the report that reached Officer Larry Dotson was that it was *Warden Arthur Tate* who said, "you do what you gotta do and we'll do what we gotta do." Williams, *Siege in Lucasville*, p. 27.

26. These words are taken verbatim from a copy of the internal communication or "kite" sent by Hasan to Warden Tate, stamped "Received, April 7, 1993."

27. Robert L. Cohen, M.D., to Staughton Lynd, Dec. 26, 2003 (emphasis added). "PPD" means purified protein derivative. The alcohol to which Muslim prisoners objected was phenol.

28. Deposition of David See, p. 54, quoted in Report of Plaintiffs' Expert Steve J. Martin, Feb. 28, 1996, p. 14, in *Morris, et al. v. Voinovich, et al.*, Civ. C-1-93-436 (S.D.Ohio 1994).

29. Transcript, *State v. Sanders*, p. 4678.

30. The warden's memo of April 8, responding to Hasan's kite, is attached to "Disturbance Cause Committee Findings, p.579. After his release on parole in 1992, "Little Rock" Reed wrote to Warden Tate criticizing the lack of religious services for Native American prisoners at Lucasville. Tate replied, using the same word he would later use to Hasan, that he resented Reed's attempts to "dictate" how to run the prison. Original Action in Habeas Corpus, *Timothy "Little Rock" Reed v. John F. Kinkela, Chief, Ohio Adult Parole Authority, et al.*, in the Supreme Court of Ohio, Case No. 98-2041, filed Oct. 5, 1998, p. 9.

31. Keith Lamar to Staughton Lynd, Jan. 2003.

32. Martin Report (see n. 28 above), p. 15.

33. "Disturbance Cause Committee Findings," Executive Summary, p. 4.

34. Martin Report, pp. 16–17, citing the depositions of the two lieutenants.

35. Keith Lamar to Staughton Lynd, Jan. 26, 2003. The quoted words are from *Macbeth*, Act I, Scene 3.

36. SOCF staffing rosters cited in Martin Report, p. 7.

CHAPTER 2

1. Testimony of Dr. David Hammer, Daily Transcript of Proceedings, May 16, 2003, p. 20; testimony of Jacalyn McCullough, Daily Transcript of Proceedings, May 19, 2003, pp. 45–55, *State v. Were II*. Namir was tried for a second time after the Supreme Court of Ohio found that he had not had a mental competency hearing during his first trial.

2. Transcript, *State v. Were*, p. 2247.

3. Ibid., p. 2250–51.

4. Ibid., pp. 2247–48.

5. Conversation between Derek Cannon and Staughton Lynd, May 21, 2003. As Cannon had foreseen, in Namir's second trial his testimony in the Cannon case was used against him to prove that he had been in L-6 at the time of Officer Vallandingham's death. Testimony of Mark Piepmeier, Daily Transcript of Proceedings, May 8, 2003, afternoon session, *State v. Were II*, pp. 4–5.

6. Transcript, *State v. Robb*, pp. 5462–63.

7. Ibid., pp. 5465–66.

8. Ibid., pp. 5472–75.

9. Ibid., pp. 5474–76.

10. Ibid., pp. 5476–78.

11. Ibid., pp. 5478–83.

12. Ibid., pp. 5483–85.

13. Hasan set forth the following account in a letter to Staughton Lynd, Mar. 31, 2003. Many of the key episodes were also described by a family member during the mitigation phase of Hasan's trial, and in an interview reported by Kristen Delguzzi, "Violent inmate: I've changed; Lucasville riot leader spent most of life in prison," *Cincinnati Enquirer*, Mar. 4, 1996.

14. Delguzzi, "Violent inmate."

15. Only live testimony can be accepted in mitigation, but George's defense team sent Ms. Bowers out in January cold and snow to meet with friends and relatives of the defendant and collect affidavits that could not be used in court. Although Ms. Bowers mailed these documents to the judge and they were made part of the record after sentencing, the jury never saw them. The most poignant of these affidavits is

her own. I have supplemented its contents from conversations with George Skatzes, especially on May 26, 2003, from his own account written in April–May 2003, and from a second affidavit by Ms. Bowers, Petition for Post-Conviction Review, *State v. Skatzes*, Exhibit 39.

16. George Skatzes to Staughton Lynd, July 29, 2003.

17. Testimony of James Rogers, Transcript, *State v. Skatzes*, Case No. 83CR-3 (Logan Cty. Ct. of Com. Pl. 1983), p. 1366.

18. Testimony of Danny Stanley, Transcript of hearing on motion for new trial, *State v. Skatzes*, Case No. 83CR-3, pp. 101–2, 107–8.

19. George Skatzes, "To Whom It May Concern," Apr. 11, 1993.

20. The following is drawn nearly verbatim from the opinion of the Ohio Supreme Court in *State v. Lamar* (2002), 95 Ohio St.3d 181, 219–21.

21. Keith Lamar to Staughton Lynd, Apr. 3, 2003.

22. Keith Lamar to Staughton Lynd, Jan. 16, 2003.

23. These additional comments are from a transcript of his remarks contained in a letter to Staughton Lynd from Keith Lamar's wife, Angela Merles Lamar, Jan. 6, 2003.

CHAPTER 3

1. John Perotti, "Lucasville: A Brief History," *Prison Legal News* (Dec. 1993), p. 9. Gary Williams, *Siege in Lucasville: The 11 Day Saga of Hostage Larry Dotson* (Bloomington: 1st Books Library, 2003), p. 13, states that after the inmates listened to their demands being broadcast on the radio by a local station, they surrendered. The prisoner identified in this source as "Eric Swafford" is Eric Swofford, #178-862.

2. Testimony of Reginald Williams, Transcript, *State v. Sanders*, p. 2129.

3. Ibid., p. 2215.

4. Testimony of Reginald Williams, Daily Transcript of Proceedings, May 6, 2003, afternoon session, p. 57, and May 7, 2003, morning session, p. 31, *State v. Were II*.

5. Testimony of Reginald Williams, Transcript, *State v. Sanders*, p. 2140.

6. Ibid., pp. 2140–41.

7. Prisoners Dennis Weaver (black), David Sommers (white), and Bruce Harris (black) were killed later.

8. Testimony of Rodger Snodgrass, Transcript, *State v. Robb*, pp. 3925–26.

9. Testimony of Inmate #1 in the anonymous history of the rebellion entitled "To Whom It May Concern," July 5, 1993, p. 8. A copy is in my possession.

10. Testimony of Inmate #2, ibid., pp. 10–11.

11. Paul Mulryan, "Eleven Days under Siege: An Insider's Account of the Lucasville Riot," *Prison Life*, n.d., pp. 32, 33.

12. Mark Colvin, *The Penitentiary in Crisis: From Accommodation to Riot in New Mexico* (Albany: State University of New York Press, 1992); Bert Useem and Peter Kimball, *States of Siege: U.S. Prison Riots, 1971–1986* (New York: Oxford University Press, 1991), pp. 104–5, 212.

13. A videotape of the exchange was entered into evidence as Exhibit 315 in *State v. Skatzes*. I have transcribed it.

14. Ibid.

15. Testimony of Sergeant Howard Hudson, Transcript, *State v. Sanders*, pp. 2719, 2721.

16. Testimony of Anthony Lavelle, Transcript, *State v. Sanders*, pp. 3632–33 (emphasis added).

17. Williams, *Siege in Lucasville*, pp. 120–21. Officer Dotson also reports that his fellow hostage, Officer Anthony Demons, stated immediately after his release on April 16 that Officer Vallandingham's death was caused by cutting off water and electricity in L block. Ibid., p. 166.

18. The sheets were apparently left hanging at the time of the surrender. Photographs of sheets with these hand-lettered messages were taken by the Ohio State Highway Patrol, turned over to defense attorneys, and entered into evidence at trials.

19. These demands appear on additional OSHP photographs. The demands are numbered, but there is no single complete list.

20. Jill Riepenhoff, "The blame game: Spokeswoman heals after war of words over guard's death," *Columbus Dispatch*, Apr. 11, 2003.

21. Williams, *Siege in Lucasville*, p. 139. Officer Dotson adds that Unwin left for her Columbus home soon after the news conference, emotionally distraught. Ibid., p. 131.

22. Testimony of Anthony Lavelle, Transcript, *State v. Sanders*, p. 3646.

23. Williams, *Siege in Lucasville*, pp. 129, 131, 143.

24. Opinion, *State v. Robb* (2000), 88 Ohio St.3d 59, 62.

25. *State v. Skatzes*, Exhibit 322A (the government's transcript of Tunnel Tape 61), pp. 2–3. There is serious disagreement as to (1) whether a meeting took place on the morning of April 15, and (2) whether Tunnel Tape 61, which purports to record what happened at the meeting, was fabricated from recordings of meetings held at other times. Here I make the assumptions most favorable to the prosecution: that a meeting occurred, and that Tunnel Tape 61 records with substantial accuracy what was said at the meeting.

26. Ibid., pp. 13–18.

27. Testimony of Anthony Lavelle, Transcript, *State v. Were*, p. 1238.

28. Testimony of Anthony Lavelle, Transcript, *State v. Skatzes*, pp. 3909, 4066–67, 4098–99.

29. Testimony of Anthony Lavelle, Transcript, *State v. Sanders*, pp. 3649–50.

30. Ibid., pp. 3786–87.

31. There was also testimony in the trials of Namir and Hasan that Hasan was in L-6 just before Officer Vallandingham was murdered and that Namir supervised the killing of the guard. However, as I shall demonstrate in Chapter 8, the key witness to this scenario—Kenneth Law—has twice stated under oath that his testimony at Namir's and Hasan's trials was false.

32. Opinion, *State v. Robb* (2000), 88 Ohio St.3d 59, 62–63.

33. Testimony of Stacey Gordon, Transcript, *State v. Robb*, p. 3529.

34. Testimony of Stacey Gordon, Transcript, *State v. Skatzes*, p. 4253.

35. Testimony of Stacey Gordon, Transcript, *State v. Robb*, p. 3530. See also Gordon's testimony, Transcript, *State v. Skatzes*, p. 4253.

36. Interview with Sergeant R. T. McGough, Tape A-194, Jan. 5, 1995, p. 15 (one and a half to two hours); Transcript, *State v. Robb*, p. 3534 (one to one and a half hours); Transcript, *State v. Skatzes*, p. 4256 (one to one and three-quarters hours); Transcript, *State v. Sanders*, p. 3462 (one to one and a half hours).

37. Testimony of Anthony Lavelle, Transcript, *State v. Skatzes*, p. 4066.

38. See also my essay "Who Killed Officer Vallandingham?" It is available on the internet at http://acluohio.org/issues/death_penalty/who_killed_officer_vallandingham.htm.

39. *State v. Skatzes*, Exhibits 295A and 296A (the government's transcript of Negotiation Tape #4, 4:51–8:20 p.m., pp. 29–30, 63, and Negotiation Tape #5, 8:23–10:50 p.m., p. 20).

40. *State v. Skatzes*, Exhibit 296A, p. 32, and Transcript, p. 2158.

41. Transcript, *State v. Skatzes*, pp. 3919, 4104, 4112–14.

42. Testimony of Brian Eskridge and Aaron Jefferson, Daily Transcript of Proceedings, May 9, 2003, pp. 69–73, and May 12, 2003, pp. 6–8, *State v. Were II*; affidavits of Brian Eskridge, Wayne Flannigan, and Aaron Jefferson, Second Petition for Post-Conviction Review, *State v. Sanders*, Exhibits 9, 10, 11.

43. Testimony of Sean Davis, Transcript, *State v. Were*, p. 1644.

44. Transcript, *State v. Skatzes*, pp. 2238, 5377–83. Inexplicably, there exists only a fragmentary record of Skatzes' negotiations during the morning of April 15, even though both the state and the prisoners were independently recording them. Sergeant Hudson read into the transcript of Skatzes' trial his notes on the conversation between Skatzes and prison negotiator Dirk Prise. Some notes were also made by persons listening to negotiations in the tunnels under L block. Ibid., pp. 2193, 2195–96, 2235–39; Exhibits A, B, C and D.

45. Ibid., pp. 2195, 2237–38, 5380–81; Exhibit 297A, p. 2; Exhibit A.

46. Testimony of Tyree Parker, Transcript, *State v. Were*, pp. 1686–88.

47. Testimony of Willie Johnson, Transcript, *State v. Robb*, p. 4651; *State v. Were*, p. 1762.

48. Testimony of Willie Johnson, Transcript, *State v. Were*, p. 1764; to the same effect, *State v. Robb*, p. 4653.

49. Testimony of Eddie Moss, Transcript, *State v. Robb*, pp. 4503–12; *State v. Were*, pp. 1808–9.

50. Testimony of Eddie Moss, Transcript, *State v. Robb*, p. 4517.

51. Testimony of Sterling Barnes, Transcript, *State v. Were*, pp. 1865–68.

52. Testimony of Greg Durkin, Daily Transcript of Proceedings, May 9, 2003, *State v. Were II*, pp. 52–53; affidavit of Greg Durkin, Second Petition for Post-Conviction Review, *State v. Sanders*, Exhibit 8.

53. Affidavit of Roy Donald, Second Petition for Post-Conviction Review, *State v. Sanders*, Exhibit 16.

54. These statements were written down in two separate pages of notes by

"Pence," submitted by R. Cunningham, in Critical Incident Communication, Apr. 15, 1993. One of these pages contains the two statements beginning "talking about" and "background voice"; it is *State v. Skatzes*, Exhibit D. The second page, containing the statement about "wasting valuable time," was not made part of the record.

55. Transcript, *State v. Sanders*, p. 5202.

CHAPTER 4

1. *State v. Skatzes*, Exhibit 309A, pp. 2–3.

2. Ratcliff testified at Skatzes' trial that his parents were in a school across the highway during the uprising, and that "every time you turned around [my mother] was collapsing." When Skatzes transmitted Ratcliff's message, "a buddy of mine . . . ran over to the school and said, as long as he's with inmate George, you might as well believe he's going to be okay. And that gave them hope and faith." Transcript, *State v. Skatzes*, pp. 5998A–5999A.

3. Prise's proposals will be found in Lucasville Telephone Negotiations (inmate tapes), Tape XIII, pp. 8–9, 12–15, as well as on the state's Negotiation Tape #12, pp. 22–30.

4. Attorney Schwartz's good work in helping to end the Lucasville standoff was recognized in Patrick Crowley, "Against All Odds," *ABA [American Bar Association] Journal* (Dec. 1993), pp. 66–69.

5. Testimony of Niki Z. Schwartz, Transcript, *State v. Robb*, pp. 5577–79.

6. Ibid., pp. 5579–84.

7. Ibid., pp. 5585–88.

8. Ibid., p. 5606. At Attica, the rebellion ended with a massive and bloody assault on the occupied recreation yard by armed forces of the State of New York. At Santa Fe, "negotiations with inmates had very little to do with the release of hostages or ending the riot." Mark Colvin, *The Penitentiary in Crisis: From Accommodation to Riot in New Mexico* (Albany: State University of New York Press, 1992), p. 191. Such negotiations as occurred are described by a prisoner who was there in W. G. Stone, *The Hate Factory* (Agoura, Calif.: Paisano Publications, 1982), pp. 160–86, and by Bert Useem and Peter Kimball, *States of Siege: U.S. Prison Riots, 1971–1986* (New York: Oxford University Press, 1991), pp. 108–9, 111.

9. Testimony of Rodger Snodgrass, Transcript, *State v. Skatzes*, pp. 4379–80; see also Testimony of John Powers, Transcript, pp. 5911–16.

10. Stipulation, Transcript, *State v. Skatzes*, p. 6058; Transcript, Testimony of Howard Hudson, p. 1858. Officer Dotson offers essentially the same account. Gary Williams, *Siege in Lucasville: The 11 Day Saga of Hostage Larry Dotson* (Bloomington: 1st Books Library, 2003), p. 65.

11. Testimony of Dwayne Johnson, Transcript, *State v. Skatzes*, pp. 5939–48. John Fryman, a prisoner assaulted by other prisoners on April 11, describes in an affidavit how Skatzes helped to save both Officer Kemper and himself:

> It had just gotten dark when I heard George's voice again. He was talking about a CO whom they were carrying. Then I heard him say to bring me too. The CO, who I later learned was Kemper, and I were left in the middle of the yard. I heard George tell the others to be careful with the CO.

Affidavit of John L. Fryman, June 17, 1998.

12. Testimony of Darrold Clark, Transcript, *State v. Skatzes*, pp. 2328–29.

13. Ibid., pp. 2380–81; see also Transcript, pp. 5152–53.

14. Testimony of Jeff Ratcliff, Transcript, *State v. Skatzes*, pp. 5995A, 5999A–6000A.

15. Ibid., pp. 5145–46, 5199.

16. Ibid., p. 6000A.

17. Testimony of Larry Dotson, Transcript, pp. 4219–20; Testimony of Jeff Ratcliff, Transcript, p. 5995A; Neg. Tape #4, Exhibit 295A, pp. 4–5; Neg. Tape #5, Exhibit 296A, p. 21; Neg. Tape #12, Exhibit 303A, p. 29, all in *State v. Skatzes*. Officer Dotson speaks of Skatzes making his rounds, offering Dotson medication that Skatzes had in his possession, and checking on Officers Dotson and Buffington every day. Williams, *Siege in Lucasville*, pp. 163–64.

18. Testimony of Tim Williams, Transcript, *State v. Skatzes*, pp. 3087, 3195.

19. Testimony of Robert Brookover, Transcript, *State v. Skatzes*, p. 3771.

20. Transcript, *State v. Were*, p. 2240.

21. Testimony of Willie Johnson, Transcript, *State v. Robb*, pp. 4661–62; Transcript, *State v. Were*, pp. 1783–84.

22. Testimony of Eddie Moss, Transcript, *State v. Robb*, pp. 4525–28; Transcript,

State v. Were, pp. 1824–25.

23. Declaration of Leroy Elmore, Aug. 26, 2002, restating in expanded form Affidavit of Leroy Elmore, Dec. 20, 1995.

24. Testimony of Miles Hogan, Transcript, *State v. Sanders*, pp. 1981–87, 2006–7.

25. Testimony of Reginald Williams, Transcript, *State v. Sanders*, p. 2148.

26. Testimony of Rodger Snodgrass, Transcript, *State v. Skatzes*, p. 2526.

27. Testimony of Howard Hudson, Daily Transcript of Proceedings, May 5, 2003, morning session, *State v. Were II*, pp. 156–59.

28. Testimony of Niki Z. Schwartz, Transcript, *State v. Sanders*, p. 5495.

29. Ibid., pp. 5496, 5526–30.

30. Ibid., p. 5491.

31. Testimony of Niki Z. Schwartz, Transcript, *State v. Robb*, pp. 5589–90.

32. Ibid., p. 5592.

33. Ibid., p. 5596.

34. Ibid., p. 5598.

35. Ibid., p. 5605.

36. Ibid., p. 5606.

37. Testimony of Howard Hudson, Daily Transcript of Proceedings, May 6, 2003, morning session, *State v. Were II*, pp. 70–71. Hudson, a sergeant at the time of the investigation, was later made a lieutenant.

38. Affidavit of John L. Fryman, June 17, 1998.

39. Affidavit of Emanuel "Buddy" Newell, Dec. 30, 1998.

CHAPTER 5

1. Testimony of Niki Z. Schwartz, Transcript, *State v. Robb*, pp. 5614–15. Reporter Robert Fitrakis determined that Assistant Special Prosecutor Daniel Hogan earned nearly a hundred thousand dollars of extra income from his work on the Lucasville cases "while at the same time working full-time as an assistant Franklin County Prosecutor." Bob Fitrakis, *The Fitrakis Files: Free Byrd and Other Cries for Justice* (Columbus: Columbus Alive Publishing, 2003), p. 31.

2. Motion for an Order to Compel Discovery, *State v. Robb*, Oct. 27, 1994; Second Petition for Post-Conviction Review, *State v. Sanders*, p. 95 and Exhibits 34

B–D. The State of Ohio spent $892,000 funding the defense in all riot-related cases, including payments for attorneys, investigators, and expert witnesses. In contrast, it paid approximately $1.4 million to the prosecution and another $1.3 million to the Ohio State Highway Patrol, the agency investigating on its behalf. Second Petition for Post-Conviction Review, *State v. Sanders*, Exhibits 34A and E.

3. Cleveland *Plain Dealer*, Apr. 25, 1993.

4. Testimony of Niki Z. Schwartz, Transcript, *State v. Robb*, pp. 5624–25.

5. Telephone interview with attorney Dale Baich, Oct. 17, 2003.

6. Niki Z. Schwartz to Chief Justice Tom Moyer, Feb. 24, 1994, p. 1.

7. Motion for Notice in Order to Challenge Array of Grand Jury, *In re Grand Jury Target Wayne Bell*, Case No. 93 CI 433 (Ct. Com. Pl. Scioto Cty.), filed Dec. 7, 1993. Application to Record All Grand Jury Proceedings, filed Dec. 8, 1993, and Motion to Dismiss Grand Jury Due to Biased Grand Jurors, filed Jan. 5, 1994, ibid.

8. Memorandum in Opposition to Motion for Notice in Order to Challenge Array of Grand Jury, Request for Sanctions, filed Dec. 13, 1993, ibid. Rule 11 states in part: "The signature of an attorney constitutes a certificate by him that he has read the pleading; that to the best of his knowledge, information and belief there is good ground to support it; and that it is not interposed for delay. If a pleading is . . . signed with intent to defeat the purpose of this rule, it may be stricken as sham and false.... For willful violation of this rule an attorney may be subject to appropriate action."

9. Memorandum in Opposition to Motion to Dismiss Grand Jury, filed Jan. 14, 1994, ibid.

10. Testimony of Niki Z. Schwartz, Transcript, *State v. Robb*, pp. 5622–23.

11. Schwartz to Chief Justice Tom Moyer, Feb. 24, 1994, pp. 2n., 2, 3.

12. Ibid., p. 5.

13. Schwartz, "To Whom It May Concern," Dec. 1, 1998; statement by attorney Richard M. Kerger, Mar. 21, 2000.

14. Petition for a Writ of Habeas Corpus in a Capital Case, *Siddique Abdullah Hasan v. Todd Ishee*, Case No. 02-MC-051 (S.D.Ohio 2003), pp. 6–8.

15. Similarly, Judge Mitchell heard testimony about Skatzes in the Robb trial, when Skatzes was not present and had no opportunity to respond.

16. Editorial, Cleveland *Plain Dealer*, Apr. 25, 1993.

17. Howard Tolley, Jr., professor of Political Science, University of Cincinnati

and Amnesty International representative in Ohio, "Hamilton County Death Sentences: Overzealous Prosecutors and Jailhouse Informants," Apr. 11, 2003. An exasperated Chief Justice Moyer declared in 1999: "Clearly, our protestations have failed to change the advocacy of some prosecutors. It is as if they intentionally engage in improper conduct, safe in the belief that this court will continue to protest with no consequences." Moyer, Ch. J., concurring and dissenting, *State v. Fears* (1999), 86 Ohio St.3d 329, 352.

18. "The Risk of Serious Error in Ohio Capital Cases," testimony of James S. Liebman before the Criminal Justice Committee of the Ohio House of Representatives in Support of H.B. 502, June 4, 2002, p. 6. The "death-sentencing rate" is the number of death verdicts for every 1,000 homicides. Ibid., p. 5.

19. Staughton Lynd, *Intellectual Origins of American Radicalism* (New York: Pantheon, 1968), pp. 120–21. Professor Jules Lobel of the University of Pittsburgh Law School describes the "deeply racist" character of antebellum Cincinnati. Ohio's "Black Laws," adopted in 1804, denied blacks the right to vote, testify in court, serve in the militia, or receive a public education. Going beyond these restrictions, Cincinnati racists practiced direct action. In 1836 a Cincinnati mob broke into the office of the abolitionist James Birney, destroyed his printing press and then "rampaged through town, systematically looting black neighborhoods." Jules Lobel, *Success Without Victory: Lost Legal Battles and the Long Road to Justice in America* (New York: New York University Press, 2003), pp. 51–52.

20. Statement by Attorney Kerger, Mar. 21, 2000. See, with citations to the record, Petition for a Writ of Habeas Corpus, *Hasan v. Ishee*, pp. 10–12.

21. Testimony of Howard Hudson, Transcript, *State v. Skatzes*, p. 1913. Accord, Daily Transcript of Proceedings, May 6, 2003, morning session, *State v. Were II*, p. 69.

22. Opening Statement of Prosecutor Gerald Krumpelbeck, Transcript, *State v. Sanders*, pp. 1224–25.

23. The panel decision later reversed by the Court of Appeals *en banc* is *United States v. Singleton*, No. 97-3178 (10th Circuit Court of Appeals, July 1, 1998), 1998 WL 350507. Attorney John Val Wachtel, counsel for appellant, describes the case in the *OACDL Vindicator* (Fall 1998), pp. 12–16.

24. Affidavit of Derek Cannon, Petition for Post-Conviction Review, *State v.*

Skatzes, Exhibit 33.

25. Affidavit of Hiawatha Frezzell, Sept. 26, 1996.

26. David "Doc" Lomache to Prosecutor Daniel Hogan, n.d., but apparently soon after a previous letter dated June 12, 1995.

27. Interview #945 (no date), Tape A-245, Transcript, pp. 92–101.

28. Testimony of Emanuel "Buddy" Newell, excerpt of proceedings, *State v. Cannon*, pp. 28–29.

29. Kevin Mayhood and Jill Riepenhoff, "Lucasville: The untold story," *Columbus Dispatch*, Apr. 6, 2003.

30. Testimony of Robert Brookover, Transcript, *State v. Robb*, p. 2569.

31. Ibid., p. 2600.

32. Ibid., pp. 2609, 2614, 2617, 2623.

33. Ibid., pp. 2632–33.

34. Ibid., pp. 2518–23.

35. Ibid., p. 2524.

36. Inter-Office Communication, From: Sergeant Howard Hudson, To: Mark Piepmeier/Special Prosecutor, Subject: Robert Brookover, July 26, 1995. The following paragraphs are also based on this source.

37. Reginald A. Wilkinson and Thomas J. Stickrath, "After the Storm: Anatomy of a Riot's Aftermath," *Corrections Management Quarterly* (1997), p. 21.

38. Testimony of Anthony Lavelle, Transcript, *State v. Skatzes*, pp. 4054–55.

39. Statement of Prosecutor Hogan, ibid., p. 4047.

40. Testimony of Howard Hudson, ibid., pp. 2215–18.

41. Rodger Snodgrass to George Skatzes, Apr. 24, 1994.

42. Anthony Lavelle to Jason Robb, Apr. 7, 1994.

43. Conversation with George Skatzes, June 20, 2003.

44. Lavelle was charged with conspiracy to commit aggravated murder on June 9, 1994, and entered into a plea bargain on June 10.

45. Testimony of Antoine Odom, Transcript, *State v. Robb*, pp. 4853–55.

46. Testimony of Anthony Lavelle, Transcript, *State v. Skatzes*, pp. 4052–53, 4160–61.

47. Testimony of Rodger Snodgrass, Transcript, ibid., pp. 4390–96 (stabbed Elder); 4477–82 and 4487–90 (tried to kill Newell); 4656 (never charged in connec-

tion with murder of Sommers); 4413–14, 4430–31, 4593–95 (helped to guard hostage officers but kidnapping charges dropped).

48. Testimony of Robert Brookover, ibid., p. 3688.

49. Closing statement of Prosecutor Hogan, ibid., p. 5751.

CHAPTER 6

1. Transcript, *State v. Skatzes*, pp. 168–69, 171–72, 178–79.

2. Ibid., pp. 224–25, 228–29, 231–32, 236, 243, 246.

3. Ibid., pp. 425–26, 429–30, 434, 437. This person was seated on the jury that found Skatzes guilty and condemned him to death.

4. Ibid., pp. 655, 657, 660–62.

5. Ibid., pp. 714, 720.

6. Ibid., pp. 729–30, 736, 742.

7. Ibid., pp. 886–87, 891, 900. Defense counsel used a peremptory challenge to prevent this person from serving on Skatzes' jury.

8. Ibid., pp. 1088–89.

9. Ibid., pp. 1089–90, 1095, 1099.

10. Ibid., pp. 1100, 1108–10. Defense counsel used a peremptory challenge to prevent this person from serving on Skatzes' jury.

11. See Ohio Revised Code § 2923.01 Conspiracy. Mumia Abu-Jamal has called my attention to provocative comments on conspiracy by some very distinguished legal minds. Clarence Darrow offered the example of a boy who steals candy and is punished for a misdemeanor, whereas two boys who *plan* to steal the candy but don't are punished for a felony. The conference of Senior Circuit Judges, chaired by Chief Justice William Howard Taft, warned that "the rules of evidence in conspiracy cases make them most difficult to try without prejudice to an innocent defendant." Supreme Court Justice and Nuremberg prosecutor Robert H. Jackson called conspiracy "that elastic, sprawling and pervasive offense [that] defies definition." Judge Learned Hand termed it the "darling of the modern prosecutor's nursery," because of the many advantages it affords the prosecution. See Donald Freed, *Agony in New Haven: The Trial of Bobby Seale[,] Erika Huggins and the Black Panther Party* (New York: Simon and Schuster, 1973), pp. 102–4.

12. Ohio Revised Code § 2923.03.

13. Transcript, *State v. Sanders*, pp. 5052–54.

14. Ibid., pp. 5225, 5227, 5232.

15. Ohio Revised Code § 2929.04 (A) (5).

16. Hasan and Namir were found not guilty of murdering prisoner Bruce Harris and guilty only of the murder of Officer Vallandingham. Several other "aggravating factors" besides course of conduct were available to justify a recommendation of the death penalty: the offense was committed while the offender was in detention, and the victim of the offense was a law enforcement officer. Ohio Revised Code § 2929.04(A)(4) and (6).

17. Transcript, *State v. Skatzes*, p. 6096.

18. Ibid., p. 5668. See to the same effect the statements of Prosecutor Hogan, ibid., pp. 5746–47, 5777, 6096–97.

19. Testimony of Rodger Snodgrass, Transcript, *State v. Robb*, pp. 3942–43.

20. Testimony of Rodger Snodgrass, Transcript, *State v. Skatzes*, pp. 4399–4400.

21. Testimony of Anthony Lavelle, Transcript, *State v. Were*, p. 1238.

22. Testimony of Anthony Lavelle, Transcript, *State v. Skatzes*, pp. 3909, 4066–67, 4098–99.

23. Testimony of Anthony Lavelle, Transcript, *State v. Sanders*, pp. 3649–50, 3786–87.

24. James Liebman, "The Risk of Serious Error in Ohio Capital Cases," testimony before the Criminal Justice Committee of the Ohio House of Representatives in Support of H.B. 502, June 4, 2002, pp. 4, 6–7.

25. Opinion of the Court of Common Pleas of Franklin County, *State v. Robb* (Apr. 17, 1995), p. 2.

26. Ibid., p. 3.

27. Opinion of the Court of Appeals of Ohio, Tenth Appellate District, *State v. Robb* (Apr. 30, 1998), p. 7.

28. *State v. Robb* (2000), 88 Ohio St.3d 59, 62.

29. Opinion of the Court of Common Pleas, *State v. Robb*, p. 1.

30. Opinion of the Court of Appeals, *State v. Robb*, p. 6.

31. *State v. Robb*, 88 Ohio St.3d 59.

32. Opinion of the Court of Common Pleas, *State v. Robb*, p. 3.

33. *State v. Robb*, 88 Ohio St.3d 59, 64.

34. Ibid.

35. Testimony of Stacey Gordon, Transcript, *State v. Robb*, pp. 3560–61.

36. There is no dispute as to these facts. See Opinion, *State v. Lamar* (2002), 95 Ohio St.3d 181, 186–88.

37. Interview #1264 with Aaron Jefferson, June 23, 1994, Tape A-190, pp. 7–12.

38. Daily Transcript of Proceedings, May 5, 2003, *State v. Were II*, pp. 17–24.

39. Opinion, *State v. Robb* (2000), 88 Ohio St.3d 59, 66–67.

40. Ibid., pp. 78–79.

41. Jason Robb to Staughton Lynd, June 18, 2003.

CHAPTER 7

1. Tom Wicker, *A Time to Die* (New York: Quadrangle, 1975), p. 169.

2. Ibid., p. 238.

3. The books presenting this "whiteness" theory of labor history are discussed and critiqued in Eric Arnesen, "Whiteness and the Historians' Imagination," *International Labor and Working-Class History*, no. 60 (Fall 2001), pp. 3–32; and Peter Kolchin, "Whiteness Studies: The New History of Race in America," *Journal of American History*, v. 89, no. 1 (June 2002), pp. 154–73.

4. "Disturbance Cause Committee Findings," Executive Summary, p. 3.

5. Editorial, Cleveland *Plain Dealer*, Apr. 25, 1993.

6. "Disturbance Cause Committee Findings," Executive Summary, p. 3.

7. Steven Douglas Looney, "Little Rock Reed: America's Most Wanted 'Fugitive from Justice,'" *Journal of Prisoners on Prisons*, v. 9, no. 1 (1998), pp. 59–60.

8. Testimony of Sergeant Howard Hudson, Transcript, *State v. Skatzes*, p. 1904.

9. Looney, "Little Rock Reed," p. 61.

10. Ibid., pp. 61–62. The law suit is *William Rogers v. Department of Corrections, et al.*, No. C-1-91-688 (S.D. Ohio).

11. Testimony of Charles Valentine, Transcript, *State v. Skatzes*, pp. 4921, 4923–24.

12. Skatzes' words are drawn from the recollection of an eyewitness now at another Ohio prison; from the testimony of Brian Michael Young in *State v. Skatzes*,

Transcript, pp. 5082–83; from the testimony of Thomas Blackmon in *State v. Were II*, Daily Transcript of Proceedings, May 9, 2003, morning session, p. 7 ("George Skatzes . . . made a statement, saying, this is . . . not a black thing. This is not a white thing. This is our thing against [the] administration"); and from Skatzes himself.

13. *State v. Skatzes*, Exhibit 309A.

14. Testimony of Sergeant Howard Hudson, Transcript, *State v. Skatzes*, pp. 1930–45, 1950.

15. Ibid., pp. 1922, 1978.

16. Ibid., pp. 1993–94.

17. The description of Skatzes' experience with African Americans is drawn from conversations with him on Nov. 10, 1999, Apr. 21, 2003, and May 27, 2003.

18. Unsworn statement of Jason Robb, *State v. Robb*, pp. 5486–88.

19. The following is drawn from a letter from Hasan to Staughton Lynd, June 26, 2003.

20. Keith Lamar to Staughton Lynd, Apr. 25, 2003.

21. George W. Skatzes, Hunger Strike Statement Form, Apr. 22, 1996.

22. "Re: Hunger Strike," signed by the Five and another Death Row prisoner, John Stojetz, and addressed to Warden Ralph Coyle, July 14, 1997.

23. Siddique Abdullah Hasan to Alice Lynd, July 26, 1998, and to Staughton Lynd, July 28, 2003.

24. Unnamed to Mr. and Mrs. Lynd, May 19, 2001.

25. Bruce Nelson tells how black longshoremen in New Orleans declined to join the International Longshoremen's and Warehousemen's Union (ILWU), believing that locally negotiated arrangements that gave blacks control of "most waterfront occupations" provided greater security than the race-neutral labor market advocated by the ILWU. Bruce Nelson, *Divided We Stand: American Workers and the Struggle for Black Equality* (Princeton: Princeton University Press, 2001), pp. 101–10. The oral histories collected by Michael Honey in *Black Workers Remember: An Oral History of Segregation, Unionism, and the Freedom Struggle* (Berkeley: University of California Press, 2001) show how blacks struggled—together with whites when possible but, more commonly, alone—to overcome Jim Crow on the shop floor. Ruth Needleman in *Black Freedom Fighters in Steel: The Struggle for Democratic Unionism* (Ithaca, N.Y.: Cornell University Press, 2003), p. 197, explains how African American steelwork-

ers in northern Indiana insisted on building separate black organizations "because they had seen their cause set aside in the name of political expediency by white unionists on the left and the right."

CHAPTER 8

1. Jerome Bruner, "Do Not Pass Go," review of David Garland, *The Culture of Control: Crime and Social Order in Contemporary Society*, in *New York Review of Books*, Sept. 25, 2003, p. 4.

2. Ibid.

3. Department of Rehabilitation and Correction, Parole Board Hearing Policy 105-PBD-03, section VI(D)(7)(d): "Any inmate with a maximum security classification or any other classification title utilized to denote the most serious security risk inmates, at the time of release eligibility, shall not be granted release."

4. The author is one of the attorneys who represented Robb, Skatzes, and a third DR-4 prisoner, Ronald Combs, in a §1983 action against employees of the Ohio Department of Rehabilitation and Correction arising from the events of September 5, 1997.

5. "Use of Force Investigation Report: Death Row 4 Riot of September 5, 1997," pp. 15–16.

6. *Austin, et al. v. Wilkinson, et al.*, 189 F.Supp.2d 719, 722–23 (N.D.Ohio 2002). The author is one of the attorneys for plaintiffs in this class action concerning conditions at the Ohio supermax.

7. Ibid., pp. 723–24 (citations to record omitted).

8. In May 2000 George Skatzes was transferred back to Death Row at the Mansfield Correctional Institution.

9. "Notice of Anticipated Length of Stay at Level Five Security Classification," Aug. 4, 2003.

10. *In re Medley*, 134 U.S. 160, 168 (1890) (describing effects of solitary confinement as practiced in the early history of the United States).

11. Transcript, *State v. Sanders*, p. 1153.

12. Ibid., pp. 5055, 5067.

13. Ibid., pp. 1398–1400, 1414. In other contexts, the state insisted on stressing

that what happened at SOCF was a riot. For example, Skatzes was not indicted for conspiracy to riot, but Prosecutor Hogan argued in the Skatzes trial: "We need to prove that there was a conspiracy to commit aggravated riot in order for a number of what would normally be hearsay statements to come into evidence." Transcript, *State v. Skatzes*, p. 4887.

14. Transcript, *State v. Sanders*, pp. 4665–66.

15. Opinion, *State v. Sanders* (2001), 92 Ohio St.3d 245, 260.

16. Transcript, *State v. Sanders*, pp. 5309.

17. Ibid., pp. 5327–28.

18. Ibid., pp. 5332.

19. Opinion, *State v. Sanders* (2001), 92 Ohio St.3d 245, 266–67, 281.

20. *Attica: The Official Report of the New York State Special Commission on Attica* (New York: Praeger, 1972), pp. 283–84.

21. Bert Useem and Peter Kimball, *States of Siege: U.S. Prison Riots, 1971–1986* (New York: Oxford University Press, 1991), p. 56; Tom Wicker, *A Time to Die* (New York: Quadrangle, 1975), pp. 309–10.

22. Reginald A. Wilkinson and Thomas J. Stickrath, "After the Storm: Anatomy of a Riot's Aftermath," *Corrections Management Quarterly* (1997), p. 21.

23. Ibid.

24. Useem and Kimball, *States of Siege*, p. 56 (emphasis added).

25. *New York Times*, Jan. 23, 1975; Apr. 8, 1975; Feb. 27, 1976.

26. Ibid., Dec. 31, 1976.

27. Judge Daniel Gaul of the Cleveland Court of Common Pleas, foreword to Mike Gray, *The Death Game: Capital Punishment and the Luck of the Draw* (Monroe, Maine: Common Courage Press, 2003), p. ix. Daniel Hogan, one of the prosecutors in the Lucasville trials, was alleged by defense counsel to have withheld the identity of an exculpatory witness in the unrelated case of Kim Hairston. "Without assigning blame, the appeals court said Hairston should get a new trial. Then, during the second trial, a key prosecution witness recanted her story. Hogan had to dismiss the charges." Jeb Phillips, "Few Ohio prosecutorial mistakes found in study," *Columbus Dispatch*, June 28, 2003.

28. Interview #104, Apr. 21, 1993, at 11:48 p.m., Tape A-19, p. 8.

29. Videotape of Anthony Lavelle, Polygraph Test of 5/27/94, pp. 94–100.

30. Affidavit of Kenneth Law, Mar. 9, 2000.

31. Affidavit of Kenneth Law, Sept. 19, 2003, Petition for Post-Conviction Review, *State v. Skatzes*, Exhibit 27 (emphasis added).

32. "Testimony at Rules Infraction Board," Jan. 18, 1996. This document contains the following verifications: "I have read the above and find that it is an accurate summary of testimony before the Rules Infraction Board," (signed) Andrea Carroll, Secretary, Rules Infraction Board; "I have read the above and certify that it is a true and accurate summary of testimony given before the Rules Infraction Board on the date written above," (signed) Sergeant Howard Hudson.

33. Assistant Special Prosecutor Hogan asserted in closing argument during the penalty phase of the Skatzes trial: "[T]hink about David Sommers, the third, the last of the three killings, the one where [Skatzes] *wielded a bat and literally beat the brains out of this man's head.*" Transcript, *State v. Skatzes*, p. 6108 (emphasis added). During the penalty phase of Aaron Jefferson's trial, Assistant Special Prosecutor Claude Crowe told the jury:

> If there was only one blow to the head of David Sommers, the strongest evidence you have [is that] this is the individual—I won't call him a human—this is the individual that administered that blow.... *If there was only one blow, he's the one that gave it.* He's the one that hit him like a steer going through the stockyard, the executioner with the pick axe, trying to put the pick through the brain.

Transcript, *State v. Jefferson*, pp. 656–57 (emphasis added).

34. Testimony of Dwayne Buckley, Excerpt of Proceedings, *State v. Cannon*, pp. 6, 14; Attorney Joseph L. Hale to Derek Cannon, Oct. 11, 1995, p. 3, reporting the comments of Judge Cox about Buckley's testimony; Judith K. Wise, Chief, Bureau of Records Management, Department of Rehabilitation and Correction, Certification of Record, Feb. 11, 2004. Derek Cannon's name does not appear on the list of prisoners in L block who surrendered on April 21, 1993.

35. The convictions for kidnapping hostage correctional officers are no more persuasive. Officer Darrold Clark asked Skatzes to remove him from L-6, the pod controlled by Muslim prisoners. Skatzes arranged with the Muslims to move Clark to the pod controlled by the Aryan Brotherhood, L-2, where he protected the guard until personally releasing him on April 15. Further, Skatzes was not involved in capturing

and restraining either prisoner Elder or Officer Vallandingham. But Skatzes was sentenced to an additional 15–25 years for "kidnapping" each.

36. Lamar's counsel has moved to reopen his appeal under Ohio Appellate Rule 26(B) and *State v. Murnahan* (1992), 63 Ohio St.3d 60. Assignment of Error No. 2 concerns the prosecutor's use of peremptory challenges "to exclude the only two African-American jurors on Mr. Lamar's venire." Counsel argues in support of this assignment that the prosecutors' reasons for excluding Mr. Ramsey and Ms. Nelson, the two African Americans, were pretextual and therefore violated *Batson v. Kentucky*, 476 U.S. 79 (1986).

37. Testimony of Dr. Patrick M. Fardal, Transcript, *State v. Skatzes*, pp. 4865, 4867, 4870–71, and Daily Transcript of Proceedings, May 5, 2003, morning session, *State v. Were II*, pp. 44, 54–56, 61. Officer Dotson observes that the preliminary autopsy report by Scioto County Coroner Tom Morris said that the cause of death was strangulation, with no other signs of torture or injuries. Gary Williams, *Siege in Lucasville: The 11 Day Saga of Hostage Larry Dotson* (Bloomington: 1st Books Library, 2003), p. 187.

38. Michael N. Nagler, *Is There No Other Way? The Search for a Nonviolent Future* (Berkeley: Berkeley Hills Books, 2001), p. 53.

39. Mumia Abu-Jamal, *Death Blossoms: Reflections from a Prisoner of Conscience* (Farmington, Pa.: Litmus Books, 1996), p. 83.

40. Interview with Keith Lamar, Sept. 25, 2003.

41. "Stop the Violence" courtesy of Keith Lamar.

INDEX

Lavelle's attempt to create a public address system in occupied cell block, 55; becomes a Muslim, 40; and beginning of uprising on April 11, 123; and crisis about TB testing at SOCF, 22–28, 163–64, 216n25; efforts to obtain effective counsel, 92–94; life story of, 35–40; at meeting in SOCF chapel on April 14, 28; not guilty of murder of Bruce Harris, 170, 229n16; as "peacemaker" during settlement negotiations, 72, 81; no physical evidence against, 97; picture of, 36; supposed plot to kill, 130; on prohibition of contacts with media, 213n6; protects hostage officers and prisoners during uprising, 80; on race, 147–48; race discrimination in selection of jury for trial of, 96; relation with George Skatzes, 107–08, 149–50; in SOCF honor block, 13; named as target by Highway Patrol, 83–84; on telephone calls by prisoners at SOCF, 215n20; tries to put on evidence about causes of uprising, 162–65; voice not heard on Tunnel Tape 61, 80–81

Hogan, Atty. Daniel: on agreement reached by Skatzes and Burchett on April 14, 65; alleged pay for work on Lucasville prosecutions, 224n1; on Lavelle's decision to inform, 106, 111; prepares Brookover as witness, 103–04; on Skatzes' noninvolvement in planning uprising, 123; states that Skatzes committed same lethal act against David Sommers that Jefferson also convicted for, 234n33

Hogan, Miles: protected by Hasan, 80

Hostages: capture of, 11, 49–52; killed at Attica, 75; Michael Hensley, 40; number of at SOCF, 11; release of on April 21, 75. See Clark, Darrold; Demons, Anthony; Dotson, Larry; Ratcliff, Jeff; Vallandingham, Robert

Hudson, Sergeant (later Lieutenant) Howard: on absence of physical evidence, 97; alleged to have targeted spokemen during investigation, 83; denies targeting spokesmen during investigation, 82–83; investigated Robert Brookover's veracity after Brookover testified, 105–06; and Officer Vallandingham's death, 5–6; on stalling by state during negotiations, 5, 55; threatened Derek Cannon and George Skatzes with death penalty if refused to "cooperate," 97–98, 107–08

Informants: encouraged by Warden Tate, 18–19; killed on April 11, 19, 50–52; and prosecution strategy, 6–7; in Lucasville prosecutions, 96–111, 208–09 (Appendix 5)

Jamal, Mumia Abu-. See Mumia Abu-Jamal

Jones, Alvin (also known as Mosi Paki), Rules Infraction Board conviction of, 170, 172–73, 234n32, 235n37

Kerger, Atty. Richard: on Hasan's efforts to obtain effective counsel, 92–94; on racial discrimination in selection of Hasan's jury, 96

Knecht, Krystof, on conditions at SOCF before uprising, 17

Lamar, Angela Merles, 8

Lamar, Keith, 11–12: befriended by George Skatzes, 148; on causes of uprising, 17, 18, 21, 28–29; drafts demands for Lucasville Five hunger strike, 149–50; exculpatory evidence withheld from, 131–32; life story of, 45–48; picture of, 45; poem by, 176; unfairness in trial of, 172

Lavelle, Anthony: becomes informant, 106–10; confesses to Leroy Elmore,

prisoners' demands in, 53–58
(Appendix 2); during April 12–15,
54–58, 63–65; and settlement of
uprising, 71–76; stalling by state
during, 5, 55

Newell, Emanuel "Buddy": assaulted
on April 21, 130; tells Highway
Patrol that Lavelle wanted to kill
hostage officers, 168; protected by
Hasan, 80; testifies to targeting of
prisoner spokesmen by Highway
Patrol, 83–84; on "snitch academy"
at Oakwood Correctional Facility,
102–03; on violence at SOCF, 14

Oakwood Correctional Facility: as
"snitch academy," 102–03

Ohio State Highway Patrol (OSHP),
6, 126, 156: exculpatory interviews
withheld, 131–32; found Robert
Brookover's trial testimony to have
been unreliable, 105–06; informed
by Lavelle that he was there when
Officer Vallandingham was murdered,
168–69; investigation procedures of,
99–102; permitted prisoner Law to
present perjured testimony, 170,
234n32; targeted prisoner spokesmen
for prosecution, 83–84; threatened
prisoners who did not "cooperate"
with death penalty, 97–102, 107–08,
169–70; told by prisoner Newell of
Lavelle's intent to kill hostage
officers, 168

Ohio State Penitentiary (OSP, "supermax"): constructed in Youngstown
as result of SOCF uprising, 158–61;
parole made impossible for prisoners
at, 157; proposals for change by prisoners at, 174–76; "real maximum
security prison" demanded by Scioto
County residents after uprising,
202–03 (Appendix 3); supermax
unit at SOCF sought by Warden
Tate before uprising, 19–20

Ohio Supreme Court. *See* Supreme
Court of Ohio

Operation Shakedown: as cause of
uprising, 156; and forced interracial
celling, 54, 57, 137–39; policies
associated with, 17–20; result of
murder of Beverly Taylor, 16; single-
celling objective not achieved, 4

Overcrowding: double-celling as cause
of uprising, 21; insurgents demand
an end to forced integrated celling,
54, 57; single-celling sought by
Operation Shakedown not achieved,
4; at SOCF before uprising, 137

Perotti, John, on history of SOCF,
14–15, 213n3

Piepmeier, Atty. Mark: pressured Ohio
State Bar Association to give priority
in assignment of counsel to prisoners
who agreed to cooperate with prosecution, 91–92; sought to prevent
prisoners' access to counsel before
indictment, 89

Prosecutorial misconduct alleged, 6–7,
168–70 (Appendixes 5 and 6): by
Hamilton County prosecutors, 95,
226n17; by prosecutor Brower,
169–70; by prosecutor Hogan,
103–04, 234n33; by prosecutor
Piepmeier, 89–92; by prosecutor
Stead, 103–04, 106

Public Defender (Office of the Ohio
Public Defender): informed participants in uprising of their rights,
88–89; prevented from representing
group interests of potential defendants, 89–91

Race and racism (Chapter 7): alleged
April 11 agreement between Muslims
and AB, 123–25; in city of Cincinnati
and Hamilton County, 96, 226n19;
contrasting racial makeup of SOCF
prisoners, SOCF correctional officers,

244 Lucasville

riots to revolutions against monarchies and empires, 13; on negotiations at Santa Fe, 222n8

Vallandingham, Officer Robert: award named for, 3; condolences offered by George Skatzes, 70–71; how killed, 172–73, 235n37; responsibility of state for death of, 5–6, 219n17; alleged role of Derek Cannon, 171–72; alleged roles of Hasan and Namir, 78–81, 169–70; who killed, 49 (Chapter 3)

Were, James (Namir Abdul Mateen). *See* Namir
Wicker, Tom, on race relations in Attica uprising, 134–35
Wilkinson, Director Reginald: credits Lavelle plea bargain as key to aggra-

vated murder convictions of Hasan, Namir, Robb and Skatzes, 106; on duration of SOCF uprising, 1, 212n2; policy prohibiting media contact with prisoners convicted of crimes related to uprising, 3, 213n6; repressive policies of after 1993, 156–61
Williams, Reginald: concerning Muslims' intentions on April 11, 49–50, 123; on Hasan's opposition to violence against Andre Stockton, 80; implicated in murder of Bruce Harris, 209 (Appendix 5)
Williams, Tim: implicated in murder of Earl Elder, 209 (Appendix 5); picture of, 99; protected by George Skatzes, 78; protected by Hasan, 80
Wiretapping: legality of, 6, 132–33; by FBI, 59, 66, 125–26; by state, 54. *See also* Tunnel Tape 61 (Appendix 1)

Staughton Lynd has been a scholar-activist all his adult life. The director of the Freedom Schools in the 1964 Mississippi Summer Project, he also is the author of a number of books, including *Intellectual Origins of American Radicalism* and *Living Inside Our Hope: A Steadfast Radical's Thoughts on Rebuilding the Movement*. His most recent book is *The New Rank and File*, edited with Alice Lynd.